In Search of Appalachia

In Search of Appalachia

Best wishes –
from Nancy Diggs

Nancy Brown Diggs

HAMILTON BOOKS
Lanham • Boulder • New York • London

Published by Hamilton Books
Hamilton Books is an imprint of The Rowman & Littlefield Publishing Group, Inc.
4501 Forbes Boulevard, Suite 200, Lanham, Maryland 20706
www.rowman.com

6 Tinworth Street, London SE11 5AL, United Kingdom

British Library Cataloguing in Publication Information Available

Library of Congress Cataloging-in-Publication Data Available

ISBN 9780761871606 (pbk. : alk. paper)
ISBN 9780761871613 (electronic)

♾️™ The paper used in this publication meets the minimum requirements of
American National Standard for Information Sciences—Permanence of Paper
for Printed Library Materials, ANSI/NISO Z39.48-1992.

Contents

Acknowledgments

My thanks to so many for lending me their expertise: the Reverend Doctor Vanessa Oliver Ward and the Reverend Doctor Wendy J. Deichmann of the Union Theological Seminary; Fred Bartenstein, the University of Dayton's country music specialist; and the faculty of the Appalachian Studies program at Sinclair Community College, among others. Thanks to history Professor Emeritus William Schuerman of the University of Dayton and to Ken Brown, experienced writer and good neighbor, for looking over parts of the manuscript.

I am grateful to everyone who steered me toward those I should meet. The late Dr. Elise André put me in touch with "Mr. Appalachia," the legendary Loyal Jones, and Dr. Carole Ganim, a congenial traveling companion, introduced me to her corner of Kentucky and some of its fascinating residents.

Thanks to all those who generously shared their stories with me, especially those, like the late Hobert Rice, who were part of the Greatest Generation, to whom we owe so much.

Introduction

L'il Abner, Beverly Hillbillies, Dukes of Hazard, Hee Haw, Deliverance, Justified, Buckwild . . .

Hillbillies, rednecks, crackers, clodhoppers, ridge-runners, stump-jumpers, briars . . .

How did millions of people who value family, honesty, loyalty, faith, independence, character and country, for whom people are more important than things, ever become pariahs in their own land? Aren't those traits that all Americans aspire to?

Was it when the writers of the early twentieth century chose to look at Appalachians as colorful outsiders, inferior because of their isolation?

Was it when the timber interests destroyed the forests, and industrial giants rationalized exploitation by saying that such primitive people had to be brought into the modern world, no matter the means?

Or was it when the government forced the exile of thousands of families from their homesteads because, after all, the people were "culturally or biologically inferior" and had to be "saved"?[1]

Or maybe it was when the media decided that the mountain people were the only group that could be safely mocked without fear of recrimination. Says John Shelton Reed, "Hillbillies appear to be the last acceptable ethnic fools."[2]

Having written several books that touched on other cultures, I thought it was time to look at one closer to my own, geographically, that is. Yes, my family roots were in Kentucky, but I was well educated, well traveled, and able to speak five languages—and so surely not like those people. But surprise! Appalachians are not like "those people" either. And those aren't the people I remember from a Kentucky childhood.

When I hear that rural accent: all those shortened "I's," the " in's" for "ing's," the southern cadence that stresses the first vowel of words of more than one syllable—INsurance, UMbrella, DEtroit—I have my Proustian moment. I'm back at my grandparents' house, a place filled with love and down-home smells: peach slices hanging over the stove to dry, coal smoke, coffee.

In the kitchen the aunts and uncles sit around the table drinking coffee, laughing and talking—or rather shouting, as they are all a little deaf—until late at night. In the morning I'll wake up in the feather bed to the sound of women's sleep-hoarsened voices and the smell of biscuits and bacon.

Summers meant the odor of kerosene, which we slathered on to keep the chiggers off before picking blackberries for Mammy's cobbler—and yes, we called her "Mammy," a term of English and possibly Irish origin long before Al Capp debased it.

In my earliest memories, she would get water from the spring, heat irons on the stove, and warn us children away from of the bucket of lye she used for making soap. In the winter we'd sneak sugar lumps from the barrel in Pappy's general store, slipping past the farmers playing checkers by the pot-bellied stove . . .

In writing *In Search of Appalachia,* I would meet many who didn't fit the stereotype, including bluegrass superstar Ricky Skaggs, millionaire businessmen, Greatest Generation veterans, educators, those who earned their doctorates and law degrees, and those who worked with their hands to feed their families. The people I met were more like *The Waltons* than the *Beverly Hillbillies,* more Sgt. York than Pvt. Gomer Pyle.

I found that people from the hills, shaped by history and geography, have many valuable qualities of which they—and we—can be proud. Appalachian culture formed many of the characteristics considered typically American today: our independence, our self-reliance, and our patriotism and dedication to service, especially military. What's more, millions of Americans still feel its influence.

What are we talking about when we say "Appalachia"? The Appalachian Regional Commission, established in 1965 to research and overcome some of the problems in the hills, designates these sections of the country as Appalachian: all of West Virginia, parts of Kentucky, Tennessee, Alabama, Georgia, North Carolina, South Carolina, Ohio, Pennsylvania, Virginia, Mississippi, Maryland and even a small part of western New York state: all the land covered by the Appalachian mountain range, which equals an area of 205,000 square miles.

With a population of over 25 million, it has as many people as all of the Scandinavian countries combined, twice as many as Greece, Belgium, Portugal, and the Czech Republic respectively, and it equals the number of people in such troublesome places as Yemen, North Korea, and Afghanistan. That's a lot of Americans to be disrespecting, and there are many more throughout the country who can claim its heritage.

Appalachian values have a long pedigree, dating back to influences centuries ago and thousands of miles away. Or we could even say eons ago, for the landscape has had a part in forming the character of those from the mountains.

In this book we'll look at some of the reasons—the sticks and carrots—which led the early immigrants to risk the perilous voyage to America, and perilous it was on tiny, crowded ships, some not much larger than a double-wide trailer. We'll explore what happened when they got here, how and why settlers moved into the mountains, how our Appalachian ancestors shaped the country, and how the traits carried from faraway places and distant eras continue to affect lives today, for better or worse.

The Appalachian people are not just the descendants of those who left the British Isles—the "huddled masses" from northern England, lowland Scotland, and Northern Ireland. The hills have long been populated by Native Americans, Germans, Italians, and other Europeans, as well as African Americans. But it is the group that constitutes the core of our culture, most of whom are Scotch-Irish, that will be the focus of this book, for that is the culture that has left its mark most indelibly on our ways—and which happens to be my heritage.

NOTES

1. Harold W. McSwain, *Appalachia: Similarities to the Third World*, (Columbus, OH: Rural Resources, Inc., 1986), 4.

2. Quoted in *Appalachia: Social Context Past and Present*, (Dubuque, IA: Kendall/Hunt, 2002), Philip J. Obermiller and Michael E. Maloney, editors, 10.

Chapter One

The Backstory

Could you take it? Two months at sea, cold, wet, hungry, and seasick. You might sleep four to a bed, with beds stacked three deep. Food would be something like "oatmeal for breakfast, a scrap of meat and cheese with a few peas and some bread or biscuit for dinner, and biscuit or bread and molasses for supper." Hardly sumptuous, but even this Spartan diet could be reduced, for "the bread and biscuit were commonly wet and moldy, the meat spoilt, and the water brackish."[1]

Records are scanty, but it appears that the mortality rate for immigrants who sailed across the Atlantic might have been a relatively low ten to fifteen percent. So let's just hope you haven't heard the horror stories about the ship that was carrying 280 Scots of whom eighty died of starvation and overcrowding, or the ship with 190 Irish immigrants of whom 100 died of starvation, or the one that arrived in Boston with only fourteen survivors out of 123 of those on board.[2]

A deadly epidemic might sweep through the passengers, and you'd be lucky to live through it. All of this in a ship of less than 300 tons, maybe eighty feet long, about twice the length of a Greyhound bus, with up to 200 passengers. Indentured servants usually traveled in the "'tween decks," a space about five feet tall.

For purposes of comparison, we can visit replicas of the Jamestown ships, which reached our shores in 1607. The "Godspeed" was 40 tons and 68' long and carried a total of 52, while the U.S.S. Constitution, a warship launched in 1797 and on view in Boston Harbor, was comparatively large—2,200 tons, 203 feet in length. But to really put this in perspective, consider the size of a typical Carnival cruise ship today, with a displacement of about 130,000 tons and a length of 1,000 feet. And instead of the spas, pools, and fancy plumbing of the latter, sanitation on an immigration ship would be—a bucket, which wouldn't stay stationary in a North Atlantic storm. The odor alone would be overwhelming, especially if you were in an unventilated lower deck.

One early immigrant from Germany, Gottlieb Mittelberger, left a vivid description of his harrowing crossing, in which he saw "many die miserably":

> "During the voyage there is on board these ships terrible misery, stench, fumes, horror, vomiting, many kinds of seasickness, fever, dysentery, headache, heat, constipation, boils, scurvy, cancer, mouth rot, and the like . . . Add to this want of provisions, hunger, thirst, frost, heat, dampness, anxiety, want, afflictions and lamentations, together with other trouble, as e.g. the lice abound so frightfully, especially on sick people, that they can be scraped off the body. The misery reaches a climax when a gale rages for two or three nights and days, so that everyone believes that the ship will go to the bottom with all human beings on board. In such visitations the people cry and pray most piteously."

Children, he added, rarely survived the voyage, and "many a time parents are compelled to see their children miserably suffer and die from hunger, thirst, and sickness, and then to see them cast into the water. I witnessed such misery in no less than thirty-two children in our ship, all of whom were thrown into the sea. The parents grieve all the more since their children find no resting place in the earth but are devoured by the monsters of the sea . . ."[3]

WHY THEY LEFT

Who were they, our adventurous forebears who settled the rugged hills of Appalachia, and what made them leave?

Most came from the British Isles, especially the borderlands of northern England and southern Scotland, and many from Scotland, the so-called Scotch-Irish, sailed from Northern Ireland, abandoning century-old Scottish settlements.

As early as Queen Elizabeth I in the sixteenth century, England's rulers had looked for ways to pacify those unruly people in Ireland. England and Ireland had been periodically at battle since the 1200s.

The borderlands, too, often caused problems, those areas above Hadrian's Wall in northern England, which marked the end of the "civilized" area once controlled by Rome. An earlier wall in Scotland separated the Lowlands from the warring clans of the Highlands.

In 1603 Queen Elizabeth died and the Protestant James I, who was also king of Scotland, succeeded to the throne. That same year two Scottish lairds in lowland Scotland bought land in Ulster, also known as Northern Ireland, and brought their countrymen to settle it. In 1607, the same year that America's Jamestown was founded, some 40,000 Scottish Presbyterians emigrated to Ulster. Also in 1607, seeing the writing on the wall, many of those of the Catholic aristocracy left Ireland for good; most headed for Spain.

What better way for the English to settle the continuing battles with Ireland than to send those from the restless borderlands, including lowland Scots, to the large English holdings in Northern Ireland? There, in what was called the Ulster Plantation, Protestant numbers would keep rebellious Catholics under control. The fact that some Irish chieftains were planning to seek help from Spain and France made it especially urgent.

Persecutions under England's later monarchs Charles II and James II, Catholic rulers who reigned successively from 1660–1688, pushed more Scottish Presbyterians to leave Catholic-controlled Scotland and join their fellow Protestants in Northern Ireland.

In 1600 a mere two percent of those in Ireland had been of Scottish or English descent; by 1640 it is estimated that some 100,000 Scots and 20,000 English were living there. But by 1700, over a quarter of Ireland's population—27 percent—could claim that they or their predecessors had come from across the Irish Sea, and almost all of them had settled in Ulster.[4] With the founding of the Plantation, "Ulsterners," says James Leyburn, "like their Scotch-Irish descendants, would feel a new freedom to strike their own bargains, a man deciding his future for himself. The passage to Ulster was a strike toward individualism."[5] Many of them would later head for America, leaving the mark of their homeland on this new world.

Ulster represented a much better life for many Scots. Now they would escape the continuing fighting and raids. For over 200 years the leadership of the country had been chaotic, leaving clan leaders to take responsibility for their own. This unsettled situation led to "a familiar pattern [that] reinforced itself in what would become the Scots-Irish character: the mistrust of central authority, the reliance on strong tribal rather than national leaders, and the willingness to take the law into one's own hands rather than waiting for a solution to come down from above."[6] In this tribal society, family loyalty was paramount, while those outside the family met with "suspicion and hostility."[7] Sound familiar?

Living conditions were rough and primitive in Scotland. Farming methods had not changed in centuries. Cleanliness was not an option, nor a goal. Houses had little furniture—hay strewn on the mud floor served as beds—and kitchens were rudimentary. Animals shared the cottage, tethered at one end.

It was this factor that would later prove to be an advantage for the settlers in the New World, but tragic for the Native Americans. According to Charles C. Mann, many animals can pass on diseases that can be transmitted to humans. "Over time," he says, "mutation lets animal diseases jump to people:

avian influenza becomes human influenza, bovine rinderpest becomes human measles, horsepox becomes human smallpox."[8] European settlers, long accustomed to the proximity of domestic animals, developed at least partial immunities to those diseases, while they spread like wildfire among the populations with whom they would later compete, for there were few domestic animals among Native Americans.

The move from Scotland to Ulster would be a big step forward, for the English had brought with them better farming methods, along with iron tools. In addition, the newcomers found more arable land where the English had drained fens and bogs.

Not that they were welcomed by the native Irish, who did not take any more kindly to this intrusion and confiscation of their lands than would Native Americans a century or so later. An uprising begun in 1641 would last more than a decade; about a seventh of the immigrant Ulster population died.[9]

And there was more trouble coming.

A Little Ice Age in the late seventeenth century resulted in years of poor harvests in Scotland. Although crops failed, the northern counties of Ireland were ideal for raising sheep, and Ireland's wool trade flourished to the point that English wool merchants suffered from the competition. So under pressure from the English king, the Irish Parliament passed the Woolens Act in 1699, which barred Irish exports beyond England and Wales. English merchants, on the other hand, were free to sell to foreign and colonial markets and free to set their own price.

The linen industry was introduced and took up part of the slack, with the help of Protestant Huguenots who came at the king's invitation. Originally from Catholic France, they had been living in Protestant Holland. But Ulster's economy had suffered a blow from which it could not recover.

Rents paid by tenant farmers rose to outrageous levels, leading to more financial woes. To add to renters' discontent, the owners were often absentee landlords who showed little interest in their property, or their tenants.

Drought, famine, severe frosts, and illness—among sheep as well as people—were further inducements to leave Ulster and head for America.

Religious persecution, the intensity of which would depend on who was in power, was always in the background. It was officially sanctioned in 1692 when, under the influence of Church of England members, the Irish Parliament, from which Catholics had long been excluded, decreed that all officers were to partake of communion at an Anglican church three times a year.

Presbyterian clergy who would not conform to Church of England practices would be disqualified as ministers, unable to teach anything about their faith in schools. When there were no ministers, Presbyterians conducted their own services in homes or crossed the sea to Scotland for baptisms and communion.[10] Presbyterians were not allowed "to hold political office, serve in the military and even bear arms."[11]

It was not the first time that Presbyterians had suffered restrictions on the practicing of their faith. Back in 1639, an oath of loyalty to the king and the established church was demanded of all those in Ireland, the so-called Black Oath. Some had returned to Scotland, where Presbyterian practices had been re-established in 1638 following the Covenanters' rebellion.

Scottish Presbyterians had long been at odds with the established Church of England. The militant Covenanters, Presbyterians who opposed the king's interference in church governance, had declared that only Jesus was the head of the church. Many were martyred in the conflict that ensued. Although the rebellion failed, it did gain some concessions for the Scottish churches, or "kirks." It was not until 1690, however, that the reign of the Protestant monarchs William and Mary brought full acceptance of the Scottish Kirk.

Now, though, disgruntled subjects had another option. Many would head for the New World: The exodus that had begun at the end of the seventeenth century grew to the point that between 1717 and 1776, over a quarter of a million Ulster-Scots—one-third of the Protestant population of Ulster—left for America.

All immigrants did not come by way of Ireland, however. Scotland and northern England, the "borderlands," sent many forth to the colonies, as did Germany and other European countries. Scotland, as well as Yorkshire and other parts of northern England, also had their share of impoverished farmers, high-rent problems and absentee landlords, but there were other factors at work in Scotland. As the number of emigrants grew to alarming numbers, the great thinkers in England debated the causes.

As the decades passed and more and more people sailed for America, the mass exodus from Britain did not go unnoticed. As one writer in Yorkshire put it in 1773, "The emigration of people from all parts of England . . . is very amazing indeed, and if no stop is put to it England will really be drained of multitudes of all sorts, also of people of considerable property; ships are daily taken up for this purpose, and the spirit of emigration daily encreases [*sic*];—America that land of promise, is their cry."[12]

Some leaders feared that "Scotland would be fatally depleted, economically as well as demographically, and that 'the continual emigrations from Ireland and Scotland will soon render our [American] colonies independent on [*sic*] the mother-country.'"[13] More than one writer envisioned a future *Planet of the Apes*-like scenario in which twentieth-century visitors would encounter nothing but wild beasts and piles of stone in London where its great buildings had previously stood.

In the aftermath of the Scottish Rebellion of 1745, clan chieftains were stripped of their authority. No longer were there close ties between landlord or tenant. Some clan leaders, having lost their traditional positions, could only hope for better in a new land.

Once clan chiefs had become mere landlords, focusing more on making their estates pay than on the welfare of their tenants, the path was smooth for The Clearances to take place in the eighteenth and nineteenth centuries. In the Highlands, the land was "cleared": farming was abandoned for the raising of sheep, which would require vast acres for grazing. Many of those living in their ancestral homeland were displaced and forced to move; why not choose America?

Dr. Samuel Johnson feared that such large numbers of emigrants would pose "some catastrophic cultural loss," and that those who left their home-lands would have no "cultural power" in the new environment.[14]

He was wrong: The Scotch-Irish in particular would become "the historic and ideological template from which modern understandings of 'American' were struck."[15]

To the "sticks" of poverty and religious persecution were added the "car-rots" of land and freedom. The British were especially eager to create a buffer zone, peopled by the Scotch-Irish, to keep French encroachment and the native population in the colonies at bay; offering land was well worth it. Recruiting agents spelled out the previously unattainable dream of landown-ership, which brought prestige and respect in England. Now the destitute could move on up.

Many chose the route of becoming indentured servants, a kind of tempo-rary slavery, but not much different from time spent in an apprenticeship. According to a record of emigrants from England and Scotland from Decem-ber 1773 to March 1776, almost half, 47.8 percent, were either indentured servants or "redemptioners," those who were committed to raise the unpaid amount of their passage within a certain time or enter into indenture.[16]

There were distinct advantages. The expensive voyage would be paid for, and after the servant worked off the debt, which usually required a commit-ment of four to seven years, he could receive payment, often in land. Those indentured were often "members of society," although of a lower rank than their masters.

Along with their faith, those Scotch-Irish who were Presbyterian brought with them a "zeal for education," a legacy of the Reformation. Teachers were much in demand in Scotch-Irish settlements, and many indentured servants found themselves employed as schoolmasters or tutors.[17]

In some cases such servants were treated as members of the family, like John Harrower, an educated but impoverished Scotsman. Fortunately for us he kept a diary recounting his experiences on a Virginia plantation, which were mostly positive. His master, Colonel William Daingerfield, was a kind and generous employer. Harrower ate with the family, received money for clothing, had his laundry done, and slept in "a very fine feather bed." Working as the schoolmaster for his master's children, he was able to earn extra money by teaching other children, as well, including those the colonel recruited. Unfortunately, he died from an unknown illness after three years, without bringing his wife and family (and servant!) to America, as he had hoped.

The young Quaker Thomas Brown, possibly my great-grandfather many times over, was typical of those early immigrants in many ways. He and his family sailed from England in order to have the freedom to worship as they pleased. No longer would they be persecuted for refusing to pay taxes to support the established Anglican church. Young Tom may have seen Quaker founder George Fox put in the stocks in his home town of Mansfield, in northern England, the cradle of the Quaker movement. Fox's crime? Attempting to preach at an Anglican church service; only priests were allowed to do that.

Long before Harrower's arrival, Tom had completed his indentured servitude with honor, had married a fellow Quaker, and was doing so well that he could build a sturdy house for his wife and family, which would eventually include nine children. The house, now privately owned and renovated, still stands in Inwood, West Virginia, and is on the National Register of Historic Places.

Obviously, from the many notices of runaway servants, not all placements were as satisfactory as Harrower's or Brown's, and many lived in slave-like conditions, but those who stuck it out would have gained their own foothold in America.

WHAT THEY FOUND

What would greet the immigrants when they arrived in the New World? For many, it was indeed the Promised Land, and one created over millions of years.

If we could fast track our geological history, the world would seem to be a restless place: continents shifting, mountains forming as the earth's crust folded and faulted, seas rushing in and then disappearing. Ancient lava flows metamorphized into gneiss, schist and granite, while heat and pressure from the collision of continental masses and other forces melted rock, sometimes causing it to "flow with a consistency like that of toothpaste," leaving a scene that can "look like the folds and swirls in a marble cake."[18]

For geologists, who can read the rocks in the same way that some read books, the Appalachians must be a real page-turner. Scientists tell us that a billion years ago there was one continent surrounded by water, a supercontinent. We can see evidence of that period in places like North Carolina's Blowing Rock and Red Top Mountain in Georgia, while spectacular outcroppings like North Carolina's Whiteside Mountain and Chimney Rock are of ancient granite, revealed by the erosion of softer rock. In some areas, mountain paths sparkle with tiny particles of mica, as if a powerful force had sprinkled diamond dust.

Put in simple terms, using the analogy of a calendar year, Kentucky's coal was being created around 2:30 P.M. on December 6. The Paleozoic period, during which many Appalachian features would emerge, would end on December 12, around 1:30 in the afternoon, and—finally—people would appear at about ten minutes before midnight on December 31.

As continents shifted, strata of rocks would be pushed over others, vertical layers would become horizontal or be forced into crazy-quilt angles. Some 750 million years ago, vast inland seas like that of the Ocoee Basin, which covered parts of the Carolinas, Tennessee, and Georgia, were created and left their mark; sediment, accumulating over millions of years, became limestone and dolomite. Over thousands of years, erosion trimmed down formerly Alpine heights.

While today, by world standards, Appalachia's mountains are not big—the highest, Mt. Mitchell in North Carolina, is a mere 6,684'—they've helped to shape the character of its population.

Photographs from space give a clear picture of accordion-pleated green velvet, whose steep slopes and deep valleys would form remote and hidden "hollers." There, settlers created their isolated communities, learning to rely upon themselves.

But there's a surprise in the landscape at Middlesboro, Kentucky, which otherwise is a typical Appalachian city. Some 300 million years ago, it's estimated, a huge meteorite struck the earth, creating a basin in which the town would later be established.

The meteorite would play a role in American history of the eighteenth century. The thrust of tectonic plates had prepared the way, and the meteorite landed in just the right place for erosion to enlarge the gap and make it easier for pioneers like Daniel Boone to head west. About three-fourths of the settlers who came to Kentucky are thought to have passed through this, the Cumberland Gap.

Not only would coal have been formed in those ancient eras, but rich deposits of copper and gold—more like a curse than a blessing—would form in ways that were not well understood until the late 1970s.

Gold would help determine the fate of the native Cherokees. Although those in the region had long known about the deposits, gold was of no use to them, but when the word spread among the white population, hordes of gold miners rushed in.

It all began when twelve-year-old Conrad Reed found a seventeen-pound gold nugget in a nearby North Carolina stream. Not knowing its value, but admiring its beauty, the family used it as a doorstop for a few years, until someone took it off to a jeweler for his opinion. In today's currency, it was worth about $160,000. Although the jeweler paid a paltry $3.50 to the family, history tells us that eventually they may have received fair value for this, the first recorded gold nugget discovered in America.

Soon the Reed gold mine was in full operation and continued to produce for another couple of decades. Although it is no longer operating, it is still possible to tour the mine today.

Greed for gold would be an impetus for President Andrew Jackson to forcibly remove the Cherokees from their homeland in the winter of 1837–38. More than a third of them, some 4,000 souls, would die on this "Trail of Tears."

And coal? It too would be a mixed blessing. Although the hill folk looked to the mines to support them, the greed of absentee mine-owners eventually led to the destruction of the land and damage to its people.

Copper and iron ore were found in abundance. What geologists called the Ocoee Basin, an ancient sea, came to be called the Copper Basin. Mid-nineteenth-century mining and smelting of the copper deposits created sulfur dioxide fumes, which in turn produced acid rain, creating a nineteenth-century Carthage: thousands of acres of land where nothing would grow. It was only after some fifty years that better methods were discovered to convert the toxic fumes into sulfuric acid for fertilizer production.

The process of change continues, as evidenced by frequent landslides, as softer rock collapses under harder layers, sliding down the steep slopes. Interstate 40, which goes through Tennessee to Asheville, North Carolina, was closed for several months in 1997 and 2009 due to massive rockfalls, as was Interstate 75 in Tennessee in 2016. A section of Newfound Gap Road, U.S. 441, the main route through the Great Smoky Mountains National Park, was destroyed by a landslide, closing the road for three months in 2013. And back in 1984, some twenty cars were trapped between two simultaneous landslides on the same road. Other geological events continue, but the pace is too slow, and our lives too short, to discern them.

Appalachia abounds in nature's gems like Tennessee's Cumberland Plateau, a wonderland of rivers and waterfalls and God's sculpture in stone: cliffs, caves, "rock houses," and natural bridges. Or the hair-raising stonefaced cliffs of North Carolina.

Take a hike in the woods for a taste of what it must have been like hundreds of years ago. A stay at a backcountry lodge like the Big South Fork's Charit

Creek Lodge is like stepping back in time. A steep walk down, with an elevation change of some 430 feet, leads to cabins warmed by wood stoves and lit by oil lamps. Our forebears would probably have used bear grease as fuel.

Perhaps the most remarkable aspect of this time travel is the lack of noise: no planes, cars, or motors of any kind, just the bird calls, the gurgling of a stream, the soft susurration of the wind, and, they tell us, the occasional yipping of coyotes. Or a bear might wander through. On a clear night it's possible to see the sky as it looked 150 years ago: a mass of stars undimmed by city light pollution, the Milky Way sweeping across.

For those early settlers, even though life wasn't easy, the new land must have seemed like a gift from God. Limestone deposits that reached the valley floors contributed to fertile soil for farmers, metal-bearing soils furthered the growth of trees like red spruce or cedar.

In summer the mountains were a palette of many shades of green, from the deep forest green of hemlock, through the brighter jade tones of maples, oaks and pine trees and oaks to pale yellow greens, with fleeting splashes of silver. Rhododendron and mountain laurel brightened dark woods with pink and white blossoms. Fall brought the kind of riotous orange, yellow and red that still attract hordes of tourists today, while the watercolor shades of spring were highlighted with redbuds, dogwood and wild azalea. The region could boast— and still does—one of the "most diverse biologies in the temperate zone": over 10,000 known species exist, "greater than in all of northern Europe."[19]

In the mountains there was ample timber for building cabins, plenty of chestnuts and other nuts to eat and provide mast for the hogs, and clear running water. Crops could grow in fertile valleys and up steep slopes, some so steep that mules couldn't pull the plows.

They might have come to a new country for a new life, but they had brought much of the old life with them, including notions of democracy fostered by the Scottish Kirk, the Presbyterian church founded by John Knox in the middle of the sixteenth century. In spite of poverty, most of the Scots who had headed for Ulster "carried with them democratic ideals growing from the Protestant Reformation of 1560."[20] The mistrust of central authority, and the propensity to take the law into one's own hand, the heritage of a long history of a clan society, accompanied the newcomers.

Not only did they bring values like independence, the closeness of families, and notions of democracy, but also ways of life. Elizabeth Hirschman, an American professor, joined hands with two British scholars, Stephen Brown of Northern Ireland and Pauline Maclaran from England, to compare artifacts of domestic life at Tennessee's Museum of Appalachia, the Ulster-American Folk Park and the Ulster Folk and Transport Museum in Ireland. They found remarkable similarities.

At odds with their Catholic neighbors, for whom religious art reflected the beauty of heaven, Calvinist emigrants had disdained anything that spoke of the visual arts. Nothing in their churches was to distract from hearing the word of God.

In the triumph of the practical over the visually pleasing, cabins in both Ulster and Appalachia were "similarly furnished." Both are "monochromatic, unadorned, and lacking in aesthetic refinements . . . It is as if the Scotch-Irish wish to view themselves—and have others view them—as a strictly no-nonsense culture, one in which any presence of frivolity, luxury, or irrational impulse is condemned."[21]

Nevertheless, the pioneer buildings at the Museum of Appalachia near Knoxville, Tennessee, together form an idyllic Brigadoon of a village. There, in the shade of ancient trees, is everything a settler might need: church, mill, barn, school, gardens, and a still. Sheep graze in the large green lawn, cows low in the pasture, and chickens run free.

There were occasions for having fun, as indicated by the musical instruments that immigrants brought with them, although settlers might have called get-togethers "play parties" instead of "dances," in order not to offend stricter Presbyterian sensibilities.

The Museum of Appalachia's extensive display of weapons: "knives, hatchets, swords, bayonets, muskets, rifles, revolvers, powder molds and bullet molds" reflect the ideology of the mountaineers' origins. "From these warrior beginnings," say the authors of *Two Continents One Culture,* "the Scotch-Irish colonists evolved into a gun-owning subculture that exists to this day."[22]

It was an ideology that would serve the country well when American colonists decided to throw off the English yoke. The Scotch-Irish made up about a third of the fighting force and are remembered for bravely standing with George Washington during that terrible Valley Forge winter of 1777-78. And let's recall that a little more than fifty years later, among those who fought and died alongside Scotch-Irish Davy Crockett at the Alamo, seventy-eight of them, almost a third, were from the Appalachian states.

A display of tools in the museum shows us the newcomers' talent for making do when needed items were hard to come by, as when a sheriff in Tennessee confiscated the container used in a still and converted it into a butter churn.

Those from the mountains still boast of the talent for using what's available to meet their needs. Former Kentuckian Elmo Garrett claims, "I can see a use for almost anything." It's hard for him to throw anything away, even though, he says, "My wife gets on to me. But she's almost like me . . ."

In his book *Kentucky Traveler,* musician Ricky Skaggs recalls that his father was a "real Mr. Fix-It": "A neighbor would call him on the phone and say, 'Hobert, our cook stove is tore up. Could you come fix it?' He'd say,

'Yeah, be over there in a little bit.' He'd grab some tools out of his toolbox and go over and get the stove fired up."[23]

Our friend Mark[24] claims it was his father's resourcefulness that saw them through hard times, in Michigan, in Ohio, and back in Kentucky. "He could do anything," he says. "He could build a house, do the electricity, install the plumbing, everything." Perhaps it is this resourcefulness that has played a part in Mark's outstanding success with his large manufacturing company. And, like his fellow business leader Sam Morgan, he has been generous in "paying it forward."

Sam's father, too, was resourceful. He literally built the log cabin which housed his family in Kentucky, with logs that he had cut down in the forest. (There will be more about Sam in a later chapter.)

Part of the reason for wanting to find a good use for what's available, in both America and in Northern Ireland, might have deep religious roots, what Brown and his fellow authors call "the Calvinist drive" to put our God-given resources to good use. And so, in both the New World and the settlers' homeland, "efficiency and productivity" were "cardinal virtues."[25]

While those in America were applying their talents to produce the tools they needed to survive, their cousins back in Ulster would apply those same qualities to help create a booming industrial Northern Ireland.

NOTES

1. Bernard Bailyn, *Voyagers to the West,* (New York: Vintage Books, 1986), 319.

2. Marilyn C. Baseler, *"Asylum for Mankind": America 1607–1800,* (Ithaca, NY: Cornell University Press, 1998), 95.

3. "Passage to America, 1750," *Eye Witness to History,* www.eyewitnesstohistory.com (2000).

4. Billy Kennedy, *The Scots-Irish in Pennsylvania and Kentucky* (Belfast: Causeway Press, 1998).

5. James G. Leyburn, *The Scotch-Irish: A Social History*, (Chapel Hill: The University of North Carolina Press, 1962), 98.

6. Jim Webb, *Born Fighting*, (New York: Broadway Books), 78.

7. Kennedy, 29.

8. Charles C. Mann, *1493: Uncovering the New World that Columbus Created,* (New York: Knopf, 2011), 98–99.

9. Leyburn, 124.

10. Ibid, 121–122.

11. Kennedy, 27.

12. Bailyn, 42.

13. Ibid, 8.

14. Ibid, 498.

15. Stephen Brown, Elizabeth Hirschman, and Pauline Maclaran, *Two Continents One Culture: The Scotch-Irish in Southern Appalachia,* Johnson City, TN: Overmountain Press, xii. Bailyn, 166.

16. Bailyn, 166.

17. Leyburn, 320.

18. Sandra H.B. Clark, "Birth of the Mountains," USGS: Science for a Changing World, pubs.usgs.gov/gip/birth/pdf. 2009.

19. Ibid, 2.

20. Brown, et al., 5.

21. Ibid, 45, 46.

22. Ibid, 61–63.

23. Ricky Skaggs with Eddie Dean, *Kentucky Traveler: My Life in Music* (New York: HarperCollins, 2013), 30.

24. Some names and details have been changed to protect privacy.

25. Browning, et al.

Chapter Two

The Industrial Age

The new age of industry that had begun in Britain in the second half of the eighteenth century was flourishing there by the 1830s. As England was enjoying its benefits, and drawbacks, in America, Appalachia's lack of transportation would hold back its progress until after the Civil War, when construction of the railroads began again in earnest.

Meanwhile, in America, with Andrew Jackson's election in 1828, the spotlight was on the common man that this rustic Tennessean represented. Ralph Waldo Emerson praised the self-reliance and individualism of Americans. Walt Whitman in *Leaves of Grass* claimed that the best of America lay in its common people: in the "fierceness of their roused resentment . . . their susceptibility to slight . . . the air they have of persons who never knew how to stand in the presence of a superior"—all aspects of the Appalachian character.

Nineteenth-century art extolled the virtues of the rural life: all those paintings of barns and cabins, of cider-makings, fiddling, and corn-husking, by people like William Sidney Mount, Frank Mayer, and George Caleb Bingham.

Bingham's painting *Daniel Boone Escorting Settlers through the Cumberland Gap* depicts those brave pioneers headed for Kentucky as a civilizing force, calm in the face of any danger. Some say the painting contains religious symbolism and that the woman on the horse, Boone's wife Rebecca, represents the Virgin Mary, reflecting America's mission to the world.

In Mayer's *Independence—the Country Squire*, the painting's subject, smoking his long-stemmed clay pipe, with his boot-clad feet resting on the rails of his porch, could have stepped right out of a Kentucky cabin.

Yet, ironically, in 1903, John R. Fox, Jr. perpetrated the "mountaineer" stereotype in his bestselling books like *The Little Shepherd of Kingdom Come* and *Trail of the Lonesome Pine*, with characters who seemed quaint and simple, who talked funny, and who were outsiders as far as the rest of

America was concerned. His books also contained scenes of violence that would become associated with mountain ways.

The Civil War, especially brutal in the border states, where neighbor fought against neighbor, and even brother against brother, enhanced the violent image. The postwar period might have been even more violent than the war itself, as there were wartime grudges to settle and wartime enmities to continue among veterans who were now well accustomed to fighting.

Feuds, especially in Kentucky, were a sign of the times. The Civil War had inured its participants to violence; ex-soldiers made use of the guerilla techniques they'd learned to apply them throughout the area as people settled scores. Thus began the vicious cycle that would be carried down through generations. There was not only the long-lasting Hatfield-McCoy war, but also others, as between the Howards and the Whites, the Frenches and the Eversoles.

Later the early mining camps added to the reputation for violence. Given the preponderance of young single men—and we know today that the brains of young males may not mature until age 30, or older—add guns, alcohol, and easily obtained cocaine, and you've got a prescription for mayhem. Add to that the fact that this was a population that had just missed the "action" of the Civil War and that also lacked the restraining influence of family, and it's no wonder that the violence in the camps more than equaled that in the Wild West.

Today we wonder if the media and video games lead to violence; in the late nineteenth century, Dime Novels took some of the blame for their adulation of gun-toting heroes.

Moonshining also added a tolerance for lawless behavior. When our newly-formed country needed money to pay off its war debts, Alexander Hamilton, Washington's Secretary of the Treasury, proposed that a tax be imposed on whiskey, and Congress voted the proposal into law back in 1791. Moonshiners refused to respect a law that they considered unfair. What one grew was one's own business, and corn was much easier to transport in its liquid form.

In spite of attempts by federal troops to enforce it, the law was met with great resistance in the so-called Whiskey Rebellion that began in western Pennsylvania, with its large population of Scotch-Irish settlers. Other areas of Appalachia found less militant ways to resist, including intimidating revenue collectors and enacting resolutions against it.

Having never been truly enforced, the excise tax was removed in 1802 by President Thomas Jefferson, no friend of Alexander Hamilton. He spoke of the latter's "vainglorious desire to exercise power and of his fiendish control over Washington's mind."[1]

While the government had reasserted federal authority, the "war" had the unforeseen consequence of pushing illegal distilleries into other areas, including Kentucky. The whiskey tax remained on the books until the 1840s, says historian John Alexander Williams, but it was never again collected in Appalachia.[2]

Not that moonshining became lawful, however, for a new tax was enforced post-Civil War, as the federal government reasserted its power.[3] Later, in the 1920s and 30s, moonshining is said to have given rise to drag-racing, inspired by moonshiners fleeing from government pursuers at high speeds. Today the worst counties for the growing and consumption of marijuana are those considered "dry," in spite of local laws, or perhaps because of them, since people have become accustomed to ignoring the law.

Gary G. talks about a visit to his hometown that illustrates the laissez-faire attitude of the region:

> A friend of mine I knew from school days is the county sheriff. I kid him.
>
> I was down there a few years ago and I walked up to him and I said, "Where would I find some moonshine?"
>
> "Moonshine? I'm the county sheriff. I don't know about that stuff!"
>
> I said, "Yes. you're the county sheriff. The reason I'm asking you is because you should know if it's going on."
>
> He cracked me up, but as he walked away from me, he said, "I can't help you, but if you talk to those two guys sitting over there, they can help you." And they did, and I got real moonshine!

Nevertheless, crime rates in Appalachia remain low compared to other regions; in 1998 West Virginia had the lowest crime rate in the country.

As for the law in general, it appears that it has not done much to protect the rights of those who live in the mountains; instead it has become more of a tool for exploitation.

The richness of minerals in the area had been known at least as early as the 1740s, but it was not until after the Civil War and the extension of the railway system that it was profitable to make use of them.

In the 1870s it was timber and iron ore that attracted speculators. At first the locals warmly welcomed the newcomers who rode into the mountains seeking timber and minerals, and who were offering cash for unused land. Owners "found such an offer hard to refuse in most rural areas, where hard money was scarce, life was difficult, and [there was lack of] opportunities," says Ronald Eller.[4]

But it was a devil's bargain, as unsophisticated landowners would learn later. "'Broad form deeds,' as they were known in eastern Kentucky, effectively transferred to the land agents all of the mineral wealth and the right to remove it by whatever means necessary. When the landowners discovered what their property was really worth, they were no longer so welcoming: "By 1900, the land agent was as likely to be met with a rifle as a 'halloo,' and he would seldom be invited inside the cabin."[5]

Perhaps the most tragic result of this virtual rape of Appalachia was the disappearance of its forest. John Alexander Williams spells out the heart-breaking figures: "As late as 1870, two-thirds of West Virginia was covered by old-growth forest, amounting to at least 10,000,000 acres. By 1900 this figure had been reduced to half; in 1910, by more than four-fifths. The virgin forest was gone, except for the pathetic remnants of a few hundred acres, by 1920."[6]

Meanwhile, Appalachia had its own version of Britain's "dark, Satanic mills." While most of the cotton mills in the thriving textile industry were in other areas, three-quarters of a million people left the mountains, a move that meant leaving everything that was familiar. In a typical mill, 60 percent of the workers were women; half were children between the ages of twelve and sixteen. Working sixty-five to seventy-two hours a week, not unusual for the time, employees lived in what we would consider substandard housing, dirty and crowded. With lint ever present in the mill, many suffered from irreversible "byssinosis," sometimes called "brown lung disease," the textile workers' counterpart to black lung disease.

The cotton mills would soon be eclipsed by King Coal, however, and then began the real exploitation of Appalachia, which would dwarf earlier land transactions contracted with an unsuspecting population.

Coal was needed to fire the machines of industry, to feed the generators of the electric power plants that were springing up, and to heat the houses of America, while coal in its coke form was used in making steel. It didn't take much of an investment to open a mine, and they sprang up everywhere in the southern mountains. Again, the outsiders came, both to operate and to work in the mines.

Early on, given the remote locations of mining camps, mine owners faced a labor shortage. Some solved the problem by using slaves, and when this was no longer possible after the Civil War, convict labor was employed, except in West Virginia, where it was not allowed.

In Tennessee, however, most of those brought in to work had been convicted of petty larceny, and in Alabama, "the overwhelming majority of convict laborers was black, many convicted for minor infractions that in some cases seem to have been placed on the books for the purpose of ensuring a steady supply of convicts to be leased," says Williams, who claims that "the system was, in effect, a postbellum extension of slavery."[7]

Those of European origin were not the only ones who lived in the Appalachian mountains. In addition to the native Cherokees, there were African Americans there from the beginning of frontier times.

"As whites moved into the mountains," says Althea Webb of Berea College, "so did free and enslaved Africans," so that by 1860, "African Americans were approximately 10 percent of the population."[8]

In addition to the slaves and prisoners forced to work in the coal mines, some black workers came of their own accord, but it was active recruiting by the coal operators that swelled their ranks, with West Virginia receiving the greatest percentage.[9] Segregated from their white co-workers, they had their own communities, and "in some mining towns black lawyers and doctors wielded a degree of political influence."[10] Black miners, however, were never promoted to positions of authority; most were relegated to be "pick miners and loaders of coal."[11] Coal operators sought a strategic balance of black, native white, and immigrant workers in attempts to play one group against other and thus ward off unionization.[12]

Nevertheless, African Americans were much better received in the mountains than in the more southern states. Here they were known as individuals rather than a nameless group of second-class citizens.

Sam Morgan, originally from Leslie County, Kentucky, owes a good part of his success to his African-American business partner, and he can count other black men among his friends. He claims that:

> They didn't have prejudice in the mountains. The prejudice was in the big cities, in Louisville and places like that. In the mountains they all lived close to each other. I mean, the white people lived close to the blacks, they worked in the coal mines with the blacks. I don't think there was hardly any discrimination.
>
> See, in the mountains, when they integrated the schools, nothing happened. They had no problems because of these boys playing athletics and stuff, so they were glad to integrate, and they all worked in the mines together and everything anyway. So there wasn't any prejudice in the mountains 'cause if people were prejudiced in the mountains, everybody considered them stupid.
>
> In Leslie County we had one black family. The man's wife died, and after our house burned down, he lived next door to us. We moved in town and rented a house. I remember I had the mumps, and he was sick, and Mother would prepare meals for him and for us and take them next door and feed him.
>
> When he died he had the largest funeral anybody had ever had in Leslie County. Everybody loved the guy. Now, I don't remember—because this was when I was a child—I don't remember what he did working. He might have worked in the timber.

Roscoe Napier's experience was similar:

> I remember one black man in town. His name was Buford Phillips . . . He went with us to Indiana to visit a brother-in-law of mine who lived in Indiana . . . My brother-in-law got sick and his brother lived in Manchester, Kentucky, near

me. His brother, I think, got Buford Phillips, who had a car, to drive us up to visit him in Indiana. He was a nice guy. He was just one of us, as far as that goes. We got along real well.[13]

Free African Americans, Greeks, Germans, Italians, Welsh—workers came from all over, finding mining and company towns more attractive than the ghettoes of eastern cities. Farmers from the area were attracted too: Mining was more predictable than farming, and while miners were given Sunday off, farmers were at work every day.

The late 1800s were an age of paternalism. Consider Dayton, Ohio's National Cash Register Company (today's NCR). Its founder and president, John H. Patterson, felt that a happy worker was a better worker. His factory buildings were well lighted and well ventilated. Inside walls were painted in cheerful colors, potted plants were added, and the grounds: lawns, trees and shrubs, were landscaped by the famed Olmsted Brothers.

Work days were short for the times: nine and a half hours for men, eight for women, and pay was equal to or more than the prevailing rates. The company cafeteria served healthful meals, and there were classes of all kinds, lectures, and religious instruction. Believing in the importance of education, Patterson instituted a kindergarten program for employees' children, since there was none in the public schools. And so the company towns of the era were not all the prisons that later generations might consider them to be.

A fourth-generation miner, Richard Koger now guides tours through his family-owned Barthell Coal Camp, near Stearns, Kentucky, which has been restored to be historically correct—down to the color of the paint—in accordance with archives at the University of Kentucky.

As coal camps went, Barthell, active from 1902 until 1948, was probably one of the better ones. The mine here employed 265 people, 200 of whom were miners underground.

One of the eighteen mines and ten mining camps run by the Stearns Company, it was equipped with a room that served as dentist's and doctor's offices, as well as mortuary, complete with embalming table. It was here that injured miners were brought. Doctors were even able to do amputations, but if a miner required more complicated surgery, he would be taken to the nearest hospital—seventy miles away in Danville, Kentucky. Doctors contracted to practice for a certain period of time at the camp in exchange for the company's paying their expenses to attend medical school.

The barbershop was the "local hangout, where the guys would get together and just sit around to tell stories." This was the only camp with a barbershop, for the company soon learned that people were so poor that they had their hair cut at home. The barber had to be a miner, too, in order to make ends meet. At the adjacent bathhouse, where hangers and baskets were provided, most of the miners would shower with their clothes, Richard says, then hang them up to dry on the line.

And, of course, there was the company store, which sold everything: clothing, hardware, staples, animal feed, including what could be ordered from Sears, Roebuck. Above the store was the scrip office, where miners would be paid in scrip, the only currency accepted at the store.

A row of company houses stretches across a hillside. As comfortable as any for that time and place, they might house families with eight or ten children, for large families were the norm. If a miner was injured and unable to work to pay the rent, the family would be evicted and replaced by other tenants. Nor was there compensation for injuries before the arrival of the unions.

Pauline Slone of Hindman, Kentucky, proudly displays a sign on her door proclaiming her to be, like Loretta Lynn, "a coal miner's daughter." Her spacious frame house is decorated in what I think of as "country cozy" style, with its displays of fine-stitched quilts and rag dolls made by her late mother-in-law, Verna Mae Slone, a local writer known for her books about Kentucky ways. Pauline, in her early seventies with gray, well-styled hair, is dressed informally in jeans and a gray and navy blue short-sleeved top. She's obviously in pain from a recent fall and regrets that she can't serve us something to eat with the usual Appalachian hospitality. Instead she insists that I take a doll-sized quilt and a rag doll made by Verna Mae Slone.

Pauline spent much of her childhood living in company towns, and although the houses they lived in were "nice," she says:

> When I think about it, I think about slavery, just because everybody was in this little mining camp, you know? Nobody beat you to work or anything like that, but that's the only thing I could describe about it.
>
> When I was smaller, my dad would ride a horse up the holler and over the mountain, and he would work, I think, for like a dollar and a half an hour in the mines, and then he'd drive his horse back at night. Sometimes he would have to work night shift, and he'd come home at like 3:00 in the morning, and my mom would have to heat the water for him to bathe, and I think a lot of that—I know it contributed to his death, but we also had part of it, too, because my mom died with pulmonary fibrosis, and she never smoked. When Dad would come home, he'd bring all that black dust back home.

It's hard to believe now that, as Loretta Lynn says in her book *Coal Miner's Daughter*, "They used to tell the miners that coal dust was good for you, that it helped ward off colds. Or they'd tell a miner that he would get sicker from dirty sheets than from working in a coal mine—lots of stupid things, but nobody knew better then." She remembers that when her father was suffering from the black lung disease that eventually killed him, "he got laid off when he couldn't work fast anymore. They just said, 'Take your shovel and go home.' No pension, no benefits, just 'go home.'"[14]

Richard Koger agrees that it was a terrible thing:

Especially a lot of times when these people got killed. There's a lot of deaths in these mines. So if they got killed, of course the family had to move out, and that's the way that young children started to work.

They started working as young as nine, ten, eleven years old. This was before child labor laws, and of course at that time there was no law saying you had to go to school. A lot of them quit school to go to work in the mines. What these miners would do, they'd take the oldest son of the family and take him in the mine with them, because chances are both of them are not going to get killed or injured at the same time, of the family.

My grandfather worked in the mine for forty-eight years. He started at age eleven. He just went to school long enough to learn to read and write a little bit, and that was it. He started out loading coal. That was his first job. He was a hard worker, and he worked his way up to foreman and then to superintendent. It was hard in the beginning for him. The reason he started out so young is that he was the oldest in the family. His father passed away, so he had to do something to take care of the family.

John Spargo, in his 1906 exposé of child labor, *The Bitter Cry of the Children,* graphically described the tasks performed at the coal breaker, "the area outside the mine where coal was graded, mostly by young children." As he writes:

Work in the coal breakers is exceedingly hard and dangerous. Crouched over the chutes, the boys sit hour after hour, picking out the pieces of slate and other refuse from the coal as it rushes past to the washers. From the cramped position they have to assume, most of them become more or less deformed and bent-backed like old men.

While coal breakers were used in the anthracite mines of Pennsylvania, they were not part of the processing of coal in bituminous mines. But other unpleasant jobs existed for child laborers in the rest of Appalachia, as well. As Spargo wrote:

From the breakers the boys graduate to the mine depths, where they become door tenders, switch boys, or mule drivers. Here, far below the surface, work is still more dangerous. At fourteen or fifteen the boys assume the same risks as the men, and are surrounded by the same perils. Nor is it in Pennsylvania only that these conditions exist. In the bituminous mines of West Virginia, boys of nine or ten are frequently employed. I met one little fellow ten years old in Mt. Carbon, W. Va., last year, who was employed as a "trap boy." Think of what it means to be a trap boy at ten years of age. It means to sit alone in a dark mine passage hour after hour, with no human soul near; to see no living creature except the mules as they pass with their loads, or a rat or two seeking to share one's meal; to stand in water or mud that covers the ankles, chilled to the marrow by the cold draughts that rush in when you open the trap door for the mules to pass through; to work for fourteen hours—waiting—opening and shutting a door—then waiting again for sixty cents; to reach the surface when all is wrapped in the mantle of night, and to fall to the earth exhausted and have to be carried away to the nearest "shack" to be revived before it is possible to walk to the farther shack called "home."[15]

Mine work was challenging enough for adults, let alone children. According to Richard Koger, "they worked ten hours a day, six days a week. Sunday was the only day off, and they did that until they got unions, which was in the mid-thirties."

The tunnel is now shored up, and the ceiling has been made much higher, but, he says, "the mine was never over five feet in any place."

"So you'd have to bend over while you were working?"

"Yeah," he said, adding that:

The seam of coal in this mine here was anywhere from two to four feet. If you were working a four-foot seam of coal, you'd have about a five-foot roof; if you were working a two-foot seam of coal, you'd have about a three-foot roof. So in this mine, none of them could ever stand up straight. They were working most of the time on their hands and knees.

And of course in the old days this was all done by hand. They were using picks and shovels, and they had hand drills, so they could drill that coal. In the beginning in 1902 when they started here, they were using black powder for blasting, and of course later on they went to dynamite.

He explained that:

In this mine from 1902 up until 1910 they worked in here with no electricity, so what they used to pull out the coal cars were miniature ponies. They had to use miniature ponies because the roof was so low. Now in some of the other mines which were taller than this, they used mules. The sad thing is they all went blind, and the reason the ponies went blind is because the company kept them corralled inside the mine. The only time they saw daylight was when they would pull a car out and back in, so eventually they would go blind.

Canaries were used to detect the methane gas. The gas is odorless and taste-less. You never know when it's building up, and it's very dangerous. If you've got a lot of methane gas and you have a spark, it could blow the whole mountain up. Now there's a couple of reasons they used canaries, because any bird would have worked because the bird was so sensitive to that gas, so what happens is they would hang these birds from the top—the gas builds up at the top first and works its way down. And once the gas starts building up, what happens is that the bird just faints. That would let the miners know that it was getting dangerous and they had to go out. They had to wait until that gas was gone before they could go back in to work.

After they got electricity, machines replaced the ponies. The machines were very powerful. They're a lot like a locomotive on a train. These things weigh eight tons each, and they would pull up to fifty tons in one trip. They would run on electricity, just like a streetcar.

Another danger for miners was the "third wire" on the ceiling that supplied the electricity. Roger held up a sample and explained: "This is the original wire that came out of this mine here. That's a half-inch copper wire, and it had 720 volts of DC going through it, so if you touched it, you were gone."

When they first got electricity in the mine, a lot of people got electrocuted just by accidentally getting against it. My grandfather always said, "Don't ever touch that third wire!"

Mining is still one of the most dangerous professions. Pauline Slone describes what happened to her daughter's husband Ronnie years ago:

My son-in-law and two of his cousins had this plan that they were going to own a mining company. One went to school for business, one went to school for marketing maybe, and Ronnie was going to do hands-on, learn everything. He was just twenty-one years old.

He went to work that day and he's the kind of person that wants to learn everything. He wasn't even supposed to go back to this certain place to work, but he went because the other man was late or something. He was working with something like an auger. Well, he put some kind of a rag around it and for some reason it started twisting and it pulled his arm off!

When he got better, he decided—he thought he couldn't do much. Well, first of all he bought a coal truck and started hauling coal, and with his coal truck he made $120,000 a year. That was like a ton of money back then.

He did that for a while, maybe one or two years, and then he went back in the mines. He could do anything. He would change tires on that big coal truck. There was nothing that stopped him from doing whatever he wanted to do. He didn't want to give up. He did learn all about the mines, and he was a foreman, I guess one of the best foremen there was around.

Hard, dirty, and dangerous work. And yet, Roger Koger claims the miners loved it. Once there was an explosion in the mine, and his grandfather, now a foreman, was caught in the fire with two other men. He told them to lie down and cover their heads, and the fire passed over them, but not without burning their clothes. Nevertheless, he was back in the mine the next day.

Outsiders came to make their fortunes in operating the mines, as well. Alexander Arthur was one of the future coal barons who arrived in Middlesboro, Kentucky, from Scotland by way of Canada. First he would turn his attention to timber resources in Tennessee, and when that venture failed after disastrous flooding, he turned his hand—unsuccessfully—to the railroad industry.

With the help of backers in England he finally realized his potential with the American Association, Ltd., which was soon joined by other companies, like the Watts Steel and Iron Syndicate, Ltd. and the South Boston Iron Works.

The boom years of 1889 and 90 were good to Middlesboro, "the Magic City," where Arthur saw to its modernizing: railroad access, streetcars, new buildings, parks, schools, a water reservoir, a luxury hotel, and more.

Leaders of industry built mansions that must have resembled today's Cumberland Manor B&B, which was built in 1890. High above the city, on Arthur Heights, residents of the 6,000-square-foot Victorian home could look down from the large brick front porch, relax in the spacious living room with its coffered ceiling, stained glass and leaded windows, or read a book in the paneled library. The elaborate wood work and hand-carved staircase also declared the affluence of the owner.

By 1895, however, the mighty city had lost its magic. With the bust came a large contingent of disappointed investors. The "native population" felt cheated, too. Mostly poor and uneducated, they were "lacking the sophistication to know the value of their land and its resources . . ." Downright fraud was perpetrated, too, including the signing of fraudulent documents by illiterate landowners. Some would find their houses burned down when they refused to sign.[16] Is it any wonder that outsiders are still not trusted?

NOTES

1. Ron Chernow, *Alexander Hamilton*, (New York: Penguin Press, 2005), 478.

2. John Alexander Williams, *Appalachia: A History,* (Chapel Hill: University of North Carolina Press, 2002), 119.

3. A family "heirloom" is a photograph of my great-grandfather Howard's still in a remote area in the woods.

4. Ronald D. Eller, *Miners, Millhands and Mountaineers: Industrialization of the Appalachian South 1880–1930,* (Knoxville: University of Tennessee Press, 1982), 54.

5. Ibid, 57.

6. Williams, 250.

7. Ibid, 221.

8. Althea Webb, "African Americans in Appalachia" www.oxfordaasc.com/public/features/achive/0213/essay.jsp (accessed March 22, 2017).

9. Eller, 169.

10. Ibid, 171.

11. Ibid, 170.

12. Ibid, 171.

13. I remember that my family also had a strong sense of fairness. When a food stand refused to serve a black man, my uncle, next in line, argued with the server and insisted that he wait on the man. My Kentucky-born father, too, exhibited a strong sense of fairness rare for the area where he was working in the deep South. As a road contractor, he insisted on paying the black workers the same as the whites, an unheard practice there. Back in the 1930s there were few schools for black students who hoped to go beyond the eighth grade. My mother's younger sister, who taught in the white school, wanted more for the young black boy she was tutoring privately. She approached the head of the school board to ask if the boy, who had so much to offer, couldn't join the other students at the white high school. She was turned down; the boy would only cease to be content with his lot in life, she was told, and possibly cause trouble.

14. Loretta Lynn, *Coal Miner's Daughter,* (New York: Knopf Doubleday, 2010), 13–14.

15. John Spargo, *The Bitter Cry of Children*, (New York: Macmillan, 1906), 163–65.

16. Ann Dudley Matheney, *The Magic City: Footnotes to the History of Middlesborough, Kentucky, and the Yellow Creek Valley*, (Middlesboro, KY: Bell County Historical Society, 2003) 166.

Chapter Three

Faith of our Fathers

It is faith that best defines the Appalachian character, says Ricky Skaggs. "In Appalachia," he explains, "we draw on the Father, the Son, and the Holy Spirit. We know that there's power in that, we know that there's deliverance in that, we know that there's life in that."

Many a Christian may say, "Give God the glory," but the bluegrass star actually lives his faith. "I love getting to do what I do, because I feel like the spirit of God that's in me can awaken a sleeping thing inside someone, a destiny or a dream or a vision that God put in their heart long before they ever was born . . ."

I met with Ricky before his performance at the Southeast Ohio Indoor Music Festival in the backstage dressing room, more like a small living room, with its comfortable high-backed chairs and end tables. Bass fiddles and mandolins lay around the room.

Wearing a light suede zippered jacket, jeans, and black gloves, he apologized for shaking hands wearing his gloves, but his hands were cold on this chilly March night. He is a big man, with the long white hair of an Old Testament prophet, but the courtly manner of a Southern gentleman. "I'm glad to be part of your book," he tells me.

Because of the many problems in Appalachia today, he says, "If you were to go up there right now, as the world would look at that, they would say, 'Where's your God? Where's your God? This God you pray to, this God you depend on, where is he? Where's he with opioid addiction? Where's he with alcoholics? Where's he [with poverty]?' But our God is our God, and we trust him."

"God is not on our time schedule," he explains. "He's out of our time. Time to him is something for us. He made time for us, and I think he created time so it wouldn't all happen at once! God respects time and understands it, but he comes in and out of our time."

He credits God with his success, especially for his good luck in being born in Kentucky.

> You know, God could have had me born in Brooklyn, but he chose to have me born in Appalachia, and I'm thankful that I'm there because I received things in Appalachia that I could never have received in Brooklyn, that I could never have received anywhere else on the whole planet.
>
> Now, I've been all over the world, and I love different cultures, I love the music, and I appreciate the music everywhere, but there's something about what God put in my heart in Appalachia that has opened doors for me all over the world. They've opened because I *am* from Appalachia and that I haven't changed. I haven't changed my appearance, I haven't changed my name—I mean, "Ricky Skaggs"—does that really sound like a stage name?

With his religion such an important part of his life, it is not surprising that he has made a study of the Great Awakenings, the religious movements of the eighteenth and early nineteenth centuries. He was especially affected by what he learned of the Second Awakening and its Kentucky revivals at the beginning of the nineteenth century. "I've studied it. It's important to me," he says.

There would be challenges, however, to ways of worship in the mountains as the centuries progressed.

RELIGION EVOLVES

At the end of the Civil War, the railroad network that Lincoln had envisioned began to expand throughout the country and into the mountains of Appalachia. Along with the trains came what the mountain people called "railroad religion," brought in by outsiders, which was, in their opinion, too cold and impersonal, too taken up with concerns of this world, rather than the world to come. Educated Yankee ministers read their carefully composed (and boring) sermons to congregations more used to the fiery, spontaneous rhetoric of mountain preachers. And why should Appalachians change their ways? After all, church practices in the mountain areas had served them well for long years.

Originally most of the pioneers were Presbyterian, a sect established by John Knox in Scotland in the late sixteenth century, which was revolutionary for its time. Christians do not need an intermediary, he preached, therefore Catholic saints are unnecessary; Christians can communicate directly with God. Churches were plain and unadorned: no Papist paintings or sculptures on view to distract from hearing the word of God. Presbyterian teaching stressed equality and independence, which would wield a strong influence on a burgeoning republic in later years.

The stern Presbyterian practices of the settlers' original homeland were soon overtaken by those of the less formal Methodist and Baptist churches. And no wonder, when we consider what an early Presbyterian service in America was like, as described by James G. Leyburn, who says that by the standards of today, they were "unconscionably long and tedious":

> In the Presbyterian tradition, the sermon—the expounding of the Word—was the central part of the service. The customary sermon lasted for an hour and a half, and was by no means a simple discourse. From long practice, the congregation knew what to expect of a preacher: if he did not develop his points logically and in order, with a firstly and secondly, and so on until "Finally, my brethren," he could hardly maintain respect. The Bible was read; prayers, sometimes as long as three-quarters of an hour, with the whole congregation standing, were offered extempore; and hymns were sung. . . . There was no musical instrument of any kind, [and] the introduction of a musical instrument was [a] radical innovation, hotly resisted until the nineteenth century.[1]

After the Revolution, Presbyterian churches continued to require educated clergy, which put them at a disadvantage when other churches were less demanding of their preachers. Methodists rushed to take advantage of the opportunities on the frontier, instituting a circuit rider system in which a preacher (like my great-great-great-grandfather the Reverend John Baird) traveled on horseback from church to church. In the face of the need for clergy, education was too time-consuming, as well as expensive. God and experience would provide everything a Methodist preacher needed.

The question of education may still arise. When Randy L., about whom we'll hear more later, left his fundamentalist church to join a more liberal, Episcopal church, he came without the formal education of which most of those in authority boast. Randy tells what happened when he was attending a training session and a well-dressed matron approached him.

> She said, "Why are you here?" I said, "I'm training for a position and this is part of the process." And she said, "No, no, no. Why are *you* here?" And I said, "I'm training for this position, and the church asked me to come up." And she said, "No, no, no, you misunderstand me. Why are *you* here?" And I said, "I don't understand what you're asking me, for some reason. I guess I'm a little confused." She said, "You have no education. The Episcopal church only sends people who are educated. You're not educated." And I said, "Well, that is true. I am not educated. But, you know, I don't believe Peter, James, and John had much education, either!"

No need for education was not the only factor that influenced the growth of Baptist and Methodist churches. The "Great Awakening," an evangelical movement that swept through Protestant Europe and North America in the 1730s and 40s brought a new awareness of personal spiritual salvation that led to their strengthening. This was followed by the Second Great Awakening, whose history so affected Ricky Skaggs, and which emphasized evangelism. This second movement was especially influential in Appalachia; the first camp meeting was held in Kentucky in 1800. Numerous emotional camp meetings and revivals would follow.

Although the Presbyterian church was still a presence, membership in Baptist and Methodist churches soared. While the Baptist church had its roots in England in the early seventeenth century, the first American Baptist church can be credited to Roger Williams in about 1638. Not only did it stress salvation through a personal relationship with God, but also stressed the independence of individual congregations. There would be no need for church hierarchy or government interference.

"Schismatics," those who had broken off from traditionalist churches, sowed the seeds for the Pentecostal movement. Those at schismatic services seemed at times to suffer muscle spasms. A contemporary writer in 1808 referred to the involuntary movements of these dissidents as "the rolling exercise, the jerks and the barks." Here is Richard McNemar's description of the "rolling exercise" that believers underwent:

> The exercise commonly began in the head which would fly backward and forward, and from side to side with a quick jolt. . . . He must necessarily go as he was stimulated whether with a violent dash on the ground and bounce from place to place like a foot-ball [*sic*], or hop around with head, legs and trunk, twitching and jolting in every direction, as if they just inevitably fly asunder. And how such could escape without injury, was no small wonder to spectators.[2]

For those who are unfamiliar with the more emotional aspects of a fundamentalist church service, it can be rather startling, even today.

Angel Asher, a college graduate who works as a paralegal, remembers her childhood with nostalgia. She says,

> I always went to a Pentecostal church, Grandma took me when I was seven. That's what I was raised in, that's what I still go to. I was at a Catholic high school, though, and I was kind of an oddity in religion class. We'd talk about one thing and the teacher would say, 'And what do *you* believe?' so that they could have that comparison.
>
> I would never take anybody from high school to church with me, because I would always think it would scare them, because we had a shoutin', run-the-pews, roll-on-the-ground kind of preacher. That to me was normal, and that's

what I'm used to, but to those who grew up in the Catholic church, it might have scared them a little bit. The stereotype that I found growing up in the Pentecostal church is that "So does that mean that you handle snakes?" And it's not true. . . . Pentecostals do not predominantly handle snakes."

West Virginia native Tim D. would agree that church can be frightening. After his father died while he was still a child and the family moved out of the holler, he says, his mother took him to visit different churches:

So she took me to this one church—Nazarene? Anyway, I was sitting at the end of the aisle, and this guy was doing his preaching, and he came up and grabbed me! He tried to get me up to the front, and I ended up going to the front, but I was crying. Well, a lot of people were crying because they thought I was saved or something. I was crying 'cause I was scared! This guy literally dragged me out of my chair, and I was scared. Needless to say I ended up not going back to that church again. . . .

I often think adults don't realize what they're doing with kids. But in our adult lives, in the military, we've gone to one church and the other. Abundant Life and the Vineyard here . . . When I was overseas, we went to a basically black church, and that was a totally "Hallelujah" different kind of thing. And Abundant Life churches, and people talking in tongues, that scared the heck out of you: "mmm-gobble-gooble-gook-ayeee!"

And I'm like—"O-kaaay . . ."

This "speaking in tongues" is an important part of some fundamentalist services. The sounds that the speaker utters have no relation to his language, and rather are considered the voice of the Holy Ghost. "Appalachian English . . . is therefore the imperfect human way of talking to and about God, while speaking in tongues is the perfect speech of God himself."[3]

Churches like the Tabernacle of the Holy Gospel in Jesus [sic] Name, just outside of Middlesboro, Kentucky, are certainly different from the mainstream. It's one of an estimated 250 churches in the Appalachians that demonstrate their faith by acting out this passage, in Mark 16: 17–18:

And these signs shall follow them that believe: in my name shall they cast out devils; they shall speak with new tongues; They shall take up serpents; And if they drink any deadly thing, it shall not hurt them; they shall lay hands on the sick, and they shall recover.

I'm accompanied by Ann Metheney, author of a masterful book on Middlesboro's history, *The Magic City*. Like me, she's never been in such a church before. Before the service started, I chatted with the people waiting outside the small wooden building. Where in the world would they find the snakes? I wondered. The woods are full of them, I learned.

"What's the thinking behind snake-handling?" I asked Dave, a young man who, like most of the men, was in jeans and a T-shirt, his with the name of a church youth group.

"It's not to test God," he said, as some people claim, but rather "it's to prove the power of God to unbelievers." (This was not the time, I decided, to ask about the previous pastor, the Reverend Jamie Coots, who died of a snakebite he refused to have treated. Instead, I expressed admiration for their strong faith.)

Dave remembers the exact date three years before when he was saved.

"But isn't it against the law to handle snakes?' I wondered.

"God's law is more important than man's law," Dave countered.

I learned, too, that the service might go on for two, even three hours, but I soon found that it was anything but boring.

The church is small, plain, with no decorations at all. There are no stained glass windows, in fact no windows at all, but a simple cross is mounted on the wall behind the podium, and on the front of the pulpit is affixed a sign: "Jesus Made the World." A placard announces that no one under eighteen will be allowed to handle snakes or drink poison, another common practice. It is also forbidden to bring in cameras, cell phones, or any kind of recording device.

Those attending, perhaps forty people, half male and half female, were very friendly. Like all women in the Pentecostal tradition, women here do not cut their hair, most curling it up in a bun, and wear long skirts with their T-shirts. A particularly friendly woman, whose hair is hanging down in tendrils that have escaped their topknot, gives me a big hug. Her accent is strictly Grand Ole Opry, and I almost expect her to say, "How-dee! I'm just so proud to be here!" in a Minnie Pearl voice.

At the beginning of the service, the congregants knelt on the floor to pray. Afterwards, as the congregation followed along with the Bibles placed on the pews, the pastor read the passage from First Corinthians in which Paul described the body as corruptible, but the spirit as incorruptible.

Then other members took the floor. One middle-aged man spoke emotionally against drugs and alcohol, striding rhythmically up and down the aisle. God had told him that one of his two nieces would die, which she did, of a drug overdose, but God saved his other niece from addiction. Satan has taken over the country, he said: mothers becoming prostitutes to support their habit, parents deserting their children and leaving them with grandmothers to raise, parents failing to teach their children the right way.

As a guitar strummed softly in the background, an elderly man in a wheelchair stated that he knew he was dying, but he was not afraid. He would be in glory. A young woman approached the front, knelt and cried as she told her story in hushed tones, and other women knelt with her to offer comfort.

Joyous music accompanied the hymns, played on guitars, drums, a keyboard, and tambourine, the latter, as well as the drums, played by energetic "Minnie," who had her own testimony to share:

On her way home from a revival on treacherous mountain roads, a sudden, ferocious rainstorm threatened to drive her car off the slick road. As lightning streaked across the sky and thunder crashed around her, she prayed. "'Lord,'" she said. "'I've been out doing your good work, and I want you to stop this storm right now' And he did!" The drive home was completed in a soft drizzle.

Bible reading, hymns and sermons on faith took up much of the two-hour service, but, alas, no one was moved by the spirit to take up the snakes, which waited ominously in flat wooden boxes on the stage. At the close of the service, I am hugged again and warmly invited to return.

In spite of the nonappearance of the snakes, it was a lively evening, as well as a moving experience. Videos of this and similar churches are readily available on the Internet. We can watch believers swing the snakes about or wrap them around their bodies.

The snakes are weakened, say animal rights workers, by being underfed, dehydrated and kept in close confinement. Therefore they are less likely to strike than a healthy snake, and their venom is weaker.

Nevertheless, deaths are far from a rare occurrence. Should someone succumb of a snakebite, however, it is not considered a failing; God had willed that this was their time to die.

George Went Hensley is the person most credited for the origin of snake-handling worship in the 1920s. He went up into the mountains, prayed for protection, and then, when a rattlesnake appeared, he was able to handle it without harm. Hensley died of a snake bite in 1955.

The practice is an offshoot of the Pentecostal movement of the early twentieth century, which, in turn, was an offshoot of Methodism, itself an offspring of the Church of England. While the Pentecostal movement actually began elsewhere in 1907, it found a warm welcome in the Uplands area, where, says Richard J. Callahan, "the Holiness and Pentecostal churches were resignified, re-charged, intensified versions of already existing local practices that were consciously engaging with new forces shaping mountain life."[4]

Mountain churches seem less concerned with broader social concerns than their fellow, mainstream Christians, who want to make the world a better place. Local churches have had enough to do to help their own parishioners, who may feel overwhelmed by the economic disasters that have affected their area.

Since personal relations are important in the Appalachian culture, it should come as no surprise that churches which have their roots in the mountains would stress a personal relationship with God and with Jesus, as our savior.

It is God who can give power to the powerless, help to the helpless. The "intense religiosity" of the Scotch-Irish which, according to Robert J. Higgs, "left a strong imprint upon the Appalachian culture," has continued unabated into modern times.[5]

Elmo Garrett was born in 1943 in the same house in which statesman Cordell Hull was born. He has written an account of what religious practices were like when he was growing up in rural Tennessee in the 1950s and how much they were a part of everyone's lives. Churches in the area would often host debates at which individuals, usually preachers, would hold forth on their interpretations of Biblical subjects. People came from miles away, often sitting in truck beds in straight-back chairs, to attend the summer events, which might last two or three hours on one to three or four nights.

It was a sociable, as well as a spiritual event, he says: "There would be more men outside in the churchyard than there would be in the house!" It would certainly have been uncomfortable in a metal-roofed building with no air conditioning. With the windows open, "There were always a multitude of flying bugs around the lights, which would sometimes get in someone's hair." Still everyone looked forward to the next meeting and "regretted when the last night came around."[6]

Loyal Jones of Kentucky's Berea College, who more than anyone can be called the grand old man of Appalachian Studies, gives his take on the matter of religion in his book *Appalachian Values:*

> What [some] outside observers fail to see is that our religion has helped to sustain us and has made life meaningful in grim situations. . . . Life in the mountains until recently did not allow for an optimistic social gospel. Hard work did not always bring a sure reward, and so perhaps some of mountain religion is more fatalistic than elsewhere. The point is to get religion—get saved—and try to keep the faith and endure, hoping for a sure reward in the hereafter.[7]

I met with Loyal at Berea College, near the center for Appalachian studies that bears his name. He is a soft-spoken gentleman, tall, gray-haired, looking much younger than the almost ninety years he claims. As we sat in the lobby of the college's Boone Tavern, we were interrupted frequently by those who wanted to chat, argue politics, or just stop by to say hello.

His book *Faith and Meaning in the Southern Uplands* is a valuable resource. He expounded on the subject:

> My interest in religion was as much as how people find meaning about the inevitable questions: why are we here, what is our purpose, what's going to happen to us? So I did a book on that by interviewing people of the non-mainline denominations primarily, explaining it as much I could in their own way, their

actual words, without interpretation, because all the Ph.D. scholars I know tend to quote the folk and then explain what they were saying!

I wrote about three churches in eastern Kentucky. They were integrated churches, primarily black, but they had white members, and the little home churches and the old Regular Baptist churches, they're predestinarian. And the Primitive Baptists, they're the most Calvinistic. The word "primitive" is used in several denominations, meaning not that they are primitive, underdeveloped people, but going back to the primitive church, the beginnings of the church.

Primitive Baptists were maligned for being the ignorant Baptists because they didn't believe in theological schools; they believed that God elevated your mind, the preacher's mind, and they're completely non-missionary, and I love them for that reason. You feel comfortable among them because they're not going to try to convert you.

The old Primitive Baptists were the first ones to stand up for the integrity of black people in the South . . .

The old Regular Baptists are more continual, and they are my absolutely most favorite Christians in a way. One of the things I used to do was take the new faculty on a tour and take them to unusual things, and they would always welcome us, and they'd say, "This is how we get along in the world." But they were so non-missionary and predestinarian that they'd say, "Well, we don't know for sure that we'll be saved. We have sweet hope in our breasts.". . .

They believe that God will save only a remnant of the fallen. When you're "raptured" off, there'll only be a saving remnant of the human race, and that's pretty dour. Calvinism is a hard religion because you don't know what's to happen to you, and it has nothing to do with your good works or your goodness as a person. It has to do with the will of God and whom he has chosen.

Well, I'm not adopting that, I'm only saying that as people in dealing with one another, they respect you but don't try to convert you, and they don't expect you to try to convert them.

Even when churches preach free will, a strong belief in fatalism exists, whether or not it springs from the Calvinist notion of predestination. Some say that the fatalism of Appalachian religion has been a factor in the lack of motivation among its followers.

The Reverend Tex Sample, professor of Church and Society at Kansas' St. Paul School of Theology, is known for his work among those he calls "hard living people," those who live on the outskirts of society. He explains that "when life is out of control, the assertion that everything is designed according to a divine plan can lead one to a strange, powerful, and ultimate sense of security and safety."[8]

Although not all church members are disadvantaged, it's a message that especially appeals to the poor. Those who feel helpless can achieve power through their religion; they can look for their reward in the hereafter, if not here on earth.

Power for the powerless was the topic of the sermon at a Pentecostal church I attended in a Dayton, Ohio, suburb. Although the parishioners are mostly transplanted Appalachians, it's obvious that this church is financially in better circumstances than the last one I attended. Services are held in a large brick sanctuary, the many cars in the parking lot look in good condition, and the churchgoers appear better dressed than in most mountain churches.

Again, people are extraordinarily friendly. Again, people kneel on the floor for prayers—but here the floor is carpeted. There are no printed programs or hymnals; the congregation knows well what to expect.

The pastor preaches in the familiar cadence of the South, punctuating his sentences with a repeated, "and I say." His emotions, too, lead him to move around the platform, doing a kind of dance, while church members call out "Amen!" or "Yes!" in encouragement.

He reminds us that there is much for which we can be grateful: the polio vaccine, the end of World War II, and freedom, but especially for Jesus' love. We are all sinners, but we can be saved, he said. Even though we are powerless, we can achieve inner power through the Holy Spirit. We are not helpless with the help of Jesus.

Not all churches that appeal to mountain people—or former ones—are so rigid. The Church on the Rock is in a lower-income neighborhood populated by Appalachian immigrants. It's led by the Reverend Linda Williams, who was ordained by the Assemblies of God but who welcomes everyone, regardless of race or sexual orientation, in every kind of dress—"Just so long as they're wearing clothes!" she jokes.

The rows of folding chairs in the simple sanctuary share space with round tables and a station for coffee and pastry. There are no hymnals or prayer books, programs, clerical robes or musical instruments. And yet the congregation heartily joins in singing lyrics that appear on a screen above the pulpit. The Reverend Williams preaches about—not fire and brimstone—but the power of love: God's love for us and our love for one another. She shows a humorous video in which people give various reasons why they don't attend church. "It's full of hypocrites," for example, to which the actor replies, "So there's always room for one more!"

When it comes to salvation, in most mountain churches there's no middle ground. It's a message of "turn or burn," as more liberal clergy say in jest: turn away from evil or you'll burn in hell. You are sinful or saved, and it's an all or nothing thing. Such churches can be very unforgiving for those who don't conform.

Randy L. grew up in a desperately poor urban Appalachian neighborhood. Only his spiritual strength helped him overcome the legacy of an abusive father and the despair of the environment. Twice he was blessed with true spiritual experiences when he was convinced God spoke to him. He describes what happened one winter day.

One morning I went out the door and it had snowed so bad that winter that they had plowed just one lane down the center of the road. I was driving a Ford Pinto wagon, and I lost control. I started spinning around in circles, and ended up on the bridge sideways. I looked out my window and there was a semi coming right at me! I didn't have time to get out. All I could do was just bow my head and say, "Father, I'm yours." And I didn't look, I just kind of held on, and I didn't hear anything. Then I looked this way—and there's no semi there! He's over here. He's on this side of me! No, I saw him there! How in the world? And a voice said, "You're welcome, my child." That's the truth. That really did happen . . .

For twenty-seven years Randy had been a faithful member of his Pentecostal church, going on mission trips to Romania, Mexico and Jamaica, preaching from the altar at home and abroad. But there was one problem. It became harder and harder for him to deny his homosexuality. He felt he was living a lie, and surely God would want him to be his true self.

Then Dennis, his long-time friend and pastor, preached a sermon and said, "You never know who's sitting next to you in the congregation. We have to love all people for who they are and where they are."

"And I thought, 'There you go! Let's talk, Dennis.'"

He laughs ironically, saying, "What he preached was not true! So he kicked me out." For when Randy came out to the congregation, not only did he receive no sympathy, but he was told that he would have to leave his church home. He was possessed by the devil!

Has he been able to forgive those who expelled him?

"They're confused," he says, "That's the way I look at it. They don't know the Word."

As for Randy, he found a new home in a more liberal church, where he has taken an important role among the clergy, working with the homeless and counseling those who are confused about their sexual orientation. And isn't helping others what Christianity should be all about?

Brother Wilson, the pastor of a country church—not Pentecostal—was an important figure in my childhood, for when we visited the grandparents in rural Kentucky, his church was the one we attended. His sermons were colorful and dramatic. It is said that once when he spoke of those sinful drinkers who rolled in the gutter, he demonstrated by rolling on the church floor.

He was a good-hearted man of the cloth, who would visit and pray with my widowed mother whenever he came to the city. But, in looking after the welfare of his flock, in his version of tough love, he was unforgiving: he sincerely wished them a better life, here and in the hereafter, and he would do everything he could to make that happen.

He was especially challenged by my grandfather's brother, whom I'll call Uncle Bill. Uncle Bill was the black sheep of the family, and a disgrace to the community with his wild ways (whatever that meant). On the rare times when Uncle Bill would go to church, Brother Wilson would admonish him that unless he came more often, his future looked bleak.

In the course of time, Uncle Bill went to his reward. As the family gathered in the church for his funeral, instead of the comforting words they expected, this was what Brother Wilson had to say, shaking his finger at the audience: "You people out there in the congregation! Don't you be like Bill Brown. He's going to hell!"

We can scoff at some of the excesses of country churches, but there is an energy, a spirit?—that is palpable, a sense of warmth and loving welcome. For those who have left Appalachia, it offers a touch of home, a meeting place for likeminded people. Sharing the strong emotions of the services makes the congregation feel even closer.

It may be significant that the members of fundamentalist churches are usually not highly educated, and they tend to see things in black and white, good and evil, God and Satan.

President Harry Truman (whose grandparents came from Kentucky) demonstrated this kind of binary thinking. Having never had the opportunity for a college education, he was noted for making quick decisions. The story goes that he complained that he was forever hearing from his legal staff, "on the one hand, this, on the other hand that," to the point that he cried, "I need a one-handed lawyer!"

Universities teach their students to see things in gray and to consider all nuances. Those who leave the mountains for a higher education may face "a disrespect for our values," as Nora Stanger did. She found that among those who pride themselves for their liberal attitudes, "there is a double standard when tolerance is considered for the Appalachian Christian. The Appalachian religion is the basis of our value system," she says. "It provides purpose and meaning in our lives. It gives security and strength during times of confusion and replenishes us when we are exhausted. My request to those in authority in universities and colleges is simply to respect the individual religious choices of your students. Don't intellectualize it. Don't analyze it. Don't ridicule it. Don't minimize it."[9]

In Columbus, Ohio, the Reverend Doctor Lee Anne Reat is the pastor of an Episcopal church that serves a low-income area, and when she hears what seems like intellectual snobbism of more liberal churches, she says:

I kind of bristle, because I have seen the depth of spirituality of people in this neighborhood who would be judged on scales of where they fall in terms of their spirituality as very—almost pre-conventional, if not conventional, and the assumption in faith development literature is that as you are more educated, you will be able to think more complexly and more conceptually, your spirituality will reflect that, and the assumption is that it is in some way higher spirituality than others.

I totally, totally disagree with that. The depth of the spirituality of people who go through the kinds of lives that folks I know have gone through and who are still deep, deep believers . . .

I think one of the differences is in the way the religion has been taught by preachers who communicate a wrathful, vengeful God and that kind of black and white thinking. In our experience with street church, especially, there's basically one sermon: "God loves you. God loves all of us," and I have had people over and over and over again say, "I've never heard that. I've never heard anyone tell me that God loves me. And you tell me that, and that's what makes you different."

Fundamentalist churches are not always about gloom and doom in this life, for members also believe in the possibility of miracles. It was a "miracle" that led Ellen Shelley and her husband to join such a church. Ellen, petite with short curly hair, dressed fashionably but comfortably in jeans, boots, and a pink ruffled scarf over her gray sweater, is Director of Health and Education at Dayton's Life Enrichment Center, which offers numerous services for those in poverty. She has received an "Outreach" award for outstanding performance of her duties. She is not one to be easily fooled, so her experience came as a great surprise:

When I was in high school I had a girlfriend who was wild, as wild as could be, and never went to church or anything like that. But she got married and had her first baby, and he ended up not being able even to sit up. By the time he was a year old, he wasn't walking, and they found out he had cerebral palsy, so they went to all the different doctors and all of that, and they had some therapy going on. They put an article in the paper, her small-town paper, in which she talked about all the people that were helping out.

Then this woman called her, and she said, "You know, God can heal your baby." She said, "Oh, is that right?" And the woman said, "Yeah, God can heal your baby. There's a guy who's going to be in town, and he's an evangelist, just go there. Talk to him. Take your baby."

She had just been to the doctor and she'd gotten shoes fit for the baby, one with one lift higher than the other, because one side of his body wasn't growing at the same speed as the other. So she went to see the evangelist, and she just stood up boldly in front of thousands of people, and she said, "I want you to heal my baby."

He said, "Well, I can't, but God can. So I want you to come back tomorrow night and I want you to fill up the front row here." It was a long row, about fifteen feet, I guess, "and God will heal your baby." She called us and both of us—my husband was a true hippie--and he just said, "OK, why not? That sounds like fun. Let's go."

So we went, and all night we watched the people throw away crutches and all these things that my grandmother talked about—I mean, she used to watch Oral Roberts. She even sent them money.

We thought it must be some kind of trickery, and I thought, "How in the world did he get all these people to act? He'd have to make millions to pay these people to do this." And all night I was just doubting, doubting, doubting. And my friend filled up two rows with people, just by asking them and calling in favors.

Finally at the end of the evening, I thought, "He's never going to call her up. He's never even going to come by or even talk to her. He just tricked her into getting us in here, hoping that we would give money, or whatever.

Then he said, "OK, I asked this lady to come back and bring her baby, and now God's going to give her a miracle." He didn't take anybody else up on stage; he just prayed over them wherever they were standing or whatever. And he took my friend up on the stage, and he sat her down, and he showed everybody the shoes that she had just purchased for a very high price. Her husband went up there with her and he was standing there, and he put the baby on her lap. The preacher showed everybody how one leg was longer than the other. He showed everybody how that was going on, but still, if I didn't know her, I still would have thought it was a trick . . . So he did that, and I thought, "Oh, boy, he's got himself into it now."

Then he prayed over the baby, and he said, "Now, throw those shoes away," and he threw them aside. He had told her to bring a pair of brand new regular shoes for the baby, because he was going to be walking. They put those regular shoes on that baby, put him down on the floor—now, mind you, he hadn't really been even been sitting up very well before this, and he had never stood on his own—and they put those shoes on that baby, and he *ran* across the stage.

I knew the mother, and that changed everything. You know how your perspective is, you think you know everything—so I had to go back over the whole evening and try to figure out—"I guess that *was* real. All those people really *weren't* acting!"

I don't know how many other lives were changed that night, from those people she brought in, because none of them were believers that I know of, but I do know that our lives were changed. My husband and I were just engaged at that point. We were getting married a month later, and as we were driving home, I said, "What do you think just happened?" And he said, "I don't know, but I want to."

Why was I given that gift? I'm not even talking about the miracle of the baby walking. I'm not talking about that miracle. Why was I given that gift? Why were my eyes opened? Why was I allowed to see that? What did he have in mind for me? . . .

The Holy Spirit—God has really been working on me with that Holy Spirit thing lately. Not wanting to speak in tongues, but just listening to the Holy Spirit or waking up each morning and wanting him to be a part of what I do each day.

In a culture in which people value relationships so highly, those with their Lord can be the most important of all.

Paul Theroux, in traveling through the South, described the role of church in the communities he visited, a description that also holds true for farther north:

"A church was more than a church," he wrote. "It was the beating heart— the vitality, the hope—of [the] community. . . . People attended church to find hope, dignity, love, consolation, fellowship, and advice."[10] And so they do in Appalachia.

NOTES

1. James G. Leyburn, *The Scotch-Irish: A Social History*, (Chapel Hill: The University of North Carolina Press, 1962), 289–90.

2. Richard McNemar, *The Kentucky Revival*, (Trumpet Press, 2012 originally published in 1808), 70.

3. Nora Stanger, *Diamonds in the Dew: An Appalachian Experience*, (Bloomington, IN: 1st Books, 2003), 54.

4. Anita Puckett, "Language and Power," *Talking Appalachian,* Amy D. Clark and Nancy M. Hayward, Eds., (Lexington, KY: University of Kentucky Press, 2013), 157.

5. Richard J. Callahan, "The Work of Class in Southern Religion," *The Journal of Southern Religion* (Vol. 13 (2011): http://jsr.fsu.edu//issues/vol13/Callahan.html, 6.

6. Robert J. Higgs, Introduction and Ed., "Chapter 1: Family and Community," *Appalachia Inside Out*, Vol. 1: Conflict and Change, (Knoxville, TN: University of Tennessee Press, 1995), 349.

7. Elmo Garrett, *Memories of rural life in the 1950s.* Unpublished memoir.

8. Loyal Jones, *Appalachian Values,* (Ashland, KY: The Jesse Stuart Foundation, 1994), 46.

9. Tex Sample, *Hard Living People & Mainstream Christians*, (Nashville, TN: Abington Press, 1992), 67.

10. Paul Theroux, *Deep South*, (New York: Houghton Mifflin Harcourt, 2015), 3.

Chapter Four

Westward with Music

In Salem, Massachusetts, tourists crowd the witch museum, the pirate museum, the psychic center, the wax museum. Busy pedestrian Essex Street is lined with shops that sell witches' capes and pointed hats to fit all ages: babies and children, even dogs! Just a short distance away, though, there's a quiet and somber place, one that calls for a quite different mood from the festivity of Salem's tourist attractions.

Near the entrance to the Old Burying Point cemetery stands the Salem Witch Trials Memorial, dedicated by Elie Wiesel, who wrote: "Only if we remember, will we be worthy of redemption." Twenty stone benches display the names of each of those executed in the hysteria of 1692. Many visitors leave flowers or notes to honor those innocent victims.

A few feet away, the cemetery is filled with ancient tombstones, whose death heads, angels' wings, funeral urns and weeping willows are almost obliterated with age. Among the fading markers, there's a different, much newer headstone that has replaced the original wooden cross. A ship in full sail is depicted above the inscription: "William Cash, Born 1625, Fife, Scotland; Died 1690, Salem, Mass.; Master Mariner. Captain & Master of Brigantine 'Good Intent.'"

Sometimes visitors leave flowers or notes here, too, and so do I. "Thank you, Captain," I write, "for making me an American. My great-grandmother was a Cash," I explain—just in case . . .

The Cash family must be typical of so many that left Britain to start over in America. Genealogists tell us that Captain William, after bringing shiploads of immigrants from his native Scotland to the new land, decided that he, too, would emigrate. Later he would bring his nephew, also named William, to America.

47

Captain Cash convinced his namesake that Massachusetts was no place for an ambitious young man. Virginia, which then included Kentucky and, of course, West Virginia, was the land of opportunity, and so young William headed to its greener pastures.

Soon the Cash family, in accord with the Biblical injunction to go forth and multiply, would spread throughout the country. Like many families of the day, they would have eight, nine, even ten or more children, and almost all would live until adulthood.

Like many of the people whom Colin Woodard calls "borderlanders" in his book *American Nations*,[1] some would take the Great Wagon Road that led from Pennsylvania down through Maryland and through the Shenandoah Valley to reach the Carolinas. Branching off the Great Wagon Road in western Virginia, the Wilderness Trail, which was marked by Daniel Boone in 1775, led through the Cumberland Gap to Kentucky and the Ohio River. After the Revolution and defeat of the region's Cherokee and Shawnee tribes, between 200,000 and 300,000 people would take this route.

Others, like my Brown forebears, would build rafts and float them down the Ohio River to reach Kentucky. Men who were not steering rode along the banks on horseback, armed in case of Indian attack. The growth in population led to Kentucky's becoming a state in 1792.

By the fourth generation, Cash descendants were among those who had moved into Kentucky, and by the sixth, Cashes had headed into Missouri and Oklahoma, Texas and Tennessee, North Carolina, Alabama, and New Mexico.

Cash men fought in the Revolutionary War, the Civil War, and all the other wars involving the country. One John Cash was a great admirer of Pancho Villa and helped supply the Mexican revolutionary with guns. At the same time, unknown to John Cash, his distant cousin Ray, the singer Johnny Cash's father, was serving on the border under General Pershing, tracking Pancho Villa in order to punish him for an incursion that claimed American lives.

To look at the Cash family history is to look at the history of America. Some would prosper; others would not. My great-grandmother Mary Elizabeth Cash and her husband Isaac Carlton did well enough to send their daughter, my grandmother, to "college," actually more like a finishing school, and to let their son leave the farm to seek gold in Alaska—which he didn't find.

I can recall as a child being dragged on a hot, dusty day to a Cash family reunion at a country church in Larue County, Kentucky. Although I found it incredibly boring, as a ten-year-old would do, I did sense that there was a certain pride in being a Cash.

Not all the numerous branches of the Cash clan did as well as those in Kentucky. Johnny Cash's great-grandfather, whose forebears had left Virginia for Georgia, lost his plantation to Sherman's troops in the Civil War. The family then left Georgia to homestead in Arkansas, farming and taking whatever work they could find when times were tough.

Charlie Louvin, a radio artist who appeared in a show in Dyess, Arkansas, remembers the young teenage Cash he encountered as "a poor kid . . . Overalls. No shirt."[2] As Johnny would say later, "Daddy had a lot, but he didn't have money." It was a hard life working in the fields and hoeing cotton, but one thing the family did have was music.[3]

From the first, the Cash family would have been familiar with the songs that Captain William had heard back in Scotland, like "Barbary Allen" or "Pretty Polly." From 1916 to 1918, Englishman Cecil Sharp, among other "songcatchers," traveled throughout Appalachia transcribing the many ballads from the old country that he felt had been preserved in mountain isolation.

There were some changes to the music in America, though. American banjo player and historian Debby McClatchy notes that "most of the one hundred or so variations of the three hundred classic ballads found in America are to do with sexual struggles from the female standpoint. . . . One is less likely to find Scottish ballads of rape and dominance, or those with men as heroes. A large percentage, perhaps almost half, of the American variations tend to be about pregnant women murdered by their boyfriends."[4]

American ballads would also be changed from the traditional ones by American churches, whose puritanical influence cleaned up the language; "repentance and doom supplanted sinful behavior."[5]

Later, up until the end of the nineteenth century, broadsheet ballads sold on the street would differ from the original British themes of love affairs and focus on manly occupations: "logging, ranching, and mining, as well as sensational topics like disasters, murder, and tragedies."[6]

Early Scotch-Irish immigrants brought the fiddle with them and the kind of dancing they had known back in Northern Ireland and Scotland. Today it exists in the form of clogging. To the basic string band of banjo and fiddle of country music, there would be added fretted dulcimer, the mandolin, guitar and autoharp, and later bass, dobro, steel guitar and drums, along with different ways of playing the instruments.

Ricky Skaggs was surprised by how much was familiar on his first trip to Ireland, he tells me:

I know the first time I ever went to Dublin, I went to this pickin', they call it a "ceili". . . . After our show was finished, we went to this place—and I tell people that when I walked in, I thought I'd died and gone to eastern Kentucky. It was so much the same—the mannerisms, the way that they were with each other, the way that mothers were making sandwiches, and giving, and making sure that people had something to eat and that someone had tea or coffee or whatever, you know. . . .

And the music—that was the thing that blew my mind!—how much of the music I understood and that I knew, but it was by different names. They might have changed the name of the thing after it came to America, you know, but how much of the music that I recognized! It was a language that I could understand, you know. It was a wonderful thing. So I know that there's something about DNA, and I know there's something about our history, where we came from that is still in there.

I mean, why was *Riverdance* such an explosion in America? It was because of the DNA of our Irish and Scottish ancestors that helped to build this country, how that just thundered and woke something up in us that had lain dormant for all these years. That's why music is so important to me. . . .

The dulcimer, however, now a feature in every handicraft shop in Appalachia, was not brought from Britain, I was disappointed to know. I loved to imagine listening to its sweet sounds among the Irish mists—but, no, it was a German import, originally called the *scheitholt*. Scotch-Irish settlers apparently encountered it along the Great Wagon and Wilderness Roads.

In spite of the low numbers of African Americans in Appalachia, compared to the Scotch-Irish, black Americans made major contributions to its music. What would bluegrass music be without the banjo? By the late eighteenth century this African import had joined the traditional fiddles as a necessary part of the string group, later to be joined by the guitar, mandolin, and bass in the twentieth century.

"Early country music unquestionably owed a great debt to black cultural traditions and imitations of black cultural traditions," says historian Jocelyn Neal, including the popular black-face minstrel shows, but black and white performers could rarely associate or perform together because of segregation.[7] In spite of Sam Morgan's assertion that there was little racial prejudice in the mountains, those in other areas felt its sting. Black and white musicians played to separate audiences, and country music had a "deep association with whiteness."[8] As late as the 1960s, because African-American artist Charley Pride's country fan base was primarily white, his manager did not distribute his photograph "for the first two years of his career."[9]

Still, on a personal level there could be close interracial relationships, as both poor whites and blacks had much in common; sometimes, says Neal, "music was the binding force."[10] As black journalist LZ Granderson says, "'I know full well the world many country artists sing about: the watering holes, eating fried chicken, going to church, God, war. When [performer] Rodney Atkins sings, "these are my people," I think: "yes they are."[11]

The kind of music that was played at community get-togethers broke into the national scene with the advent of radio. Bristol, Tennessee, calls itself the "birthplace of country music," but a more apt name would be the place where the "Big Bang" of the genre took place, for there had been mountain music performances before.

In the summer of 1927 the Victor Talking Machine Company held sessions to record musicians in the area, including Jimmie Rodgers and the renowned Carter Family. The Victor company's Ralph Peer knew a good thing when he saw it. Soon, under Peer's direction, what early on was called "hillbilly music" was reaching into every home. In addition to Jimmie Rodgers and the Carter Family, artists like Charlie Poole and Fiddlin' John Carson went out over the airwaves.

Radio Bristol is still on the air, now as part of the Birthplace of Country Music Museum, a gem of a little museum and a Smithsonian affiliate. (The telephone number, appropriately, is 573–*1927*.) There I met with producer Kris Truelsen in his crowded office, where festival posters lined the walls and where two other staff members were hard at work at their computers.

Kris, blue-eyed and mustached, was wearing the kind of flat cap popular in the 1920s. His string band, Bill and the Belles, reflects the music of that time, as well as the diversity that country music represents, as their website informs us. Kris not only sings but plays a mean guitar.

The museum is filled with twenty-first century technology to take us back to those early days of radio. Surrounded by sound, you can choose which artist you want to hear, try your hand at achieving new sounds at the mixing stations or perform yourself at the sing-along station. Among other experiences, you can listen to John Carter Cash, the son of June Carter and Johnny Cash, narrate a video about his grandmother, Maybelle Carter, and the famous family she headed.

The Carter family, even though their own home life was not without its problems, was noted for the wholesome image it projected, one of home, family, and religion. Church music was an important part of their repertoire.

Religious music prevailed among what was heard in Appalachia, which is not surprising, given the importance of faith in people's lives. Here, too, there is strong evidence of African-American influence. According to Debby McClatchy, "There were three types of religious music: ballads, hymns, and revival spiritual songs. The latter directly arose out of the call and response of the African song tradition. These were popularized among the white inhabitants after the revival circuit started in Kentucky in 1800."[12]

Bill Monroe, known as the father of bluegrass, acknowledged the influence of black blues guitarist Arnold Shultz on his musical style. In the mid-1940s, Monroe's Blue Grass Boys included fiddler Chubby Wise and bassist Cedric Rainwater, along with Earl Scruggs and Lester Flatt, who would later become famous in their own right.

"Like jazz, bluegrass tunes are arranged around a lead (head) instrument, with other instruments performing breakout melody solos (lead)," Ritchie and

Orr explain in their book *Wayfaring Strangers*.[13] Bluegrass is noted for the "high lonesome" sound of its vocals, for its up-tempo, and for the traditionally acoustic string instruments: guitar, banjo, mandolin, stand-up bass and fiddle.

I got a quick tutorial on bluegrass, the crown jewel of country music, from the reigning prince, Ricky Skaggs, whose family, like the Cashes, can trace its lineage back to frontier times. Henry Skaggs and his brothers were some of the first white people to enter the Cumberland Gap region and what is now Kentucky, as recorded by Daniel Boone's fellow explorer Dr. Thomas Walker. Ricky explains that it's the sound of the banjo

That distinguishes bluegrass music from any other kind of music . . . When Earl Scruggs came and joined Bill Monroe's band in 1945, December of 1945, that's when all of the fiddles fit in the cog and they all then worked together as a unit, because Mr. Monroe was a great mandolin player, and Lester Flatt was a great lead singer, played rhythm and guitar and sang with Mr. Monroe. Had Chubby Wise on the fiddle. He was already established there, and they had a bass player. They had a banjo player named "Stringbean," David Akeman—he was another Kentuckian—but he played a more old-style that had been played for years.

But when Earl Scruggs came, he had this rhythm in his playing in his right hand, when he added the third finger. It wasn't his invention necessarily but he perfected it. It came out of North Carolina, around Shelby, where he was born and raised. There were two or three older guys over there that were playing, a guy named Snuffy Jenkins, and Smith Hammett, but there were another couple of guys over there that were playing that style of that three-fingered roll. Snuffy Jenkins was an amazing banjo player. He was much older than Earl, but Earl listened to his playing, and I think Earl had been practicing, trying to find that third finger, and then it finally, you know, kind of fell in as he was playing. But he was young enough and innovative enough that he took that and really perfected that and created a whole new vocabulary of banjo rolls, banjo styles, forward, reverse, all kinds of different things.

Snuffy Jenkins did comedy. He was on the radio over there and had records out and things like that, but he was a very accomplished banjo player. So that sound came into fullness in 1946—December of '45. But '46 was that first year that they went to Chicago and did those historic recordings, so really it was kind of birthed in '45, in December, but the baby started to grow in '46, and '47, the two years when they were building those fans.

"I know the banjo came from Africa. Where did the mandolin come from?" I ask.

I think probably Italy. It went through a lot of transformations over the years. The Gibson Company started making mandolins that were not the big "belly-style" mandolins--they had styles in Italy that you'd have to play out here [he demonstrates] because they had this oval back. They're beautifully made, but they're as hard as heck to hold onto, especially for a fat boy. You couldn't hold them! They just rolled everywhere, but Gibson started making a flatter-back mandolin, and then there were mandolin orchestras, which were very much for the hierarchy, so to speak.

Of course the industrial revolution was going on in the teens and twenties and all of that, and so they had mandolin orchestras that were like violin orchestras but they were written for mandolin, so they made mandolins, mandolas, mandocellos, just like they make violins, violas, and cellos. So that was music of the teens, twenties and thirties, and then they started to dissipate a bit. But those mandolins that were made in the twenties are the ones that we all kind of love the sound of. . . . You know, Bill Monroe was walking down the street in Miami, Florida, and he found a mandolin that was made in 1923, during that heyday of Gibson's finest mandolins. He looked in the window of a barber shop and there was this mandolin for sale. It was already twenty or twenty-one years old at the time he bought it, but it was in mint condition, just beautiful. So he bought it because it had a little bit longer-scale neck than what he was playing, and that became his partner in music for the rest of his life. He played that particular mandolin, his songwriting increased, his mandolin playing increased, and it inspired him to be the player that he was. So it's funny how one instrument can just inspire you so much—

"What's your instrument then?"

Well, mandolin, that was my first instrument. I mean as much guitar and banjo and fiddle as I play, those are great. I love them, but mandolin was my first instrument so it's my first love, and I think that's the one that I—of course I'm playing it more now that I'm back to playing bluegrass fulltime. I've got mandolin players in my band that I think are a lot better than I am, but they're stuck with me because I rent the bus!

It was the mandolin that started Ricky on his long and successful career, when at age six he first appeared on stage with Bill Monroe in the small town of Martha, Kentucky: "That night really changed my life, you know." Coincidentally, when researching his family background, he discovered that the town had been named for his eighth great-grandmother, Martha Skaggs, a full-blooded Cherokee: "such a revelation!"

As decades passed and the population grew exponentially, Appalachians sought their fortunes in new areas. Kentucky, north-central Tennessee and southwestern Illinois were colonized by 1800. Thirty years later, says Colin Woodard, "borderlanders" were in control of northern Alabama, most of Tennessee, the Ozarks of Arkansas, and the Mississippi Valley of southern Illinois and Missouri. By 1850 they were moving into Texas, bringing along their Appalachian accents.[14] Later oil booms in Oklahoma and Texas and logging in the Far West would draw more Appalachians to those areas, as in the case of a large number of Cash family members who headed for Texas.

Wherever they went, the newcomers would carry their music with them, and it would mutate as it went. In her book *Country Music: A Cultural and Stylistic History,* Jocelyn R. Neal makes a valiant effort to categorize country music. She comes up with 24 permutations, and that doesn't even include Cajun country![15]

In the Southwest it would be influenced by the music of Mexico and cowboy songs, and, in Texas, by the polkas so popular with the large German community there, Kris Truelsen tells me.

The Great Depression and the Dust Bowl of the 1930s caused many to seek a better life in California, especially those who came from drought-stricken areas like Oklahoma and parts of Colorado, Kansas, and Texas. Then in the forties it was wartime industries that attracted young workers to the Southwest and California, where they were drawn to the many dance halls and their honky-tonk music. Ernest Tubb, Hank Williams and Kitty Wells were best known in this field. From honky-tonk there arose in California the "Bakersfield sound" with its "chug-a-chug" rhythm and use of electric guitar and bass, which was popularized by Buck Owens and Merle Haggard.

When Appalachians headed for the big cities of the North in the fifties, businesses that offered music were quick to take advantage of the new audiences.

Taverns regularly booked bands advertised as being 'hillbilly' in the [Chicago area] *Edgewater-Uptown News*. Tex Carter's Lounge advertised as the "New Hillbilly Heaven" booked Russell Morris billed as "The Hillbilly's Friend." Groups like The Westernaires was also noted for its hillbilly and mountain music with groups like The Alabama Jukeboxes in these taverns were filled with western and hillbilly music. . . . By 1965, over 50 percent of the records sold in Chicago were country western, and at least one radio station had switched to a country format.[16]

Johnny Cash was there, performing at the long-closed Rivoli Theatre, which had reopened as a country dance hall, along with Buck Owens and Ray Price. The lyrics of such performers had special meaning for homesick migrants.

Meanwhile, back in the mountains, country music was still being performed, and Nashville's Grand Ole Opry was the pinnacle for any star wannabe. Influenced by mainstream pop in the early 1960s, the "Nashville Sound" was smoother and more sophisticated, the staging more glitzy and sophisticated than what had come before. Jim Reeves, Patsy Cline and Eddy Arnold rose to fame.

Still, in order to be considered country music, it had to have some connection to previous incarnations; fans rebelled if it got too far from tradition. So in the late sixties and early seventies, what's known as "classic country," which blends Nashville Sound with Bakersfield, honky-tonk, and shades of bluegrass, prevailed. Dolly Parton, the Oak Ridge Boys, Kenny Rogers, Loretta Lynn, and Tammy Wynette were among the stars.

The seventies also saw the emergence of Southern rock, another kind of "country" music, while the decade also gave rise to the "Outlaw" movement, when artists gained independence from Nashville's control. Musicians like Waylon Jennings, Willie Nelson, and former Rhodes scholar Kris Kristofferson, as music expert Michael Furmanovsky tells me, "grew their hair long, grew beards, and smoked pot" in order to appeal to the new hippie, or counterculture audience.

The very popular Johnny Cash, however, can't be pigeonholed. His long career covered a vast range: rockabilly, outlaw, gospel. . . . To make classification even more difficult, artists would wander in and out of the pop music field, too.

When the movie *Urban Cowboy* came out in 1980, starring John Travolta, it brought about new interest in country music, and especially in the kind of dancing shown in the film. In 2000, *O Brother, Where Art Thou,* loosely based on Homer's *Odyssey*, brought about a revival of interest in traditional country music, a "roots revival."

Country music did not exist in a vacuum isolated from the rest of the country. With 9/11 came an emphasis on patriotism, religious faith, and family. An economic downturn brings an emphasis on the plight of those who work hard for a living.

With all the variety, we may wonder just how to define country music. Webster's dictionary keeps it simple: it's "a form of popular music which derives from the rural folk music of the southeastern and southwestern U.S., characterized by string-band instrumentation."[17] But that doesn't include the storytelling character, or how it relates to everyday life, or how the artists differentiate the music from other genres through: "the use of Southern vocal accents, verbal interjections, and particular techniques of playing their instruments," that Neal mentions. She adds that "its underlying philosophy" is based on "Protestant, evangelical theology."[18]

Country music fans also have a unique relationship with the artists, whom they think of as one of their own. Loretta Lynn writes of the closeness she feels toward her fans, and how she credits them with much of her success. She shows her appreciation by hosting a dinner at a hotel for her fan club presidents, of which there are many, at the annual Fan Fair convention. It's a time when she moves out of her house and into a motel, because the fans "just pop into the kitchen while we're sitting around."[19] Can you imagine that happening with, say, Frank Sinatra?

We can wonder why country music is as popular as it is. In America's far-flung mines, logging camps, and industrial cities, those transplanted from the hills would welcome this touch of home. The many ballads reflected the lives of these working-class people, especially the honky-tonk songs, which so often speak of loneliness in the big city.

The Reverend Lee Ann Reat, an Episcopal priest in a Columbus inner suburb with many Appalachian transplants, wonders about its popularity. She's a fan herself, claiming that she has "a lot of that Appalachian culture embedded in me," thanks to her southern Ohio roots. She loves to travel to the mountains of southern Appalachia, to North Carolina and Georgia, where "they've really held on to the dance, the music, the religion of the mountains . . ."

She looks to the sociologist Reverend Tex Sample for explanations, since, she says, he has written several books on "hard-living people, and how the music reflects the lives of people and their hardships. Country music is based on the life today: hardworking people that live on the margins, that live tough lives, and the music reflects that. I think that that really is perhaps a way of coping in a very positive way, if we can put it out there, we can objectify it in some way . . ."

Whatever the reason, country music is now popular throughout America and beyond. Australia has its own country music tradition, with a similar background of cowboys, blue-collar workers, and wide-open spaces. Country music festivals are held every year in France, the Czech Republic and Scandinavia, and there is an enthusiastic following in Japan.

At Japan's Kyoto Opry and the city's Honky Tonk bar and restaurant, you can hear such stars as Tex Nakashima, the Nashville Cats, or Shino & Beans, some wearing the traditional cowboy hats and boots. Over fifty country music festivals are held every year in that country.

Why is it, I wondered, that our music is so popular there? I posed this question to Ricky Skaggs, whose concerts have drawn huge crowds in Japan. "The Japanese have been infatuated since the reconstruction that we helped them with after World War II," he replied.

As hard as that may have been for the elder ones, I think, the young children grew up thinking good things about America, how we were there and we helped them rebuild and all that. But then that generation had children, and then in the fifties and sixties with rock and roll, everything American—Coca Cola, everything about America, hot rods, guitars, music, all of that . . .

One of the things that they have loved about it, I think, is just the sounds of country music, you know, the harmonies, the fiddles, and all that stuff. They were very much impressed by those sounds. And there's an instrument that they play, it's a native instrument that sounds so much like a banjo when it's struck. I'm trying to think of the name—"the shamisen"?—and it's got three or four strings on it and it's got a long neck. They play it with something almost like a pick, some sort of thing, and it has the sound of a banjo.

Michael Furmanovsky is an unlikely expert on American country music in Japan. Having been born in Zimbabwe of Lithuanian Jewish heritage, he grew up in England, has lived in America, and now teaches at Kyoto's Ryukoku University.

Before I met with Michael in the lobby of Kyoto's New Miyako Hotel, he told me I would recognize him by his brown clothes and his "brown hair with some gray." He has been fascinated with American music since he first heard Emmylou Harris in England in 1976: "a life-changing moment," he says.

Later, over tempura at a restaurant in one of the city's ubiquitous shopping centers, he explained why American music became such an item in Japanese culture.

He, like Ricky Skaggs, credited its popularity to the post-war period, when all things American were positive: "The Japanese wanted American baseball, they wanted American movies, they wanted American music." He has written how the adoption of American culture was encouraged by the Occupation as a way to further democratize the population.[20]

In addition, many of the occupying forces were from the South, and, like other Appalachian transplants, they longed for the music of home. The Japanese were happy to oblige. The fifties were the heyday of country music popularity in Japan.

A stream of American music has continued to reach Japan's shores, although, in much the same way that its genres were affected as it moved to other areas, it has become more suited to Japanese tastes.

Japanese pop music of all kinds reflects the powerful influence of Misa Watanabe, who controls Japanese music trends with an iron fist. Now in her late eighties, this "living national treasure," runs Watanabe Productions, aka "Nabepro," one of Japan's two major talent agencies.

In 1961, when country music began to be replaced by Elvis Presley-like rockabilly, she arranged a rockabilly festival that incurred the wrath of parents and the organizations like the PTA, who feared such music would steer Japanese youth into delinquency. The result? Great publicity for Watanabe's business.

When the Beatles pushed Elvis aside, Watanabe formed Beatles-lookalike groups, "made them cuter and sweeter," and taught them to sing in Japanese, as well as English. Lyrics sung in Japanese were preferred by the uneducated, while the more affluent and better educated preferred the real thing. In Japan, says Michael, all music is tied to generations, much as it is in America, and also to socio-economics.

The next generation—those "long-haired, pot-smoking hippies"—sought the authenticity of British and American rock. "You're just an imitation," was their reaction to Watanabe's would-be idols and their "plastic, not authentic" music. Country music, on the other hand, was out of date, "watered down," until the genre's "outlaws" appeared, like Willie Nelson and Waylon Jennings. They countered the Nashville image of the mid-sixties'—"fake" glitzy and "de-mountainized"—with a tough one of their own. Now there was "Americana:" a country/folk/rock style.

Bluegrass came late to Japan, and again, much as in America, it has also attracted the well-educated and affluent: "professors, scientists, and the like, mostly retired people" who get together every week to play. But there's one difference in Japan: amateur groups keep a very narrow focus. If they play Fabulous Four songs, that is all they ever play. Or if it's the Beatles they cover, they won't consider Led Zeppelin, the Rolling Stones, or any other group, says Michael.

If Mrs. Watenabe has one failing in her long career, he adds, it has been her "lack of sensibility" to the R&B and soul music that came out of the South or from Chicago, like that of Ray Charles and Otis Redding. To the music industry's detriment, she has been unable to incorporate into Japanese pop those African-American elements that have so enriched American pop music, as well as country. It's a thesis he'll be exploring and writing about soon.

No longer as popular as it was in the fifties, Western country music still has its dedicated fans. Thousands of devotees, many dressed as cowboys, attend the Country Gold Music Festivals in Kumamoto organized by Japan's own cowboy star Charlie Nagatani.

Johnny Cash also performed before large audiences in Japan, but it was his visits to Scotland in the 1970s that he found most meaningful.

According to a story in *The Guardian*, in the late 1970s Cash was returning to the States and found that his seatmate was Major Michael Crichton-Stuart, the "hereditary keeper of Falkland Palace in the Kingdom of Fife on the east side of Scotland." When the singer mentioned that he had heard that his ancestors came from Scotland, Crichton-Stuart confirmed that there were places with the Cash name in Fife.

This led to Johnny's meeting with a genealogist, who told him of the Cash clan's twelfth-century origins in the Strathmiglo area of Fife, traced back the generations to the niece of Malcolm IV, and spoke of Capt. William Cash's emigration to America.

For Johnny Cash, it was an almost spiritual connection. He would visit Scotland at least three more times, and after his death, his daughter Rosanne would continue the connection, making frequent visits to Fife.

According to Rosanne Cash, "'Going further back into our Celtic past made [my father] realise that this was where he derived his tone of voice, the mournful quality of his music, and it was that sense of place and time that was passed on to him and then on to me.'"[21]

And so the story of the Cash family has come full circle.

NOTES

1. Colin Woodard, *American Nations*, (New York: Viking, 2011)

2. Nicholas Dawidoff, *In the Country of Country,* (New York: Pantheon/Random House, 1997), 141.

3. Johnny Cash with Patrick Carr, *Cash: The Autobiography*, (San Francisco: HarperSanFrancisco, 1997), 4.

4. Debby McClatchy, "Appalachian Traditional Music: A Short History," http://www.mustrad.org.uk/articles/appalch.htm. (accessed February 18, 2018).

5. Ibid., 3.

6. Ibid.

7. Jocelyn R. Neal, *Country Music: A Cultural and Stylistic History,* (Oxford: Oxford University Press, 2013), 60.

8. Ibid.

9. Ibid., 267.

10. Ibid., 60.

11. Ibid., 467.

12. Ibid., 4.

13. Fiona Ritchie and Doug Orr, *Wayfaring Strangers*, (Chapel Hill: University of North Carolina Press, 2014), 268.

14. Woodard, 189–90.

15. Neal, Jocelyn R. *Country Music: A Cultural and Stylistic History*, (Oxford: Oxford University Press, 2013), xxii.

16. Roger Guy, *From Diversity to Unity*, (Lanham, MD: Lexington Books, 2007), 73.

17. *Webster's New World Dictionary*, 3rd ed., s.v. "country music."

18. Neal, xxi.

19. Loretta Lynn with George Vecsey, *Coal Miner's Daughter*, (New York: Random House, 1976), 87.

20. Michael Furmanovsky, "American Country Music in Japan: Lost Piece in the Popular Music History," *Popular Music and Society,* July 2008.

21. Sarfraz Manzoor, "Scottish roots of Johnny Cash, the man in black tartan," *The Guardian,* 6 February 2010.

Chapter Five

The Twentieth Century

King Coal, Exiles, and the Greatest Generation

When there was a bust, like that of the 1890s, surely a boom would follow, as it did in the early twentieth century. With World War I looming on the horizon, miners' wages rose to the highest levels ever: in 1900 in the seventy-two mines in the Middlesboro, Kentucky, area, miners could make as much as $70 a month or more. To put this in perspective, to rent a company house cost $1.00 to $7.00 a month, medical care was $1.00 a month, and fuel, $.50 a month.[1]

World War I brought unprecedented growth in coal mining. Ronald Eller reports how the boom affected eastern Kentucky: in 1916 there were sixteen mines in Floyd County; in 1920 there were sixty-two, while the number of mines in Pike County went from eight to forty-five. In half a dozen counties in the region, most of the population was employed by the mines.[2]

As the demand for coal grew higher, so did the demand for workers. Large numbers of European immigrants and African Americans from the deep South joined with Appalachian natives, reaching a total of 700,000 or more miners working in nearly 12,000 mines.

But a post-war bust would follow, when Europe could once again produce its own coal. The Great Depression came early to the mountains; coal production fell sharply after 1927. What is more, the introduction of machines to replace human labor would foreshadow the even greater mechanization of the forties and fifties that would lead so many to leave their mountain homes.

These were the decades of the "mine wars," when unionists and mine operators violently clashed in virtual battles with rifles, pistols, machine guns—even bombs. The United Mine Workers of America (UMWA) by 1900 was one of the most successful unions in the country, with coal miners recruited from Pennsylvania to Illinois—but not in West Virginia. It was in that state that "between 1890 and 1912, miners . . . suffered the highest death rate in America."[3]

The state was fertile ground for unionization, and the district UMWA leader, Frank Keeney, encouraged by an aging Mary Harris "Mother" Jones, stepped up to the plate. In January 1920, bushy-browed, scowling John L. Lewis, the new head of the union, would seek to organize every mine in southern West Virginia. Keeney aimed to crack the hardest nuts: Mingo, McDowell, and Logan Counties.

A few months later a group of company detectives attempted to evict strikers near the town of Matewan. Following a confrontation with the pro-union chief of police, Sid Hatfield, a shoot-out erupted in which Matewan's mayor, two townspeople and seven detectives died. The "Matewan Massacre" fired up more miners to join the union; Hatfield was considered a hero.

When Hatfield was murdered by mine guards in 1921, thousands of miners gathered at the state capitol, ready to fight for vengeance and their rights in Mingo County. Logan County Sheriff Don Chafin, in the pockets of the coal operators, assembled an army of 3,000 men, and the "Battle of Blair Mountain" ensued. When the U.S. Army was called in, the miners who were arrested, many of whom were World War I vets, felt betrayed. Many were charged with murder and treason, including Frank Keeney, but eventually all but one was acquitted.

Finally, under New Deal legislation, private police forces were outlawed, and the rights of miners to form a union were recognized in 1935.

For Loyal Jones, the revered educator from Berea College who was born in 1928, the unions were a personal matter: "My brothers all went to the cotton mills," he says. "I was the youngest, and my oldest brother was twenty-four years older than I was, but he went to the cotton mills and was involved in the strike of 1929."

He describes the turbulent period of the 1920's:

The Communists came in after the United Mine Workers sort of abandoned eastern Kentucky and tried to do the same thing here. They were stupid enough to think that they could get all their values installed, meaning getting rid of Jesus and integrating everybody and that sort of thing. They failed in North Carolina— all the Baptists and all in love with Jesus. So my brother stayed with the mill. My sister-in-law joined the union, went to New York City to raise money for it and everything.

There were two murders: the chief of police was killed and a strike leader named Ella May Wiggins. She was a ballad singer who started making up mill songs like Aunt Polly Jackson and these other people.

My brother was one of the people indicted for conspiracy to murder her. It was actually a melee that they were trying to break up, and she was shot. He was exonerated, of course, and I didn't know who did it, but recently a young woman, a teacher friend of my daughter in Asheville, wrote a book about it. . . .

I came to the conclusion in writing a review of her book for the *Appalachian Journal* that things changed between 1929 and 2015 in terms of income dispar- ity and wages and where the money rests and who is at a disadvantage, and I blame the corporations for destroying the union after World War II.

It created the middle class. Workers could afford to buy the cars that Henry Ford envisioned when he raised their wages to $5 an hour so they could also buy a Model T Ford . . .

The Great Depression hit Appalachia especially hard. With ailing indus- tries no longer buying coal, the mountain economy was devastated. There was still the family farm—if its workers hadn't left for "public work" else- where. Many had become part-time farmers, depending on their outside work to support the family.

With all the zeal of nineteenth-century missionaries who sought to bring civilization to a backward people, the U.S. Government stepped in. Times were desperate; people were starving. For better or worse, those working with federal agencies—the Forest Service, the Park Service, the TVA—"had not the slightest doubt of their duty to bring mountain life up to twentieth-century standards whether the mountaineers involved wanted this or not."[4]

Public sentiment was influenced by writers like Horace Kephart, whose book Our *Southern Highlanders* was published in 1913. The woodsman and writer from 1903 until 1907 lived alone in an isolated cabin, where he had gone with the hope of overcoming alcoholism. He recorded his impressions as he ex- plored the wilderness. As for the men of the mountains, he wrote, "Generally they are lean-faced, sallow, level-browed, with rather high cheek-bones . . . Many wear habitually a sullen scowl, hateful and suspicious, which, in men of combative age, and often in the old women, is sinister and vindictive."[5]

With the rationalization that, after all, it was for their own good, authori- ties displaced 5,665 dwellers to make room for the Great Smoky Mountains National Park; 500 families were expelled in establishing the Shenandoah National Park, and TVA projects alone required the removal of 6,600 fami- lies. The descendants of those forced from their homes in the Shenandoah area are still vocal in their resentment.

Numbers like these are statistics; tragedy lies in the stories of individuals. In his book *Cades Cove: The Life and Death of a Southern Appalachian Com- munity 1818–1937*, Durwood Dunn describes the injustice, which he calls "Death by Eminent Domain," when one small community was destroyed to establish the Great Smoky Mountains National Park: "The real tragedy for the cove people was that they were forced to sell and move during the midst of the Great Depression. Many owned substantial homes, some equipped with running water and electricity furnished by a Delco battery system. . . ."[6]

As Dunn argues, they were not

The wretched, backward creatures living in depravity and degradation as represented by Horace Kephart. Rather they were, in the final analysis representative of the mainstream of nineteenth-and twentieth-century American culture and society from whence they came: ordinary, decent citizens who often reacted collectively—and within their limitations, courageously and responsibly—to the enormous fluctuation, social change, and political disruption surrounding their lives. . . .[7]

The exile was all the more devastating to a people so closely tied to the land, both emotionally and financially. As a community steeped in knowledge of another exiled population, they must have recalled this psalm: "By the rivers of Babylon, there we sat down, yea, we wept when we remembered Zion. . . . How shall we sing the Lord's song in a foreign land?"

It was especially hard for the elderly to become isolated from family and friends, Dunn writes, like Uncle Noah Burchfield, "one of the community's most beloved patriarchs. This gentle old man refused in 1932 to even sign a petition against the park takeover," trusting the government to treat him fairly. His faith was misplaced: he would receive "$9,000, . . . less than their own minimum estimate of $11,620," a sum which he would lose in its entirety in a bank failure.[8]

As though to justify the expulsion of its residents, Cades Cove was stripped of anything resembling modern: "All modern structures, particularly numerous homes of frame construction, were obliterated. The single guiding principle was that anything which might remotely suggest progress or advancement beyond the most primitive stages should be destroyed. A sort of pioneer primitivism alone survived the cove structures left standing."[9]

"Ironically," says Eller, "actions taken by the federal government in the 1930s further complicated the desperate conditions in the mountains. Not only did the new social welfare legislation shift the region's dependency onto the federal government, but expanded programs of land acquisition undertaken by the government also displaced hundreds of additional families from the land." Victims of eminent domain, many felt that "the government was delivering the final blow to the region's independence and traditional way of life."[10]

The boom years of World War II saw many leaving the mountains to make their fortunes in the thriving war industries. Mechanization of the mines would lead to less need for human labor, and while industry was stagnant in the mountains, it was booming in the cities of the Midwest. The family farm was too small and not productive enough to support all of the family, so many headed for the cities.

Between 1940 and the end of the 1960s, an estimated three to five million Appalachians left the region in search of work. With the rising wartime and postwar demands in the automobile, tire, and steel industries, these mountain people flooded into booming cities like Detroit, Flint, Chicago, Gary, Akron, Cincinnati, and Dayton.

Leaving home could be a wrenching experience, even for young men who thought it was a great adventure. Many remember, with nostalgia, that the 1930s were hard, but happy times back home.

Daryl S. remembers that, because they had no refrigeration, "we'd kill about four or five hogs over the winter, one or two at a time, and we'd eat out of the smokehouse and the cellar. We canned a lot, too, and we had chickens. We always had a good team of horses. Maybe Dad had one because he kept it to log with, when he got a timber job."

Those who tilled the soil remember working on steep hillsides where only corn would grow, using a "hillside plow," as Daryl recalls. "You've got to one end, you kick the lever, flip it, and go back. You can't go around in a rectangle."

We would carry water from the spring, which was to the side and back of the cemetery. . . My great-grandfather came out of Preston—he was a hardheaded sort—he had that well drilled and they got down so deep they went through sulfur. A lot of times in that area up there you'd get sulfur or salt, and he wouldn't let them go any deeper, and they kept the salt water. Mother wouldn't even drink coffee made out of that, but it was no problem washing clothes in it. She'd put the water in this big black kettle put the water on the fire outside, wash the clothes in it, then rinse them in cold water, dried them by hand and hung them on the line.

My grandfather had a little store. When I was a kid, you got salt and sugar and flour and meal, things like that. We didn't buy a lot out of the store. I know 90 percent of the time we ate out of the cellar and the smokehouse.

Daryl's younger sister has fond memories of that store: "There was candy and colas and Pepsi. Pepsi, that's what I remember. Every night, almost every night of our lives, Daddy and I would walk over there and get a carton and we'd take them back to the house. After dinner we'd either have popcorn or peanut butter and crackers, something—we'd have a snack, you know." There were other treats, too, like taffy made from sorghum, which they'd "pull and pull" and enjoy with friends.

Hobert Rice looks back with fondness at his upbringing:

HOBERT RICE'S STORY

Hobert, ninety-two, who grew up in Elliott County, Kentucky, is now retired and lives with his wife in suburban Dayton, Ohio. He remembers that:

We were the poorest of the poor, but we didn't know that. There was love in that family. There were eight children, four girls and four boys. We were raised on a farm in Elliot County, Kentucky, on a little creek called Newcombe.

Everybody worked on the farm, including my mother. She was a schoolteacher, she was a midwife, and we went horseback all over. Our transportation was horses, which did all the work on the farm, and we had a saddle horse, and that was the transportation. We at one time had a seven-gaited horse, and you could ride that thing and just sit there in the saddle and it was just like riding in a Cadillac.

When I was a young boy, I went to school. I'll tell you how "easy" it was. I walked two miles every day going to high school. The county got the money to build the school. It was back in the WPA days. I walked two miles and caught a school bus and then I rode the bus to go to school. It took us two hours and the school was in Sandy Hook, which was the county seat in that county. So if I missed the bus, I walked the short way—crossed two mountains, up one and down the other. And I didn't walk, I ran! And I would get paid twenty-five cents for helping clean the school.

The farm is still in the family. Nobody's living in it, but some of it is taken care of. The old barn is falling down but the home—they keep it up. It belongs to my younger sister. I had a couple of acres 'cause I wanted something to say was mine, but it wasn't nothing but a big expense, so I gave it to my nephew. He was the only one we knew that wanted it. We wanted to keep it in the family. His son will keep it, too. It'll never be out of our family. It'll stay within the family.

We have a reunion at the farm every year, even though nobody lives there now. The original house was torn down and a new one built. The land is in the family. It's still home to the family.

I guess in those days they didn't have electricity, and it was all coal lamps. Then the R.E.A. came through there and they got plumbing. Nobody else had anything either, but we had love in that family and we was raised up pretty strict. My mother was very strict.

My mom would work in the field until maybe about 11:00 in time to go in and get dinner—get something to eat—and after dinner she'd come back to the field and work. The whole family worked like that.

I've got a niece that ran the background on the family, and I want to tell you this. We were on a vacation and we were on the Blue Ridge Parkway in Virginia and we stopped over for a pullover. There was a plaque there that said, "The last buffalo killed in this area was in 1908 by Joseph H. Rice."

That was probably a relation. There were three brothers that come from Virginia and bought all of this land on one side of the river for two and a half miles, I think, and they paid twenty-five cents an acre for it, and it kept coming down through the generations. It was my father, and his father and mother—I've got the original first deed in there, a copy of it. I don't remember the date on it, though, that laid out the deal. You should see the penmanship.

When World War II started, I remember where I was and what I was doing. It was about 4:00 in the afternoon and I was at home and heard it on the radio.

I stayed in school until I was seventeen and my dad got me a bogus birth certificate, because I wasn't old enough, and a friend and me went to Baltimore, Maryland, and went to work in a shipyard. We was building liberty ships . . . When I first started working in the shipyard, they was getting a ship out every month. By the time I left there, they was getting one out every eight days. I learned welding there and then became a pipe fitter at Frigidaire. That's where I learned my trade.

I lost one brother in the war. I had joined the Marines and was going out to San Diego and saw them loading two caskets in Chicago. It wasn't until later that I recognized one of the escorts who had brought my brother home. My brother had been getting ready to go overseas and went and played a fast game of pick-up ball and then went and took a cold shower, and he died.

At that time, I didn't know that. So I went along to San Diego to boot camp and when I got there, there was a telegram waiting back for me.

Back in those days you had to have priority to take a flight, and I did get out of there on a plane and got to New Mexico. Then I had to get off because there was some officer who had a higher priority than I had. So I got a train there and came back to Louisville, and my brother-in-law got a bus down to Louisville and went to Morehead, Kentucky, where my brother-in-law and sister lived. I recognized the escort when I got back there.

After that I went back to the Marines. They called us "Rough Riders." I went to the South Pacific. I went to Okinawa, and that was the last battle of World War II. That was the last one. In fact, we was on a boat ready to go back up into Japan, and we went to the northern part of China. I was just a little guy, in my early twenties.

They had a prison camp up in the northern part of China, and I was in reconnaissance. We were the first ones to a camp for American P.O.W.s. I carried a very skinny guy on a stretcher, and the man asked for my name. He said, "I'll never forget that."

Over a year later I was at a base in North Carolina and somebody called my name. I looked, and there were a couple of marines and this guy was in his dress clothes. He was in a uniform with a lot of stripes on his sleeve. He said, "Do you remember me?" I said, "No, sir, I don't." And he says, "Do you remember picking up a guy in China on a stretcher?" That was the guy on the stretcher! After all that time, you know.

After the war I did my last year of high school and went to the University of Kentucky on the G.I Bill. I couldn't make it on that. That was in 1948, so I left and came here to get a job at Frigidaire, and that's when I met my wife.

At Frigidaire I was working a punch press. I went to school to keep up with all that. I worked thirty-four and a half years at pipe-fitting: plumbing, heating and pipe-fitting, for different companies. For the last nine years I worked at Rieck Services, which did mechanical contracting.

Hobert regrets that many of the younger generation are not doing as well as their forebears. Take the drug scene. Hobert's wife Emma, who was a case worker at a mental health facility, knows about drug problems. She says that a relative's ex-husband, even though "he was intelligent and as good a worker as anything," was one of the many who have become addicted to drugs.

He adds that:

It happens in the best of families. In our trade we had some guys that was on drugs. Mr. Rieck's minister asked me to take on someone who had problems. And I said, "Mr. Rieck, you don't know him." He looked at me and he said, "Hobert, you'd give a guy a chance, wouldn't you?" And when he put it that way, I said, "Go ahead and bring him around."

The first day he showed up before work time, and the next day I think he was at work on time, but the third day he was late, and he was leaving early all the time. We was out at the VA hospital when they built that. I was over all the heating that's out there at that hospital, and so I would go the time in the afternoon, and as soon as I left the building, he left. I wasn't aware until somebody told me about it. If I had a routine, he had it down pat. And he come to me on about the fourth day and said, "Hobert, I've got a job in Florida, and if you can get my money, I'd like to go to that job." I said, "I think I can help you." I got a check for him.

When he looked at it, he said, "You know, that's not right." I said, "What's wrong with it?" He said, "They took taxes out of my check." And he said, "I don't pay taxes." I said, "On your way out, you go over there to the office and explain that to them." And that's the last I heard of him.

After I retired, I went to work for myself, for about fifteen years, until I had my first heart attack.

Roscoe Napier also looks back on a childhood that was lacking in material things, but rich in love and close family ties:

ROSCOE NAPIER'S STORY

Roscoe, ninety-two, and his younger wife live in a comfortable duplex. Roscoe has painted the interior himself and it is a bright and cheery yellow. All the years away from Kentucky have not diminished his "down home" Kentucky accent. Where he grew up, large families were the norm:

I had an uncle who had fifteen children and on my mother's side—I think there were fifteen on her side of the family, to start with. A couple of them died young, but one of her brothers, Uncle Robert, he had fifteen children. And me and my brother—the one that got killed in the service—we started counting our first cousins, way back in the late thirties, and we had over one hundred first cousins.

It must have been a challenge to feed such large families, but Roscoe says:

Well, they just lived on a mountain farm and raised a lot of beans and corn. They ground their own meal and raised their own potatoes and everything they needed to eat. They raised big gardens and canned a lot of stuff, and they got by. They didn't have no money, but they didn't worry about nothing.

I had five sisters and three brothers, and I'm the only one left. My mother was uneducated, and she was a good woman. She never was out of the county, I don't think, but she raised nine children, and she raised a big garden. She raised beans and corn and potatoes, and she'd get out and work like a man, out in the sun, hoeing all that stuff and taking care of it, and then canning it and putting it away.

She made sauerkraut out of cabbage and she'd pickle corn in a big barrel—put a flat rock in a pillowcase and hold it under the saltwater—and she'd can all kinds of fruit and vegetables. We had a warming closet built by the side of the fireplace. We had a fireplace out in the middle of the house, and we had this warming closet. She'd can most of her stuff in half-a-gallon fruit jars—big jars—and some in quarts, 'cause we had a big family, took a lot to feed us all.

We killed hogs every fall. We'd usually kill five or six pigs, and we had a smokehouse. We'd put the meat in the smokehouse, used hickory wood, green hickory wood to smoke this meat. We had smoked bacon, smoked ham, smoked shoulders, and she'd can a lot of this sausage. Yeah, man, that was good sausage. That was real sausage!

We had a little bit of bottomland, but some of the farm was on a hillside. We used just a straight plow with a mule pulling it around the hillside, but it didn't do a very good job, so we had to do most of it with a hoe. That straight plow—it didn't kill too many weeds, like a turner plow would.

It was steep. We had to pull a sled on the side of the hill to gather corn. We had corn on the mountainside. That was about the only thing we could raise on that mountainside, was corn. And then we would cut all the tops from the ears up and tie them and shuck them and keep them to feed the cattle and the horses in the wintertime.

We usually had a couple of cows and maybe a calf or two and then we had two horses and a mule most of the time. We had barnyard chickens, and we'd get eggs, and those old hens would hatch out chickens, and they'd raise them from babies on up.

We didn't have nothing to worry about. Everybody was friendly, everybody loved everybody. We didn't have to lock the doors or the windows or nothing. When we'd go away to church or something, the house would be open. We'd never have nothing that nobody would want anyway, unless it was something to eat.

I grew up in Clay County, Kentucky, near the Red Bird Mission. There wasn't no town. It was way out in the country. It was about twenty miles away from town, but there wasn't no roads, just old wagon roads up and down by a creek, and the road crossed across the creek several times along the way, until they got the WPA to come in there and build the roads. This would have been in the thirties.

As for medical services, "we had the Frontier Nursing Service. Somebody'd run and get the nurse and bring her back. They'd come to the home. They'd come to the home and catch babies."

Nurses would ride horseback to otherwise inaccessible areas, delivering babies, treating ailments, and giving immunizations. They could also treat emergencies at their headquarters, a log building now serving as a B&B.

Roscoe remembers when he was treated there as a child:

They're the ones that sewed my finger back on when my brother chopped it off, with a chopping ax! Me and my older brother, he was sawing wood, and my younger brother, he was aggravating us that he had to ax it, hacking around on this block. We sat down to rest on the block of wood and I put my hand to keep him from chopping close to me, and he come down on my hand!

It was hanging right here on the side. It was cut through the nail, it went all the way through, it went straight through into the block. I was running around there screaming. I must have been about eight, nine years old, and he was two years younger than I. And one of the neighbors come down. My dad and mother was gone someplace. They wasn't home.

We had a couple of horses in the barn, and this neighbor come down and he got one of the horses and put the saddle on it and took me up to the Frontier Nursing Service and they stitched it up for me. They gave us two cookies for not crying. I remember that. It was about two miles from where we lived up to the Frontier Nursing Service. And that was the only doctor there was within twenty miles.

Our transportation was horses. I remember back when they had a church service in a little one-room schoolhouse, maybe twice a month, and these old preachers come from different places, and they would ride horses in there and hitch them up outside. Everybody rode horses, and some people, they'd bring the whole family in a wagon, and they had these straight-backed chairs sitting on a flatbed wagon, and they would ride them over in a wagon.

They didn't have Sunday School. The kids didn't know anything about the Bible. And they preached out of the New Testament, and I didn't know much about God. I'd heard about God, but I didn't know God. I didn't understand nothing about God, but a lot of times when I was out in the woods squirrel hunting—I started squirrel hunting when I was about eight or nine years old—I remember praying, "Lord, save me!" Save my soul—I didn't want to go to hell. I'd heard there was a heaven to go to and a hell to go to, and some of these old preachers, you know, told you enough about it to get you to understand there was a heaven and a hell, but I didn't understand too much about being a sinner, and I had sinned against God.

I didn't understand that too much, but I'd pray at different times," Lord, save me, and forgive me of all my sins." I wanted to go to heaven, and I'd say, "Lord, if you've saved me, shake a limb on that tree there so I'll know." See, I wanted a sign to know that he'd heard me and that he did save me, but there was no sign given. After I got to reading the Bible later on I realized there ain't no sign given like that. You're saved by grace and faith, and that's not of yourself. That's a gift of God, not of works that any man should boast about. That's the Baptist message. You are saved by grace through faith, but even that grace and faith is not of yourself. It's a gift of God, and none of your works . . .

My dad was a good Christian, and I had a good upbringing. Here's what my dad always said: Somebody would say, "Are you going to do this or that tomorrow?" And he'd say, "If it's God's will." He always put God first. My mother got saved later in life.

When I got saved, fifteen years after I got out of the service, I started going to Sunday school every week. I never missed a Sunday for three years, so I learned a lot about the word of God because we studied it every week. Every time we'd meet we'd study the Bible.

When I was growing up—of course I know people have changed over the years—but if people got sick in the neighborhood, several neighbors would come and sit up with them all night long and encourage them.

And if somebody died, they did the same thing. They'd sit up all night with the corpse, and they didn't take nobody to the funeral homes. We had an old man that made the wooden casket and a wooden box to bury them in, but they never was embalmed or anything. They just buried them that way, but all that changed over the years. You know, you've got to embalm 'em and do all this other stuff now.

I never did go to high school, didn't make it to high school. I never was a very good reader but I was good on my figures. I take care of my bank account and write checks and do all of that. My wife won't do it.

We didn't have too much educating in my neighborhood. They finally built— they had a high school at Flat Creek and all the girls and boys that lived close there, most of them would walk to school, because they didn't have no school buses running. You couldn't have got a school bus up and down there 'cause the roads wasn't that good. The poor kids, they never got much education.

But one thing I did was carry the mail horseback, up and down Red Bird, that's the reason I knew everybody within fifteen miles around. And I knew their nicknames. I knew all of the old people, old, old people, that was born maybe before 1850, old people. My dad was born in 1883. But I knew people a lot older than he was.

There was a lot of poor people that lived on this creek, called Little Creek, that ran into the Red Bird River. There were two old people who lived up the creek, and I think they lived on a dirt floor. Just had a log cabin, never had a floor in the house. I knew several like that, just had a dirt floor. That's how poor they were. They just daubed the cracks with mud. They built a log house and they took clay dirt and filled the cracks with mud, and it'd dry up and fall out sometimes.

When I carried the mail, you know, there was several post offices. I lived close to Markham post office, and I had to go up to the end of the route to start out, which was about three miles, up close to Red Bird, up towards Bethany, and this post office was called Spring Creek Post Office. The next one down the road was Flat Creek post office, and the one close to where I lived was called Markham Post Office, and the one down the road was called Peabody Post Office. I'd deliver the mail to people's boxes in between the post offices. But not too many people had boxes, only the ones that had a little money. Most poor people didn't have mailboxes; they would walk to the post office, which we did.

I remember when I started carrying the mail, they had to swear you in, but I wasn't old enough to carry the mail really, when I started. This lady named Dorie Rowley was the postmaster and she swore me in that morning. She said, "How old are you?" And I said—I lied to her—I said, "I'm fifteen," but I was fourteen!

She said, "You're supposed to be sixteen to carry the mail." And I said, "Well, I didn't know that." She said, "Well, you can carry it today, since you're here." She'd let me carry the mail that day. Well, the next day I went back and just kept a-carrying it. She didn't say no more about it.

I got ninety-seven cents a day. Ninety-seven cents a day for six days a week! I think the route, the way I went, was about thirty-two miles a day on horseback. And we had the parcel post. We didn't carry just first-class mail. The first-class mailbag was a little handful. It wasn't much, because there wasn't very many letters being mailed back then. You could mail a letter for three cents, I think, when I was carrying mail. Everybody ordered their goods, their clothes, their shoes, their everything through the mail order. Sears Roebuck, Montgomery Ward, Spiegel's. They had Spiegel catalogs, Montgomery Ward, Sears Roebuck; you had to order stuff from Atlanta.

And there was some people that ordered baby chickens, live chickens. Couldn't put them in a mail sack. I usually had five or six full sacks of parcel post to hang across my saddle, and sometimes I'd have to walk and drive the mule or horse, walk behind it. You couldn't sit on them with all that mail on the saddle. They'd feel the saddle then.

It wasn't all work when Roscoe was young. He remembers childhood games like drop the handkerchief, and later,

We'd have parties and make candy. The boys would buy all the sugar and the girls would make the candy. We'd have a 'working' with all the neighborhood boys and girls. We'd hoe a whole field of corn out and then we'd dance all night, square dance. We couldn't see a movie because we were too far from town. I didn't see a movie until I was about eighteen, nineteen years old.

I worked a little while in Dayton before I got drafted into the service. I worked at Kroger's dairy and I worked at Sunshine Biscuit Company.

I was in World War II during the invasion of France. See, we went over on the Queen Elizabeth, big ocean-liner. They had about five bunks high, and there was 22,000. That's how big the ship was.

My older brother died in the Battle of the Bulge. I was on the coast of France on Omaha Beach for twenty-one days and nights, shooting at German dive bombers.

I was scared! My knees were shaking. I thought I was going to die. I didn't know if I'd live through it or not. There were mines floating in the water, sea mines to sink ships. Our small ship was tied on the side of a Polish ship loaded with six hundred tons of TNT on it, and these mines floating . . . We had Army rifles, in case we would have to hit the beach with the Army, and we had packs, Army packs, just in case we had to hit the beach, so we were shooting at these mines floating in the water in the daytime, but at night, our fighter planes that was protecting us would go back to England, and here come the German dive bombers, and they was over us all night every night. I never got to sleep hardly at all. I was scared, hungry, tired . . .

After the war I left Kentucky to get some work. There wasn't no public work down there. That would have been 1947. I got out of the service in 1946 and I helped my dad on the farm there through '46, and then the first of '47 I came to Dayton. My cousin and I had hired in at the end of the year and started working the first of January, 1947.

I lived on East Second Street in a boarding house when I first came. It was a lot different from where I came from, but Uncle Charlie Morgan was boarding there, and I took up with him, and boarded there where he boarded.

In Dayton I did different things. I built refrigerators and I built stoves. But after I went up to Harrison Radiators, we built air-conditioners for automobiles. I would run the tests on them. Some of them we'd run for 200 hours to see if they'd hold up, and if they broke down, we'd tear them down to see what caused them to break down. My younger brother and I worked together at Harrison Radiator in the same department. We ran a computer computing these little parts that went in these compressors. It was Harrison Radiators where I retired from. I enjoyed working.

I noticed an ad in the *Kentucky Explorer* that Ike Bowling had had inserted that he was looking for information on the Bowling family. I happened to have some research that my uncle had done on the Bowling name, but it was about another branch of the family. Nevertheless, I took that opportunity to see what ancestry.com had to say about Ike's family history and, warming to the chase, I was able to trace it back to the early seventeenth century. I took my findings along when I had a chance to talk to Ike a few days later.

ICEM "IKE" BOWLING'S STORY

Ike, who is eighty-four, is proud of having served his country. When I met him, he was wearing a "U.S. Navy" baseball cap. At his front door there is a decal declaring that this is the home of someone who served. Ike, like his friend Roscoe Napier, is from Clay County, Kentucky. He has done some genealogy research and has developed a keen interest in history.

My ancestors came down in Kentucky through the Cumberland Gap or down the river from Pennsylvania. They came down the Wilderness Trail. There's a lot of the Civil War history in that area. In Clay County, near Manchester, they had the salt mines. They made salt, and it was very important. They used to make it and ship it. The Confederates first came through and got some and later on the Union came and wound up destroying the salt well, put people out of business.

Ike tells me a little about his own history in the mountains:

I first went to a one-room schoolhouse there, where my aunt taught. We walked. They had them pretty close together, the schools. Sometimes we'd have to cross the river, cross it on a boat, the only way to get across. We had a pot-bellied stove in there . . . We didn't have a well, where I went to school, so we had to go to the neighbor's to get our water. Some kids never had shoes.

On our farm we raised tobacco. Tobacco was a money crop, and we were allotted a certain amount to grow, and we'd harvest it in the fall . . . We had some flat bottomland, but there were mountains around. You weren't allowed much, maybe a half acre. Bigger farms had an acre. I can remember when we started raising it. It was about in the late forties. A lot of people, if they didn't want to raise it, they'd lease it out to another farmer. In the eastern part of the state, back in the national forest there, they're growing marijuana. A lot of things change.

When Ike was in high school, the Korean War broke out, and he knew he'd be doing obligatory service, but first he headed to Dayton for a job at Frigidaire. He says:

You know, after World War II, all the guys were coming home and there was no work back home. Either you worked in the coal mines or—there wasn't enough land to farm to make a living. Of course some of them made it, but about all that was available was coal mines or logging timber, so they came north, where they were crying for people. They'd take you off the street and put you to work.

I had brothers here. Two brothers came up. They were in World War II. Roscoe, he came up about that time. He was one of the first ones that came up. I was about eighteen, and it was an adventure. Quit school and came up here and wanted to go to work. There were a lot of us here. I come up here and I brought my clothes and things in a paper box. A lot of us was like that when we came here and got jobs. I don't know what you'd call it: a bunch of guys that know each other, associate and run around some. A lot of them have passed on now.

I got laid off, couldn't get a job and didn't want to get drafted, so I decided I'd just join the Navy. I was on a destroyer, two different destroyers, from 1952 to 1956. I was in Japan twice, we went to China, Hong Kong . . . We were in Korea, offshore, but I didn't go through much combat. We were doing escort— we escorted the bigger ships. We had significant sonar . . . We could track subs and throw depth charges on the subs. . . .

I've often wondered what it would have been like if I'd stayed in. I did four years. They tried to get me to stay in, but It's hard if you want to start a family. I could have joined the Navy Reserve, I guess.

I went back to school and studied business things, like accounting, and public speaking, and I did good. I was working toward an Associate's Degree and lacked a few credits. Didn't do it.

After I got out, I got a job at NCR and worked there about fifteen years after the Navy. They went down the tube so I went into business. Ran a business about six or seven years, home improvement. Then I got a job at General Motors, and that's where I stayed until retirement. I got a job in the power center, powerhouse, because that's what I did in the Navy.

Ike is not a big fan of government handouts. "I'm a conservative type," he says. "I've always believed in working and making your way in the world. Your word's your bond. If you made a trade with somebody, you'd give them a handshake, and that's it. You'd do it on a handshake.

"My dream when I was real young was to own a house and a decent car all paid for and I'd have no debts."

Ike has achieved his dream; now he can look back on a life well lived. Sam Morgan, too, can be proud of what he has accomplished.

SAM MORGAN'S STORY

Sam is one of the most financially successful businessmen in our area; he claims to know many former Kentuckians in his tax bracket. He has been generous with his good fortune, donating to charitable organizations and funding scholarships for students of Appalachian background. Sam has the deep voice of a big man, and he has kept his Kentucky accent, which sounds like "family" to me.

Dressed in a monogrammed short-sleeved shirt and shorts, Sam is very much at home in his new house on its many acres in exurbia. From the large living room we can see the lake he has had created and stocked.

His is a true Horatio Alger story, given what his life was like as a child in Kentucky. Fortunately he has some photographs to illustrate. Some of them he owes to a magazine article in the 1940s that featured the Frontier Nursing Service.

There's a picture of his young, beautiful mother being visited by the nurse as she lies in bed holding a baby. As he says, "Everybody was born at home down there. You know, the Frontier Nursing Service." He explains that the bed in the photograph was a cornhusk bed: "They'd take the shucks off the corn cobs and stuff the mattress." He also calls my attention to the fact that instead of wallpaper, newspapers cover the walls.

Another photograph, taken in 1940, he thinks, shows a nurse on horseback near the front of the family's log cabin. The Morgan children are assembled on the porch.

"Look at the steps on that house," Sam says. "No guard rails. That was our log cabin. My dad pulled the logs out of the mountains and built that house and filled the cracks in with mud."

Sam shows me another photograph, possibly from the thirties: "This is a school," he says, "and this is my aunt who was a first-year teacher. She went to college at Transylvania, and this is my dad with the 'school bus'—this mule-drawn cart back then. What they did, they'd go through the mountains with a couple of mules and pick up the kids and bring them to school. This was in Leslie County."

Sam's parents met at an event right out of the classic movie *Sergeant York:*

Back then they'd have these dances where the women would fix a meal, like fried chicken or pies, and the fellows would go and bid on it. That's the way they met. He had four sisters and two brothers. There were seven of them, and there were seven in our family. His parents sent him away to boarding school so he could go to college, but he didn't like it, and he came back home. He only stayed a short time, but all his sisters had college educations. They went to school up in Transylvania, which was a well-known school in Kentucky . . .

My mother couldn't read or write, because she was from a large family and her dad died when she was a youngster. She hired herself out to work for people, and she'd wash clothes in the creeks with a washboard, and she said she had one pair of shoes. They'd have holes in 'em, and she'd put cardboard in the bottom. She said many times the cardboard would freeze to the stones. Everybody knew she was a fantastic woman.

We came to Dayton in 1943. My dad worked two jobs, you know, tried to get us over the hump, and we lived out in what they call "Hell's Half Acre." I took [my friend] out there. He could not believe where we came from.

They don't call it "Hell's Half Acre" anymore . . . The house is still standing and it was a double, about as wide as my sunroom out here, so you can imagine three sections of that room. Listen to this: it was split down the middle. They were doubles! And we had one side with five kids and Mom and Dad when we first lived there.

Then we rented the rest of the house and opened it up, and us four boys, we slept four to a bed, two at the head, two at the foot. And then in 1948 we moved down to Clinton Street, down by Stivers High School.

How in the world, I wondered, did Sam ever get a start, coming from poverty like that.

Well, I started working when I was eleven years old. I worked at Saul's Car Wash. And that's the first car wash in Dayton, and what happened was, I started out sweeping cars out, you know, whisking cars. They didn't have vacuum sweepers then, so you had to do that, and if you got a car with a lot of hair and stuff in it, you just had a mess. I'd work ten hours on Saturday, at eleven years old, and I'd work seven hours on Sundays. I started out at thirty-five cents an hour and then I got fifty cents.

The Sauls had one daughter, and she was grown and gone. They really liked me, so eventually I ended up being the cashier and sort of half managing the place when I was about thirteen. Things were tough, and I would take the money home and give part of it to my family to help buy groceries. . . . I was always the one that was a worker. I worked from the time I was eleven. Nobody ever bought me a stitch of clothes from the time I was eleven years old. Even today I pick my own clothes. I don't ask for anything.

I think one of the things, people say to me, "Where are you from?" I say, "I'm from Kentucky, but I grew up in Ohio." I think you have a loyalty to Kentucky for some reason or another. I don't have any loyalty to the University of Kentucky or the schools down there, but the state. You take pride in the fact that you're from Kentucky and what you were able to accomplish under adverse circumstances. . . .

My mother always pushed us. I wasn't a good student, because I was always working and messing around. I didn't study. I never did homework in my life.

What happened was, back in Kentucky, Mother was down at the river washing our clothes, by hand, of course, and she looked up and the house was on fire. By the time she got to it, everything had burned up. We were down to the clothes that us kids had on our backs, and Dad was up there working at General Motors and trying to make a little money.

When he had five children, the war came along, and he volunteered to go in the service, but he had a heart murmur and he couldn't go. All the people around us in eastern Kentucky and Hyden, where we're from, I don't think any of them got drafted. I think they all volunteered. I mean, they're very loyal. They're tough people. They're nice people, but you don't push them around. They're really nice people.

A lot of them from the mountains, they went in the service and stayed, because it was a permanent job for them, and there were a lot of highly decorated people from Kentucky in World War II.

This country offers so many opportunities, and like I said, I'd work seventeen hours Saturday and Sunday, and then I would go shine shoes, up there on East Fifth Street. I had a shoeshine box. I'd go home and take a bath, and I'd get off at 6:00, and by 7:30 I was up shining shoes, and I'd shine shoes until about 10:30 at night.

I would do that, and also during the week I had a newspaper route downtown. I'd walk downtown from out there by Stivers High School, right down to Fourth and Main. I had the corner selling newspapers.

I've never been to college. I shouldn't say I never went. I went to the University of Dayton and took some accounting courses and aced them. No, I didn't have a really good solid education. And it's my fault, you know. My mother was always saying, "You have to get educated to survive," and I'd go to class and take easy courses. I was tired a lot of times. That's the reason today I've got somebody else doing [everything]. [My wife] Carol, she came up on a farm and she's always doing things around here, but I say, "Hey, you do it. I'm not doing it. I've done my share."

"I know it took a lot of hard work, but there must have been some opportunities," I say. Sam replies.

Well, I feel I made my own opportunities, then I capitalized on 'em. I got involved in a thing called—it's like the *Trading Post* here in Dayton. There was four of us started one in Louisville, Kentucky. We put in $750 apiece, we put in $3,000 and in 1987 we sold it for $5 million.

They sold it for $4 million and I went in and negotiated another million, so I got a check for $1,200,000. I had a fourth of it, and what happened was, the reason I didn't have a check for $1,250,00, 'cause that makes the $5 million, was they kept $50,000 back and paid us 12 percent interest. They paid a fifth of it each year for five years, so you wouldn't compete. There was no way I wasn't going to compete.

I didn't know what to do, because Ernie Green and I had started our business, and it was starting to go pretty good. We started as an outsourcer to General Motors. See, I'm the one that set all that up, and General Motors wanted me to have a minority partner, and [African-American NFL star] Ernie Green had played football at Louisville, where my brother played basketball, and I knew him from that, his reputation and everything. He was working for International Management, so he and Paul Warfield and I started a company called GWM, which was a coal brokerage. Green-Warfield-Morgan. To start that business, I just went down to Kentucky and started talking to people down there I knew.

We sold coal to General Motors to run their plants, and then that gave us an opportunity, and I got in some people at GM that liked us, and they had an outsourcing at Inland and that's the way we started. We were doing engine mounts, motor mounts. We were buying them, and coating them and putting a stake in them and shipping them to General Motors and they were selling them as a finished product. . . . We started in 1981, and we started the coal brokerage three years before that, so Ernie Green and I have been together thirty-eight years.

In our family, my dad worked all the time, and my mother was the leader. She came from a very, very poor family, just the complete opposite of what he did, and there was some resentment against my dad on the part of his folks, from his mother, not his dad, his dad died—because she was poor and everything. But anyway, they would put her in jail today if she was alive, because if we did something bad, she'd take a switch and beat our ass—I mean beat our ass! And when Dad come home, she'd say, "That one, that one." They'd get a whipping from it. They would wear your butt out! I think it was instilled by her, and backed up by him . . .

Mom was a mountain woman, boy, I never seen her back up in my life, with anybody, anything. Oh, there was discipline! You'd suffer if you got out of line, from what Mother would do!

Sam laughs at the memories and adds:

When we lived in the house down on Clinton Street . . . the boys would stretch out on the couch and read, and Mother would come by, and she'd say, "Look, if you're tired, go to bed, don't lay out on the couch. We've only got one," because people have a tendency to read and drop papers on the floor. That's the first time. The second time she told you, that broom would hit you on the side of your head, the broom part, the soft part, and she'd say, "I mean it. Now you get your butt upstairs."

Anyone who ever met Mae Morgan would never doubt that she was strong in many ways, with the reputation of helping those of her fellow immigrants in need. "Feeding the neighborhood," was how one Kentuckian transplant put it.

As Sam approaches his eighties, he's still turning his thoughts to the future and how our country could be improved.

One thing I would do, I would start taxing all those big foundations, like the Gates, the Buffett's—all the money that they send out of the country, which usually ends up in bad hands, anyway, which is the majority of that money. They send it to third-nation countries, and that's all tax-free dollars, so I've been working with [U.S. Rep.] Mike Turner on this. I would tax that 50 percent if it went out of the country. I would take that money, as long as it's used in this country, such as the Appalachian mountains now, because they've devastated the coal industry, and help those people, bring industry there, and do things in this country, and that money would be tax-free.

You take that money and you go into the mountains and you work with people like our company or other companies that are successful and say, "If you put in new plants, and stuff that you're doing in Mexico and that you're doing in China—you take this money and build these plants, which is a big percentage of the cost, and you can run them five years, ten years. Anything that you've been doing out of the country, you can take that and manufacture tax-free until you get that business on a solid basis. Take the cash and build the plants and create jobs here in America."

You're bringing the jobs back instead of taking them out. So much of this money—even Gates's son said they take it like to Africa, and he said, "Everything you're doing there is wrong." And he's a farmer.

You've got all that corruption over there and a few benefit, but the majority stay the same. So that would be tax-free dollars if they do it in this country; if they take it out, minimum of 50 percent. And it would make a huge difference, a huge impact.

And you do the same things, not in the inner city, but you do it on the outer perimeter of the inner city to bring employees and get the black people back to work, and you'll cut the damn welfare. Companies don't want to be in the inner city because of all the destruction, and we've had a pattern of that, so if you bring it out on the edges, then you can control it.

Look, you wouldn't put a factory in downtown Baltimore, because of what they've gone through. So get on the outer edges, and then you start bringing these people in there, and you train them, and you give them a salary, because most people have enough pride, except for the ones that have been on welfare for so long, and you pay them a livable wage . . .

There are a lot of companies our size that are doing well, and we have people who know how to run plants. We're bringing jobs back from China right now at our plants for things that are being done out of the country, because of the management and the way we're doing things . . .

Sam is a great admirer of a program that has been instituted in Kansas in which forty thousand people have been removed from welfare and put to work in good paying jobs. It is his hope that such a program could be established throughout the country.

"You've got to get people to work," he says, for it's important that people have the pride that comes from being employed. "If you don't, you're going to kill the pride," he says, adding that "I think the real wealthy people should pay a lot more money in taxes. I'm a Republican and I say that!"

Ike Bowling, Roscoe Napier, Hobert Rice, and Sam Morgan's parents were part of the Great Migration from the mountains. Seven million people were forced to leave their homeland between 1940 and 1992 to find jobs elsewhere. Between 1950 and 1960, says one researcher, 60 percent of those working in the mines lost their jobs; about one-fifth of the population—1.5 million people—left Appalachia.[11] It was what Deborah Hicks calls "one of the largest population shifts in American history."[12] Chad Berry, who heads the Appalachian Studies program at Berea College, cites even more dramatic figures: by 1950, he claims, about five million people had left the hills.[13]

"In some respects," says Jeff Biggers, "the great migration from Appalachia might be the region's most important contribution to industrial America. Beyond its natural resources, Southern Appalachia has literally peopled the midwestern factories, and other corners of the nation's industries with its very inhabitants and their mountain culture—and their traditions of labor battles and resistance, independence and resilience, music and literature."[14]

Along with their old cars and battered suitcases, or in some cases, boxes and paper bags, the immigrants brought with them their age-old values, including pride—values that were likely to be misunderstood in their new environment.

NOTES

1. Ann Dudley Matheney, *The Magic City: Footnotes to the History of Middlesborough, Kentucky, and the Yellow Creek Valley*, (Middlesboro, KY: Bell County Historical Society, 2003), 307.

2. Ronald D.Eller, *Miners, Millhands and Mountaineers*, 155.

3. Introduction, "The Mine Wars," *American Experience: TV's most-watched history series*, PBS.org, 1.

4. John Alexander Williams, *Appalachia: A History*, (Chapel Hill: University of North Carolina Press), 301.

5. Horace Kephart, *Our Southern Highlanders*, (Knoxville: University of Tennessee Press, 1913), 287–88.

6. Durwood Dunn, *Cades Cove: The Life and Death of a Southern Appalachian Community 1818–1937*, (Knoxville: University of Tennessee Press, 1989, 13th printing 2015), 251.

7. Ibid., 256.

8. Ibid., 252–53.

9. Ibid., 256.

10. Eller, 240.

11. Alessandro Portelli, *They Say in Harlan County: An Oral History*, (Oxford: Oxford University Press, 2001).

12. Deborah Hicks, *The Road Out: A Teacher's Odyssey in Poor America*, (Berkeley: University of California Press, 2013), 19.

13. Chad Berry, *Southern Migrants, Northern Exiles*, (Urbana: University of Illinois Press, 2000).

14. Jeff Biggers, *The United States of Appalachia*, (Oxford: Oxford University Press, 2011), 164–65.

Chapter Six

Values

Wouldn't it be great if, to paraphrase Martin Luther King, Jr, we would judge others by the strength of their character rather than by the size of their pocketbooks? And that's what Appalachians do.

"We're person-oriented," says Dr. Tess Little.

We like stories, we're social, we like family, we like being with people, we like talking. People are more important to us than things. In mainstream, things are more important than people: "my big fancy car, my big fancy house"—you know, "I've got nice clothes," and that means something. It doesn't mean crap to us. We'll live in little hovels and invest all our money in people. Right?

We just talk a lot, among family members and people we trust. You know, we share. Interruptions are accepted. In my family everybody talks over everybody. And I really have trouble with that, trying to keep my mouth shut, and I know that that's mainstream culture and I need to do that, but I really find it tough.

Schedules are not very important. If I'm talking to you and something comes up, and there's a meeting down there, and we're talking about something really good, then I will talk with you and I will run late to the meeting. I've really worked hard on that, too. In fact, I set my alarm today so that I wouldn't do that, because I know that's one of my shortcomings, because I know that I have to fit into this world when I'm here. When I go home, I fit into an Appalachian world.

I met with Tess at the snack bar of Sinclair Community College, where she has been teaching Appalachian Studies for more than twenty years. A Renaissance woman, she is also an artist and sculptor who has won numerous awards in art, as well as in education and public service.

She is perhaps best known for developing "REACH Across Dayton—"REACH" is an acronym for "Realizing Ethnic Awareness and Cultural

Heritage"— in order to create mutual understanding among those who differ culturally.

The program is truly Tess's baby, conceived over twenty-three years ago after she convinced the dean, after several yearly attempts, that this was a program worth having.

"So I went out and put together a conference," she says." I didn't have any money, but being a typical Appalachian, you don't need money. You can do things. I found a free room, people who would come and talk for free about Appalachians, talk about African Americans." With Appalachian ingenuity, she gathered all the resources necessary.

One hundred sixty people came to that first conference, including the community's Appalachian leaders—"but they wouldn't sit down. They stood in the back with their arms folded and watched. They just wanted to make sure that they weren't going to be taken advantage of, because Appalachian people have been truly exploited, and they wanted to make sure that this young whippersnapper—I was all of thirty or so—they wanted to make sure that I knew what I was talking about. And I passed!"

Today more than 300 people attend the annual event, which features conferences, art exhibits, community art projects, musical performances, and many other activities. Willis "Bing" Davis, a well-known African-American artist, now is co-coordinator with Tess.

When it comes to material possessions, retired serviceman Tim D. almost echoes Tess when he says, "At least when I was growing up, and to some respect today, 'things' are not that big a deal. You know, a lot of people don't have good jobs, and they don't have a lot of things, but it doesn't bother them, either. It's not that big a deal, it's just the way life is."

This "the-way-life-is" fatalism, closely tied in with religious thought, is a common Appalachian trait, which, to Tess Little, "is acceptance, that this is the way the world is. Mainstream rationalism says, 'We can go out and make changes and we can make it happen, by golly!' And really life's a mixture."

In this respect, Appalachians differ from mainstream Americans, who are noted for their optimism. Immigrants from Mexico may arrive here with a fatalistic attitude, but within a generation or two they have embraced this upbeat outlook. Appalachian traditional culture doesn't change so quickly.

Mountain folks may take a fatalistic view, but they do try to tweak it a little. Look for the good luck: find a four-leaf clover, make a wish when you set right a turned-up hem—and consider all the superstitions that keep bad luck away. If you come in one door, you'll have to go out by the same one. Forgot something? If you return for it, you'll have to sit down and count to ten. I still cringe when I see a hat on a bed, and heaven help us if a bird flies in the house.

Loyal Jones, the beloved soft-spoken professor emeritus at Berea University, called on the experience and wisdom of his many years in the field to produce his book *Appalachian Values.*[1] Of course, at the top of the list is religion, a subject he has explored and written about extensively. He agrees that relationships with people, as well as with God, are of prime importance.

> If you grew up rural, you knew your neighbors, and you not only knew their names and who they were related to, you knew what their values were, and what church they went to and what their politics were, and you made a point of knowing it.
>
> Part of Southern story-telling, which irritates the Northerners, is that if we're telling the story, anytime we mention somebody, we're bound to stop and tell you who they are too, so the person who isn't half listening doesn't know who the story's about. But all of that's being lost, along with the modesty and humility that came out of that old Calvinist religion of "Don't think too highly of yourself."
>
> I think we're losing these traits that I value so much about people, and especially that about subduing the ego: "Everything's not about me." And I think it's helpful, not only in just human relations, but even . . . I've thought about it a lot and I've spoken to groups on mental health and one thing and another. . . .
>
> Tim O'Brien, a bluegrass singer, said the best way to ingratiate yourself with an audience is to make fun of yourself, sort of show a bit of humility to them or a little bit of ridiculousness, comic . . .
>
> I observed that with that wonderful old congressman from the Ozarks, Brooks Hayes. He was a wonderful man, but he was jocular, and I saw him perform at the Humanities Congress.
>
> Once he was telling Ozark jokes and everybody laughed until the tears were running down, and before they knew what had happened he had switched to Roosevelt's New Deal—he was a strong supporter of Roosevelt and his programs to alleviate rural poverty—and before they knew what was happening, he was talking about the government actually helping people, and I looked around, and people were still weeping, but with a new sentiment, you understand.
>
> I learned something profound there, I think. I see us losing these sorts of things. We're all so efficient today, we don't have time to get acquainted. We get right down to talking, and I've been kind of an amateur folklorist, collecting stories and songs and so forth, and I know you have to sit down and get acquainted and get people to know that you really care about them and you're not just going to run off and try to make a buck, or you have a new song to sing or whatever it is, you know.

When it comes to those all-important personal relationships, one should at least appear to be modest, as Loyal describes.

> If I ask a fiddler to play, he may say, "Oh, I've got this old arthritis in my hands, and my strings are dead, and I don't know whether this thing's in tune or not."

He says all that before he plays, and he might play flawlessly, but why not? He's warned me that he might not be as good as I might think he is, but if he's better than I think he is, then he's way ahead, you know.

I grew up with my mother saying, "You're as good as anybody else, but no better." That leveling thing was strong in the mountains and I think probably throughout the country in rural areas, and therefore "Don't think you're the center of things, and pay attention to the needs of others, not just your own." The whole point in life is maybe to have an amiable relationship with people rather than to make yourself the center of things. . . . There's competition in the mainstream. You don't find that so much here. People wait to be asked, so I say, discount part of this humility and reticence. It's part of the manners system. They may know how well they can do something, but they're not going to promote themselves.

When [ballad collector] Cecil Sharp came to the mountains from England [in 1916], he was looking for people who knew the English folk songs and ballads. He wasn't interested in the native ballads. He was trying to prove something, that here he'd found a place where people were singing the old songs that people had abandoned in England.

But, you know, there's a limit to that sort of thing. The people didn't volunteer to play music for him, so he went away thinking there was not a musical strings band. People played the banjo and the violin—there weren't many guitars back then—but when he collected square dance tunes and everything here, he put English jig tunes rather than the music as it derived from European music. I mean the old tunes like "Soldier's Joy" and so forth were very old, but he didn't hear the tradition because the people didn't say, "Oh, you like my singing. Would you like to hear me play the fiddle?" They would wait to be asked.

He had many prejudices against the mountain people and thought that other than the ballads, they were pretty crude, but they remembered the old ballads. He set kind of a tone with the early folklorists that somehow the ballads were so important that [not just anybody could collect them], but when Miss Petty, who had gone to Vassar, collected from one of the persons I admired, Josiah Thompson, who came to the settlement school with his ballads—when he sang them for her, she sent him to Kittridge at Harvard, who was also a balladmonger. He published them in the *Journal of American Folklore* in 1907, but credited them to Miss Petty, rather than to the little boy who actually sang them.

Loyal laughs as he adds, "It was considered that these things were actually so precious that it took an educated person to certify them!"

Mike Maloney, the "go-to" person on Appalachia in the Cincinnati area and the author of many publications on the culture, says,

I know what Loyal means when he talks about a sense of modesty. In my youth and to some degree today, I'm sure, an Appalachian preacher would spend the first five minutes of his sermon—and I've seen black preachers do this, too—spend the first five minutes of his sermon apologizing: "Oh, I'm not in good voice today, but I feel I should be here," you know. Speaking coaches say, 'Never, never, put yourself down,' but these preachers start very low key, and five minutes later, they're shouting!

He laughs and adds "It may even be a false modesty, but people expect it. I think maybe working-class people don't like it when you brag and put on airs. We have all kinds of expressions that condemn being other than modest, and preachers know that, so how can you say that is not a characteristic in that culture?"

Mike cautions that there are Appalachian men and women "who are braggarts, who do have big egos and pontificate," and so he hesitates to accept Loyal's trait list as applying to everyone; rather, we should consider them characteristics that "Appalachians ought to have and should aspire to . . . "

Rana Peake speaks of how those working in the community must be aware of what people deem important and agrees that modesty and humility are values that play a large part in dealing with others.

When meeting with Ricky Skaggs, I mentioned how admirable it was that he had never let his phenomenal success go to his head. Echoing Loyal Jones almost word for word, he replied, "Well, my mama taught me a long time ago that 'you're no better than anyone; you're as good as they are, but you're no better than they are!'"

Retired serviceman Tim D. was disappointed that his family didn't rejoice in his success in the military, where he had obtained the highest rank in the Air Force for enlisted men, that of chief master sergeant. Did they think he was "gettin' above his raisin'"? Was he failing to show humility when he spoke of his promotions?

I met with Tim in his comfortable house in suburban Dayton. He was wearing a sweatshirt with the logo of a West Virginia college team, apparently still loyal to his home state. While we talked at the dining room table, his grandson worked on his homework in the kitchen.

We were surrounded by numerous mementoes from Tim's assignments in Europe: Swarovski crystal, Hummel figurines, landscape paintings, Venetian glass, an inlaid table from Italy, a cuckoo clock from Germany, Lladro pottery, and much more. It's a far cry from his childhood home. He shares his experiences:

TIM D.'S STORY

I had a lot of frustrations with how my family acts, like for example it seemed like my accomplishments—to me they were accomplishments, when I would get promoted in the military, or I'd get a degree or something along that line, it seemed like a lot of my relatives felt like I was bragging.

It wasn't my intention at all to "put on airs." It's just that I got this job, I'm working on this, but I don't know what else . . . I felt like they thought I was a snob or something. And all we were doing was just talking about that I got things done. You'd think that in a normal family people would be really proud of you. It just didn't feel that way.

My mother—my mother is very quiet. She rarely says a word or two. Conversations are like "yes," "no," or "How's the weather," that kind of thing. You have to pry a conversation out of her, and I was just real frustrated with all that. I was like "Heck, you know, I broke out of the sticks, I was the first one in my family to go to college, the first one to do this kind of stuff," and I would have thought everybody would be all proud and happy, but it didn't seem like that kind of a life was a priority to them. That was an adjustment.

Then I read this book—I don't remember the name of it—they talked about that kind of stuff, and it was about what the Appalachian mentality was, like for example with my mother: I left home; she didn't. I can't get her to come visit me, but it's expected that I go there, because that's the homeland, that's the home where she's from, so it's: "When are you coming home? Why don't you come this way?"

I've got a brother who lives there, thank goodness, and helps take care of her, but he hasn't been here since I retired from the military, that's quite a few years ago. They won't leave that state and come this direction, and it's not like we're fighting or anything. That book kind of made me feel better about it. It's like that was home, I left home and they didn't, so that's just the way it is, I guess.

Actually how I got out of there was I went to a computer programming school. I was probably as big a hick as anybody, so to speak. Everybody likes to make fun of people from West Virginia and all that stuff—I was probably a junior in high school, maybe even a senior, before I really had any thought about what I was going to do. School was not even a consideration. I wasn't like, "Man, I've got to get good grades to go to college." College wasn't even thought of, wasn't even a discussion from the people I ran with or with my friends.

So this guy came to the high school. He had this little test, where you pick a picture, "What does this box look like if it was unfolded?" and all this kind of stuff, and he said, "You'd be good at computer programming. People who do this kind of stuff are good at computer programming." And I said. "Well, yeah, I've never really thought of it."

As it turned out there was another guy in my senior class, he did it, and so we decided that we were going to this course in Silver Spring, Maryland. They talked us into it, and it was government funded and all this kind of a deal. It was called Lear Siegler Institute for Computer Programming. What happened is the school went defunct. . . .

While I was there the draft was still going on, and my draft number was something like 36, and I really don't know how that works, but some of the guys around you, you know how they talk, they said, "Well, for your Small Hometown, USA that's going to be like one or two." I'm like "I don't want to go in the Army." I thought about the Navy with all those crackerjack outfits and all that. In that place where we were at in Maryland, all the recruiters were lined up in the same building, so I went in to talk to the guy in the Navy.

At the time I had really bad teeth, 'cause I never really took care of my teeth when I was little, so I was going to get false teeth. So here I was, a hot-headed teenager, and the recruiter guy, he just looked at me and he says, "The Navy's not going to fix your teeth." Of course I just got an immediate attitude, and I said, "I never asked you to fix my damn teeth!" and I walked right out the door and went next door and signed up for the Air Force, and I was there almost twenty-nine years. And they did fix my teeth! . . .

I had bad teeth because I never brushed them or took care of them, to be honest with you. That wasn't a priority back then. . . . It might have been different this day and. age, because instead of trying to get them fixed, I chose to pull them out. Nineteen years old and I had all false teeth.

[In my town] there was literally nobody who went to college. I take that back—one of my mother's sisters, she got out and got more education. . . . The kids in my town were just like "You grow up, you do what you want to do." Some are in coal mines, working with the local grocery stores, Walmart's: "Ooh! We finally got a Walmart, a Macdonald, so our town's really getting up there now!"

There were places like Union Carbide, but in the sticks up where I was from, coal mines were the things. There are a lot of mines going still.

I wanted to tell you, I grew up in a holler, and literally, the road was so bad. You had to go down, really down a little hill. My granddad had a house at the bottom of the hill; one of his daughters lived at the top of the hill. If you turned up the hill the other way, you've got to go across a little bitty creek and up the hill to the house where I grew up.

My youngest memories, we didn't have any running water. One of my chores was to go down to the creek and fill up a bucket of water or two and take it up the house, or bring in coal or wood for the fire. One of the first things I learned was how to pack a fire for the night so it wouldn't go out. We were there until my dad was killed, when I was eleven, and we had advanced to the point where we had a well, dug a well right behind the house, and my mother had one of these pumps in the kitchen that was connected to the well.

That was it: a wood-burning stove for cooking with. We did our baths standing in a No. 10 washtub behind this other stove in the other room, to take "spot baths," whatever you like to call it. Again, heated the house with coal, one of the rooms had aluminum on the roof so you could hear the rain hitting it. The house was literally backed right up to the woods. We had to walk through the woods one way to get to the pig trough, where we raised pigs, and then down the other way—they eventually moved the pig up back that way, and the chicken coop . . .

I told you that even if I was doing good, it was kind of like I was bragging. I didn't know how to take it. Even with my mother, although she would say that was good or whatever, I kind of got the feeling that it just didn't mean that much to her, that I'd graduated cum laude or whatever, that I'd already gotten my master's degree, that I'd gotten promoted to chief master sergeant, which is the highest enlisted grade that you can get. So those kinds of things that I was talking about, it was like it was coming across like I was all cocky or, like I said, I guess you just don't brag about those kind of things, and I guess that's what I was doing, was bragging, but I wanted them to know what was happening, what was going on.

I have a master's in early education, but none of my degrees were the same. My associate's degree was in military food administration, because I worked in the hospital with dieticians with military, and my bachelor's was business management, and then I went to early education, thinking that I wanted to be an elementary school teacher, and that didn't work out for several reasons, and I ended up getting a job at the base museum [the National Museum of the United States Air Force], where I work now, and I've been there for the last ten years now.

One of the recent ways that I've changed is when I would go home for a visit, it was such a slow pace of life. People are just sitting around, and it's quiet. . . .

Along with modesty, "neighborliness" is listed among Loyal Jones' Appalachian values, but it may mean something different to a Northerner, as Dr. Janice Wilson found out. "Maybe I can tell you a couple of stories that would highlight the difference," she says.

In Appalachia, there is a kind of banding together around tragedy. In my third year I had roomed with a girl from Berea—she was a close friend. She got married a year before I did. I was first married and I was teaching at the high school, right across the street. She had married an older man—not that much older, he was only thirty, but I went to school one day and discovered that he had died during the night.

My first impulse was to go. She was going to need me. But I didn't have a car, and my husband needed the car that day. So I went to the principal's office and said, "I need to leave. It's my free period. I'd like to leave because I need to see Janet. Connor just died. Oh, my goodness."

They said, "Are you sure you should intrude?" And so I borrowed a car from a friend, and I went to their house. But they found that inappropriate.

And then, we had neighbors who lived next door, in our first little house, and the wife died, I guess. Or there was some tragic happening. They had two children, and they came home. I made a dish and took it over to them, and they were very surprised.

We had both moved here, and they lived about six houses down the street. When she died, I baked banana bread, and my husband and I both walked to their house and delivered the bread. We thought we would give our condolences and stay five minutes. Well, we never got in the door. They came to the door and they looked confused on what to do, so we told them how sorry we were, I gave them the bread, and they took the bread and closed the door.

The Midwesterners had such a reputation for friendliness and hospitality, but compared to that kind of opening the doors to everybody that I grew up with and you probably grew up with, it's not anywhere near that.

The Appalachian spirit of hospitality is still alive and well, she says, especially in those who keep holiday traditions.

When I visited my cousins in Detroit, it was going back home, right there in the middle of Detroit. The houses were decorated as you might expect, probably better, but in the same style. The meals were always extravagant, and the women always kept their role.

I have one cousin in Detroit and, when my aunt was still alive, I spent a lot of time with her, because about the time my mother died in 2000 her health started to deteriorate. She was always like a mother to me, so I started to go up, two or three times a year. We'd spend Thanksgiving usually at my cousin's house, and her mother and a couple of women from the home county in West Virginia would be there. Everybody would come in and there would be loads of food—a turkey, a ham, maybe some spareribs, and six or eight vegetables, and four pies and three cakes, and pickles and relishes, I mean just a huge spread, because that's how the women cooked.

"Because we're human," says Rana Peake, "we bring our own experiences into whatever situation, and, if you're not familiar with this particular culture, it's just natural to think that everybody has the same values and cultural system that you come from." She adds:

I learned very quickly that that is not the case, and we need to be very conscientious when we work with the community, because especially in the Appalachian community, relationships are everything. And so if you don't take the time to build that relationship, all of the things that you're trying to accomplish, whether they're for the greater good or not, are not going to happen, because you haven't taken the time to build that relationship with that family or that school. And the same goes for the schools, even their structures.

Like for instance I'll work with a school in the Appalachian community, and even though maybe the teachers or the principal may not be Appalachian, the nature of how a child's school is run is often steeped in Appalachian values and culture. It's very much--it takes a long time—they're very cautious of people coming in and wanting to be and "I'm here to help" and that kind of thing. So in the same way that I have to build one-on-one relationships with people, I had to do that same thing, because I was seeing those same values bubbling up in the system. It's very interesting.

Honesty is another characteristic that is highly honored, which can lead to the impression of a lack of commitment. As Tess Little says:

Our word is our honor. My mother, to this day—my mother is 83—and I will say, "Mom, are you going to come Christmas? We're going to have Christmas at 4:30, and are you going to come?"

"If I can."

"Well, Mother, why don't you say you'll come, 'Yes, you can.'"

"No, I can't. What if something happens, and I can't come."

That used to bother me, that my own mother wouldn't say—of course, my mother's never missed a Christmas, but she would never say, "Yes, I'm going to come," and finally, when I understood that it was her word of honor and if she broke it, then she's lying, so she couldn't say for sure that she would come, because she wasn't positively sure that she would come. That's her word of honor.

Does that ever sound familiar! Mother, who did indeed have health problems, would always respond with the proviso that she might or might not be able to come: "depending on how I feel."

This hesitation to commit has followed Tess into her professional life.

My husband has this rule, too, this cultural rule. When I started REACH, I was going to do it for one year, and the college came to me and said, "Tess, we want a commitment for three years."

Well, being a little more into mainstream culture than my husband was, I went home and I said, "Honey, they want me to do it for three years," and he said, "Oh—how do you even know where you'll be in three years? How do you know you'll even be alive in three years? How can you do that in three years? How can you say that you'll do that for three years? You don't even know what's going to happen in three years."

I said, "Jim, I've watched these people, and let me tell you what they do. They say, "Yes we'll do it for three years,' and if something happens, they say, "Oh, I have to back out of this. I can't do it." And I said, "And that's OK for them."

So that keeps us down, because we won't make the plans, because we can't be sure.

Like Rana Peake, Tess concludes that "it's only natural to think that everybody has the same values and cultural system that you come from," although that isn't always the case.

That was a statement that resonated with me. Long ago in college I volunteered for a sorority project on which I was partnered with another young woman. When the project was completed, even though I had done essentially all the work, I humbly let her acknowledge the thanks, thinking she'd give me credit where credit was due. Apparently we were not on the same cultural wave length, because she didn't. (*Bitch!*) I also learned that Appalachians have long memories.

There is another side of the coin, too, for, as Weller says, "Such person-oriented behavior among mountain people tends to make them supersensitive to presumed slights or criticisms of their behavior."[2]

Was this sensitivity a factor in Walter G's "Don't tread on me" reaction to what he considered an encroachment on his rights? The Pennsylvania transplant from Kentucky complains that companies will do anything if they can get away with it.

For years here we had Comcast television. There was a little T.V. company here and I hooked up on it, and then Comcast bought them out. When they come down the road, they wanted to run the cable underground, but not through my property! I came out of the house—I happened to be there, it was a Saturday—and the guy's got one of them big saws.

I had just put a new driveway in, asphalt driveway, and he started cutting through my driveway for that cable. I said, "What are you doing?"

He said, "We're going to run the cable down through here."

I said, "You're not running it through *my* yard, through my property."

He says, "Well, we're a public utility!"

I says, "That's news to me."

"What do you mean that's news to you?" he says. "Comcast is one of the—"

I said, "Yeah, and they walk on people if they can." I said, "You're not bringing that cable through my property underground." I said, "You can go across the road, you can go across the street, but you're not coming through my property!"

That put them in a stall. They said, "But we're a public utility!" I said, "No, you're not a public utility. Comcast is governed by the communications; it's not a public utility." He said, "What?" I said, "That's right. Show me a letter that you are a public utility and you can come through my property, but right now, if you start with that saw, I'm going to start with buckshot!"

They didn't come through my property. They moved up the street and took the cable back across to come back across the street. There wasn't nobody during the summer and autumn. There wasn't nobody there during the week. In fact, they run a cable across the overhead on a piece of property behind.

I bought the ground because people were making a landfill out of it, and every time I come out on the porch, I could see that landfill. I bought the ground, I paid to clean it up, they run a cable across it without asking.

I went down and I took a pair of cutters. I went down and where it first hit my property, I cut the line, and at the other end I cut it, rolled it up and threw it away. And I ain't never heard nothing more about it!

"As former rural plain folk living in the urban North," says Chad Berry, "southerners brought their worldviews with them. One of the elements of this worldview was honor, which a typical southern migrant . . . would go to great lengths to preserve."[3]

Is it a sense of honor that demands that we not ask for help? That often-praised self-reliance and independence has a downside. Kathy Rowell of Sinclair College recognizes that she has a real problem with asking for help, a problem that we share, even though we know it can hold us back.

"I make my friends so angry," she says, "because you don't ask for help. If you do, it would be just from family, like I'll call my mom and ask her for help, but I'd have to pretty desperate—we're self-reliant. And I help people all the time, but I cannot ask for help, and it makes my friends angry. People get upset with me. They're like, 'You help us all the time,' but I just cannot do it. It's impossible for me."

"Oh, no," Tess Little agrees, "We don't network. That networking crap that they teach us—to learn that and think about that—because that's weakness. Yes, we would love to help somebody, but you're not going to ask for help."

Not asking for help is a mindset that extends to family problems; you don't invite outsiders to share in things that involve your kin, even though that family might be dysfunctional.

Of all the values that Appalachians hold dear, "family" is the most important; the framework on which their lives are built. As in my extended family history, you find a job for the alcoholic brother, you help the loser nephew out with his car payments, you move in with a cousin, maybe, if you need post-operative care, or your sister takes you in if you leave your abusive husband. Or, as in Linda Williams' family, as a twenty-year-old newlywed, you adopt your half-brother's troubled ten-year-old son.

Even though it might be necessary to move from the old homestead, your heart belongs in the country, and you return as often as you can, even when you're working in the city, for "making a living must never interfere with [family] obligations."[4]

In Appalachia, says Tess Little, "usually when the families got together, the men would go off and talk by themselves, and the women would talk. It was a segregated thing. The women went in the kitchen and talked, and the men went outside and talked, and the children ran around and played . . ."

It seems that in public, it's usually the man that voices an opinion, while his wife stays quiet. As in Japan, however, what happens in public may be very different from what goes on in the home.

So who runs the family? There are those, like Ronnie Day, who say unequivocally that Appalachian culture "is a patriarchy."[5] But is that true?

"No," says Tess Little. "It's really matriarchal, but the men thought they were the bosses, and the women would let them think that, and they'd just smile . . . It's a matriarchal culture with a veneer that made the man think he was in control. That works, but it's manipulative," she thinks, and something she does not wish to emulate.

"The mother is at the center of the family," says Carol C. Stephens of Western Carolina University, "and "the mother's position is one of the most power in the home. She has tremendous responsibilities, including the health of the family and she works hard, but she is also the one who is in charge at home."[6]

In my own family, Mammy was considered "feisty," horrifying her children in her eighties by climbing on a ladder to hang wallpaper. She must have had a strong, independent nature to have led her to marry Pappy. Not quite eighteen, the only child of Catholic parents in a close-knit, Catholic community, she told her parents she would be staying with her cousin, took the horse and buggy, crossed the flooding creek, and eloped with my Methodist grandfather.

"Oh, my mother ran the show," Rose Dwight remembers. "Because my grandfather had all these girls, they were expected to work as hard as any man [at his slaughterhouse], so they had to carry a quarter of a beef or whatever. When my mother was sixteen, she took her older sister's driver's license and drove a truck from West Virginia to Detroit to get a load of cattle. All of those women in her family were tough like that. She would say, "I want go to New York and see my sister," so she and I would go to New York on the train . . . My mother and father lived in separate worlds."

Rose Dwight, who has a master's degree in education, claims her mother was "a wheeler and a dealer." When Rose was supposed to go to a one-room schoolhouse, her mother paid tuition with rationing stamps for her to attend another school and "bribed the bus driver to take me to that bigger school over the mountains," she says. "She always wanted me to take dancing lessons; she wanted me to be special. I ended up playing an accordian because that would make me different. She just always had these things going on. I remember looking at other people—I've always had nice school dresses, because she made them all . . ."

It was not always a comfortable position for Rose to be in, because "I was aware that there were these differences; in that culture you had to be very homogeneous. If you acted like you were a big dog, you would have been ostracized in a minute."

Rose had many role models of strong women in her family: "One was the first woman with a pilot's license, one was Miss Charleston, another was an educator and got a Ph.D. and worked for a publisher, another was a good singer and went to Juilliard . . ."

When Sheila Taylor's parents were unable to care for her, it was her grandmother who took charge, and "Mamaw, she ruled the roost," she recalls. "The women were the ones that were at home running everything. The men went out to work, and maybe when they came in, they might have been the ultimate authority, but really the women ran everything. When you think about it, the cooking, the cleaning, the ironing, the kids—they made the world go 'round."

We don't have to look far to find other examples of strong women. Janice's mother saw that her children's future was limited if they stayed in the mountains. "My mother was stronger on this than most parents," Janice says, "but I grew up knowing that—one of my expectations was that—I would get out of there and find someplace better, because my mother told us that all the time. She said, 'When you grow up, go somewhere out of these mountains where you'll have a chance and you can have a better life.'"

Babies and small children were—and are—loved and indulged.

Horace Kephart noted back in 1913 that "most mountaineers are indulgent, super-indulgent parents . . . The boys, especially, grow up with little restraint beyond their own natural sense of filial duty. Little children are allowed to eat and drink anything they want—green fruit, adulterated candy, fresh cider, no matter what—to the limit of repletion. . . ."[7]

Over fifty years later, Jack Weller would say much the same thing: "While the child is still a baby and does not object to being an adult's toy, he is part of the world of his parent," cuddled and adored, but "as children grow, they are more and more allowed to form their own reference group, and parents cease to play with them as they mature beyond infancy. . . Girls are expected to become little mothers, and boys are given a great deal of freedom . . ."[8]

"Mountain children are reared impulsively," he adds. "Discipline is meted out with no concern about how the child will react as a child. In such an adult-centered society, children's feelings are not given great weight. When they misbehave, they are punished—and it is always physical punishment. . . . [9] And justice is swift.

As country singer Charlie Louvin says about the whipping he got for lying and skipping school, "Today that's called child abuse; back then it's called raisin' children."[10]

When children reach a certain age—as early as eight, according to Dr. Carol Baugh, they are expected to make their own decisions. Dr. Baugh, of Sinclair College's Appalachian Studies Department and past president of the national Appalachian Studies Association, says, "The Appalachian culture is very indulgent and loving until the child is eight years old, and then he is 'thrown out in the street.' The child has to fend for himself and learn from his own mistakes with little guidance from parents."

As an example, she recalls that her father would let her stay up past her 10:00 bedtime and let her see how hard it was for her to get up in the morning.

While Carol doesn't literally mean a child is thrown out in the street, that is what happened to Dr. Vivian Blevins' father when he reached twelve. After his mother died and his father abandoned the family, he was taken in by a foster family at age four. Eight years later the family kicked him out, saying, "You're on your own now." Fortunately he had an older brother who was an electrician, so he was able to live with him and learn his trade.

Vivian remembers her childhood training on a more positive note, however. "My mother always said from the time I was little, 'I trust you to do what is right and make your own decisions.' She never said, 'Come in at this time. Do this, don't do this.' She said, 'I trust you to make your own decisions.' From when I was very young, I was very independent in terms of making my own decisions, very independent. It also makes you responsible. If you make your own decisions, you're responsible for them."

While giving children responsibility at an early age might have been necessary on the farm, it would not be an advantage in an urban setting. In fact, some claim it is a detriment to the child's development.

In his classic *Yesterday's People,* Jack E. Weller writes, "This training, based as it is on the fear of punishment, builds into the child either a resentment toward or a fear of authority of any kind."[11]

It can also lead to consequences in adolescence, especially among boys. "For example," says Weller, "any boy who does well in school, or who studies hard, or who sets goals for his life which he tells the group about, becomes the object of ridicule; he either succumbs to the pressure or else is dropped from the group altogether. By this means a group solidarity is maintained. . . . Adolescent society, in short, is very much unguided by experienced adults."[12]

All people love their children," says Tess Little, the sociologist from Sinclair College, "but there are different ways of child raising. When I was young, and in most of America, we turned our children loose and let them go out and experiment and find out, and now we don't.

Generally across America, we watch them: helicopter parents.

But what does the culture do?—like for instance in my culture, you didn't send your child to college, the child would go out and work his way through college, whereas in mainstream culture, they felt like it was the parents' obligation to send the child to college. I had friends who said, 'When I went to college, my parents paid for it,' but my parents didn't have the money, but even if they had had the money, that wasn't in the cards. It was the belief that a child should figure out how to get through college on his own. So that's a cultural belief, a cultural norm. We all have those, and we don't even know we have them, because we're raised with them. We think everybody has those cultural norms.

Education was OK, but not so important when there was work on the farm and in mines. What is more, getting to school was a hardship for many. Even today it is not always easy to attain when schools are hard to get to.

We found this out after my husband and I visited Thurmond, West Virginia, the site of the film *Matewan.* We could backtrack, or, according to the map, we could take the road uphill, a "shortcut" that should eventually lead to the highway. The narrow road on the side of the cliff was rutted and became even more narrow, until the spot where almost half the pavement had slid down the mountainside.

Eventually we came to the "town" of Thayer, West Virginia, marked with a wooden sign, and passed two or three rundown shacks, a dilapidated trailer that may or may not have been occupied, and an abandoned wooden church, a dried wreath hanging on the door. Here the road forked, one rutted, unpaved track going sharply uphill, the other going downhill to a tiny railway station; neither looked navigable.

The group of young people we met who were going up and down the hill on an ATV confirmed that the uphill way required a four-wheel drive and we'd better not attempt it. I asked how the young girl among them, who looked to be about ten, ever got to school.

"Well, she misses a lot," said her big sister, "and when the floods washed away the road, they had to open up a road along the railroad track so we could get out."

It is surprising how many parents—mothers, especially, do make sure that their children get an education, like Michael Maloney's mother. Michael, now an authority on Appalachia, and his widowed mother worked hard to have him succeed. There are reports that other mothers and grandmothers sold jams and handmade items in order to afford for their children to go to school.

It is surprising how many of those children of the mountains have been educated through their own or their family's efforts. Many of those interviewed did attend college, at least for a period of time, as did their siblings and children. Education seemed more acceptable for women; men were supposed to do "real work."

Dr. Vivian Blevins, whose orphaned father worked as an electrician for a coal mine, was one of four children, all of whom received graduate degrees. Vivian, for example, worked "thirty or forty hours a week" at Kroger's while at the university, while others of an older generation took advantage of the G.I. Bill.

When it comes to education, Rana Peake of Sinclair Community College notes the conflicting emotions.

When you're from the mountains, it is not even a part of your vision, because that's not part of the world that you live in. Appalachians are very practical, very pragmatic. Education is valued as long as it—but how is it going to impact the sustainability of our family? I want to be trained to do something so that I can support my family, because Appalachians, we take care of our own.

One interesting thing that emerged from a study conducted at the college was that there's very much a push-pull with higher education. Parents were incredibly proud that their kid was going to college. You know, 'Johnny's going off to college!' They were really proud, but at the same time, 'Don't get above your raisin'. There was often a pull from family and friends to come back home.

As Alessandro Portelli says, "Education does not always rank very high in the priorities of mountain families. 'Getting above one's raising' is a serious infraction in a culture based on equality and solidarity."[13] Parents fear that their children will think that they are smarter than those who raised them.

I can remember hearing how anxious my mother's cousin's parents were when he went off to college. They worried that it might have changed him and were relieved when he came back home for the first time, walked in, sat in his favorite overstuffed chair, and asked, "What's for supper?" With relief, they told the rest of family that he was "still the same old Wesley Roy Brooks"—which became one of our little family sayings: If you went somewhere or did something special, upon return it was said that you were, hopefully, "still the same old Wesley Roy Brooks."

The journalist Hodding Carter once wrote that it is a parent's duty to give their children "roots" and "wings." Mountain children may find themselves well rooted, but the wings to leave the nest are more likely to be clipped.

Oddly, in some respects Appalachian ways seem more Japanese than mainstream American, perhaps because both are traditional societies: the separate lives the parents live, the same power of the mother in the home, the same nonconfrontational and indirect communication, the same "high context culture" in which people understand each other almost without needing language, the same respect for modesty, as evidenced by the Japanese saying: "The nail that sticks out gets hammered down." The same indulgence of young children followed by their assuming of responsibility at an early age, but in the Japanese case it's the schools that apply the screws.

Melissa is a typical Midwesterner whose husband Higashi is Japanese. She speaks of the mainstream American family she grew up in: "I love them, but they've got their own minds and they're doing their own thing, and there's not that 'I have to be there for them' idea. . . . You have each other, but you go and leave for different homes, and that's it." From Higashi's perspective, she says, her upbringing was like being raised in "a litter of puppies."[14] It's too bad he has yet to meet an Appalachian family.

For those who fear the traditional ways will be lost, the Reverend Linda Williams has some reassuring words, using this analogy:

My great-grandmother was a profound Christian, and so was my great-grandfather. Now this trickle-down effect: my grandfather wasn't; my grandmother was to a degree. It's like using a teabag. You start with a strong teabag and you have a little strong tea, you put it in the second cup, and it's OK, you put it in the third one, and it's not very good, but then you're all used to drinking bad tea. You don't know you're drinking bad tea, so you have that trickle-down effect, 'cause my values are not the same values that part of my family has, or even my son,—but you know what? They respect it. That's where you see the difference.

And the Appalachian people, when they see something, when they finally see you are you are, that you're real, there is a respect that they give you, and it's fantastic.

NOTES

1. Loyal Jones, *Appalachian Values*, (Ashland, KY: Jesse Stuart Foundation, 1994).

2. Jack E.Weller, *Yesterday's People,* (Lexington: University of Kentucky Press, 1965), 53.

3. Chad Berry, *Southern Migrants, Northern Exiles*, (Urbana: University of Illinois Press, 2000), 139.

4. Obermiller and Maloney, 347.

5. Ronnie Day, "Pride and Poverty: An Impressionistic View of the Family in the Cumberlands of Appalachia," *Appalachia Inside Out* (Knoxville: University of Tennessee Press, 1995), 371.

6. Carol C. Stephens, "Culturally Relevant Preventive Health Care for Southern Appalachian Women," *Appalachian Cultural Competency,* Susan E. Keefe, ed., (Knoxville: University of Tennessee Press, 2005), 209.

7. Horace Kephart, *Our Southern Highlanders*, (Knoxville: University of Tennessee Press, 2013), 334.

8. Weller, 64.

9. Ibid, 65.

10. Nicholas Dawidoff, *In the Country of Country,* (New York: Pantheon/Random House, 1997), 138–39.

11. Ibid., 66.

12. Ibid., 69.

13. Alessandro Portelli, *They Say in Harlan County: An Oral History*, (Oxford: Oxford University Press, 2011), 297.

14. Nancy Brown Diggs, *Looking Beyond the Mask*, (Albany; NY: State University of New York Press, 2001), 68–69.

Grave marker with inscription: "William Cash, Born 1625, Fife, Scotland; Died 1690, Salem, Mass.; Master Mariner. Captain & Master of Brigantine 'Good Intent.'" Old Burying Point, Salem, MA. Photograph by author.

John Willis Scott and "Jennie" Howard Scott ("Mammy" and "Pappy"). Circa 1895. Author's family photograph.

John Willis Scott and "Jennie" Howard Scott ("Mammy" and "Pappy"). Circa 1922. Source unknown. Author's family photograph.

Author's great-grandfather Henry Howard's still. Date unknown. Author's family photograph.

"School bus," driven by Sam Morgan's father William. The teacher, Sam's Aunt Gladys, stands at the schoolhouse door, a Frontier Nurse on horseback at the right. 1930s. Courtesy of Sam Morgan.

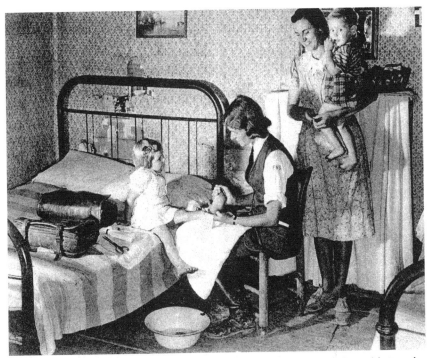

Sam Morgan's sister Sally and mother Mae, holding his brother Charles, with Frontier Nurse. Original caption: "Out of the Night and the Dangerous Ways Comes an Angel of Mercy." July, 1942. Courtesy of *National Geographic*.

Chapter Seven

Strangers in a Strange Land

"[The] southern hillbilly migrants, who have descended on Chicago like a plague of locusts in the last few years, have the lowest standard of living and moral code [if any] . . ." wrote Norma Lee Browning in the *Chicago Tribune* in 1957.[1]

Moving from their mountain homes to the cities meant a better life financially for most Appalachians, but there was an emotional price to pay, for they and their children would be anything but welcome.

With mining jobs decreasing in the 1950s, many headed for Akron's rubber plants or Michigan's booming industries. Native Michiganders referred to Ypsilanti as "Ypsi-tucky," a pejorative term that the immigrants would eventually embrace with pride. The three "R's" for the mountain folk were called: "reading, 'riting, and Route 23," the road back home.

Wanda P., in her late seventies, remembers her nine years as a child in Detroit, until her father lost his job and the family moved back to Kentucky.

"They never did send me to school up there," she says. "I guess those black people up there were mean to them, and Mom said, 'David, those colored kids were throwing cinder blocks at them!'—at my sisters, the older ones. They could have hurt them. She said she was afraid to send me to school, because I was so skinny. . ."

With the stress of the new environment, far from family and facing hostility, many of the newcomers developed health problems. Rhoda H. Halperin and Jennifer Reiter-Purtill investigated the problem of "nerves"—anxiety and depression—among urban Appalachians. They found more severe cases than they would have expected in a non-urban area "because the adaptive systems such as family-based support networks have been destroyed."[2]

Although many Appalachians went far afield, most preferred to stay close enough to home that they could go back frequently. Those migrating from eastern Kentucky headed for the closest industrialized cities: Cincinnati, Hamilton, and Dayton, while those from West Virginia were more likely to go to Columbus, Cleveland, Akron, and Canton.[3] The Miami Valley, which extends from north of Cincinnati through Hamilton, Middletown, and Dayton, "gained proportionately more southern white newcomers than any other extended area in the North."[4]

They settled in neighborhoods like Cincinnati's Lower Price Hill or Dayton's East End, where beachheads had been established by earlier transplants, in much the same way that immigrants do today. There, as in Chicago, they sought to be close to those from home. If they were close to family members, so much the better, for then they were sure to find help if they needed it.

In Chicago, the more put-downs, stereotyping and ethnic jokes they endured from the locals, the more they banded together in a "defensive response." A "group consciousness" was created.[5] And the more they kept to themselves, the less outsiders could understand them.

Not only did they face the hostility of the native community, says Roger Guy, but "anyone with a southern accent was likely to face police."[6] Not unlike in the early mining camps, men would gather in the local "hillbilly tavern," where they would drink too much, get in fights, and end up in a confrontation with the police. In her exposé of Chicago's Uptown in the 1950s, Browning wrote: "Skid row dives, opium parlors, and assorted other dens of iniquity collectively are as safe as Sunday school picnics compared with the joints taken over by clans of fightin', feudin', Southern hillbillies and their shootin' cousins."[7]

A contemporary social worker noted the "paranoia" of the police, which led them to "excessive and unnecessary" violence, brutality, and harassment.[8] He added that the police were beating our [southern] people in the head for no damn reason—just because they had a southern accent. They'd see them on the street corner and be just down right violent.'"[9]

As newcomers continue to arrive from poverty-stricken areas of Appalachia, long-held hostility still surfaces. Rose Dwight, known as the "go-to" person for anything about Appalachian culture, was shocked when she was working in the education department of Planned Parenthood. She says:

> While attending a teen pregnancy prevention workshop led by a presenter who was a teacher in the Dayton Public Schools, I asked her where all the white East End girls in the program were.
>
> In a flash she said, "You know those girls; they get pregnant because it means they won't have to go to school."
>
> Those were my people she was talking about!—third- and fourth-generation-Appalachians who have really fallen on hard times. I became so angry at her

comment that I almost blacked out. When I left that meeting, I was determined to find out the story of these neglected girls.

I went everywhere on the East Side and interviewed people at libraries, churches, service providers, landromats, etc. I was possessed. I read everything I could about the Appalachian culture. . . .

It was Rose who directed me to community leader Sheila Taylor. When I met with Sheila at a local coffee shop, she had just had extensive dental surgery, joking that she didn't want to fit the stereotype of an Appalachian with bad teeth. Sheila, who says she was born in 1952 but looks much younger, has made remarkable progress since a childhood of poverty.

Somewhere along the line, she has lost any mountain accent she might have had. When I mention the prejudice that often comes with the accent, she thinks colleges are just being realistic when they work to rid students of their accents. "What they're trying to do is say. 'With that accent, you're not going to go anywhere because people won't hire you.'"

She says to me, "You have an accent yourself."

"A little bit."

"A little bit? You think you've got a little bit. When I talked to you on the phone, I knew right away. I thought, 'This woman's writing about Appalachia. Where's she from?'"

Well, maybe I did lay it on more than usual.

Sheila talks about being "put down" because of her accent and claims she has always felt like "a stranger in a strange land" after moving from a mining town to the city. In Kentucky they lived in a company town, where most of her family worked for the mines in the skilled trades. They lived in houses owned by the mine, did their shopping at the company store. When her maternal grandfather died, the family had to move to a smaller house, so "they were kind of owned by the mine . . . but my mother saw beauty in the mountains, rather than what she owned."

As mining became less prosperous in the mountains, manufacturing elsewhere was booming, and the companies wanted to hire them "because they were good workers."

Sheila recalls that with a mother too ill from depression to care for the children and "self-medicating" with alcohol, and a loving but alcoholic father, she looked to her "Mamaw" as the mainstay of the family.

SHELIA TAYLOR'S STORY

My sister wrote Mamaw, who lived here in Dayton, my mother's mother. My sister was like twelve years old when they moved up here and let her know how things were. So one morning my grandmother and my Uncle Hugh showed up in a big car and packed all of us up, leaving my dad, who was not there at the time, and moved us to Dayton. Because family takes care of family, I stayed with my Aunt Vera, my mom's twin sister, and my sister and brother stayed with Mamaw and Uncle Hugh for a year.

So my mother got out of treatment. She was out at Dayton State Hospital, did shock treatment and my mom's family then started looking around for where she was going to be. We were out of school for the summer. It was important for my mom's family that we finish the school year, too. But see, that's not necessarily the case, because this is my story.

What would happen is that my mother got very little child support, because that's how it was. She supported us on the child support, and my grandmother—she was another very Appalachian person.

We would go to Mamaw's every Sunday, and they would bring us groceries. Mamaw would shop during the week, and she would buy for herself, my uncle, and us, and she was always certain there was fresh fruit. She always made sure we had something sweet, and she would get the staples to help us get through the week. She had a huge garden, too . . .

Being an Appalachian child that came from a dysfunctional family and having a grandmother who said, "Go downstairs and get me a poke," and my mother having a very strong Appalachian accent, we were thrown into government housing, very poor.

My worst experience was the school system, and how people perceived us to be, because first of all people thought, "Your family lives in houses that aren't taken care of, they have trashy cars all parked out front in the yard." The perception as that you were from lazy Appalachians, briars, who won't work, who have cars sitting in front of the yard, you know, the whole attitude. We live way back in the mountains, you know.

So we go into the school system, and probably by that point, I had lived in five, six places, and I was in second grade. And not just in six different houses, but in six different areas, and my stability was the people, knowing that Mamaw was still out there, who was very, very Appalachian in terms of her speech, but see, she was also a very smart woman. She only had a third-grade education, but she knew what was going on in the Vietnam War.

She read every article. They got the newspaper, they got magazines, they did read, they did expose themselves to what was going on, they were very knowledgeable about presidential elections, those kinds of things.

When we moved to Parkside [subsidized housing], I was in the second grade. My mother was very upset because I kept bringing home coloring papers instead of school work and things like that. She went up to the school and she was trying to explain to the teacher that I was already ahead—I was like a year advanced. I had already had what they were teaching in the second grade. . . . They treated my mother very poorly because of her extremely strong accent. They just weren't attentive to our needs at all.

We had very poor teachers. We had an algebra teacher who was a football coach, and he started the class by saying, "Read the book and if you have any questions, come up and talk to me."

Well, by that time—I followed the rules, OK? And I started reading the book, and I don't understand. By the time I get up out of my chair to go up, the class is already in line. Well, the class was divided. Lunchtime was in the middle, and so by the time it was my turn, it was lunchtime, and when we got back, it was too late, because I was shy and backward. I tried to get a girl in the class to help me, and she did. . . .

My husband and his brothers went to the Catholic schools to an environment that taught them how to teach themselves. That's what I think about the Catholic schools: They teach you to learn, and then you can learn. They'd not just throw memory at you. We got into rote memory. . . .

When I was twelve years old, the lady across the street that I'd been babysitting for became pregnant with her third son, and when she went into the hospital, I took care of her children. Now the welfare system had a lady who came in from 8:00 to 4:00. She would start dinner. So I went across the street, finished up dinner, gave the two little boys a bath and put them to bed, and stayed the night. And then in the morning the lady came, and then I went home, at twelve years old! I got paid, I thought, a lot of money for that. I lived across the street and that was the only reason my mom would allow me to do that. But see, young kids could do more. They were given the responsibility to do more.

I think Appalachians are like that. You love the little kids, you just love the little kids. So I decided to go to school to study early childhood education, and it took me forever to get that degree!

Work at different places, marriage, and the birth of a daughter intervened. She then worked shifts, including the night shift, at the Daybreak Center for homeless teens, her husband sharing parental responsibility. Her love for children would eventually lead her to open her own day care center. Today she works as a clerk at the Municipal Court and serves as vice president of the Dayton School Board, where she's in a position to make sure other children are treated better than she was.

SPEAKING APPALACHIAN

"He studied her with a confusion she recognized. She was well accustomed to watching Yankee brains grind their gears, attempting to reconcile a hillbilly accent with signs of a serious education," Barbara Kingsolver writes in her book *The Prodigal Summer.*[10]

Perhaps "prejudice" is a better word than "discrimination," for Appalachians are "prejudged" by their origins and, especially, by their accents.

The most distinguishing feature may be the "i" sound, for example, as in "my" or "time," which is sometimes transcribed as "ah," but that's not quite it. My cousins and I would jokingly imitate L'il Abner's "ah" words, not realizing that what Al Capp was making fun of was the way *we* spoke!

Appalachian English, with all its regional differences in accent, vocabulary, and grammar has a long pedigree. Although it used to be said that Appalachians were speaking primarily Elizabethan English, that theory has long been discredited.

It is better thought of as "colonial" or "eighteenth-century English," says Michael Montgomery of the University of South Carolina. He confirms, not surprisingly, that the greatest influence on the speech of Appalachia is Scotch-Irish, of which Pennsylvania shows the most evidence.[11]

Vocabulary is important in tracing the path of languages, but, according to John B. Rehder, the author of *Appalachian Folkways*, "grammatical traits are thought to be deeper, stronger evidence." Of Michael Montgomery's forty grammatical usages that are considered "reliable diagnostic traits, . . . seventeen are Scotch-Irish, four are southern British, thirteen are general British, and six are uncertain."[12]

What was once the language of history's leaders, lairds, and landlords is now considered that of losers. "Isn't it ironic," says Michael E. Maloney, author of numerous publications on Appalachia, "because what we find out is that we're mostly pre-revolutionary and have real American pedigrees. You know, my daughter could join the DAR. She wouldn't, but the fact is that we have pedigrees that a lot of Americans would kill for, and yet we've been laughed at and scorned and made fun of."

"How," Loyal Jones wonders, "are people affected by vicious stereotypes and by being classed as inferior because of their accents or manner?"[13] How it must damage immigrants to learn that the way they and their family speak is not acceptable and that their way of life is the object of ridicule!"

Amie Sparks Ball, then a graduate student at Eastern Kentucky University, researched employer attitudes and found that, not only are those who speak with the accent of Appalachia discriminated against in their hiring, but the dialect affects their performance appraisals and perceptions of their leadership qualities.[14]

Dr. Judy Hennessey, superintendent of the award-winning Dayton Early College Academy schools, was once advised not to tell anyone that she was from Kentucky when she went to apply for a job, or she might not be hired.

Jane Leigh ran into the problem of discrimination when she began to teach in Oakwood, an upscale suburb of Dayton. The father of a student told her that he was concerned that children would acquire her Tennessee accent and end up "talking the way you do."

She replied, "Well, you know, no kid has ever gone out of my classes talking like me unless he came in here talking like me. And I believe if I were you, I'd just relax and not worry about it!"

In spite of this point against her in the father's mind, she had a successful teaching career in Oakwood for many years before retiring.

Such prejudice rankles Angel Asher, a paralegal and a graduate of Wright State University. She says, "I have found that if I'm not careful about how I say things and my mannerisms that people automatically assume that I'm not intelligent, because of my Appalachian roots—and I've said this time and time again—I'm not going to apologize for where I came from and the roots I have, because they've made me who I am."

Her mother Diana Watkins adds that "I do think that lots of folks think Appalachian people are poor and uneducated—"

"—poor, dumb hillbillies," Angel adds.

"That's not true. That's not correct. Even if we go back years and years ago with our family, what we know is we come from a family of very hardworking, very humble people who did not expect anything, and with a lot of pride took care of things."

Ricky Skaggs moved from Cordell, Kentucky, to West Jefferson, Ohio, near Columbus, when his mother wanted to be with her much-loved ailing father. Until Ricky's grandfather retired, he had worked as a night watchman at the Darby Dan Farm, where the wealthy Galbraith family raised race horses.

Ricky, too, faced discrimination, but he was lucky, as he describes.

We moved up there, and so I had to go to school—I think I started my ninth grade, high school. So anyway, when I got there, people were calling me "Hey, Hillbilly!" because of my accent, you know, and it didn't bother me too much. I mean it kind of did, but you know what? I had a couple of guys—their mom and dad was from West Virginia and they ran the roost up there in high school. And it was like, "Hey, 'Hill'! What's up, man?" They loved the fact that I'd bring my fiddle to school or bring my guitar to school, and they really, really loved me, and it was like they would crack a head if someone came up and tried to—you know.

Rose Dwight, the expert on Appalachian culture, has focused her career on helping others understand their Appalachian neighbors through teaching at Dayton's Sinclair Community College and lecturing on the subject. Surprisingly, it was in West Virginia that she first faced prejudice:

"I went to college in Marshall in Huntington for two years, and I was really, really bored," she says. "So I decided that I wanted to go to West Virginia University, so I did, but it was an awful experience. People just really made fun of my country accent."

"How could that be?" I wondered.

"Well, at that time, in 1958, it was full of Polish folks from Pennsylvania. They could come down there and they could go cheaper than they could at the University of Pittsburgh or Penn State. And I was really depressed . . ."

Dr. Vivian Blevins recalls moving from Kentucky to Toledo, Ohio, at age thirteen. Although she was already a sophomore, she was placed in an English class for slow learners, since it was assumed that any Appalachian child would be behind. When she quickly advanced, she was moved to a class of average students. From there it wasn't long until she was in the college prep classes and well on her way to her M.A. from Eastern Kentucky University and a Ph.D. from Ohio State. Having been the president/chancellor of colleges in Kentucky, Texas, California, and Missouri, she now teaches writing and American literature at Edison State Community College. Among other pursuits, she writes a weekly column for seven newspapers in three states and continues to receive awards for her many accomplishments.

I would describe Dr. Blevins as a "presence." She wears her long blond hair in a ponytail to the side, and, she says, she loves jewelry. I would think she was an artist, but rather she is an award-winning educator.

Coming from West Virginia, Janice Wilson was shocked at the reception she received in Xenia, Ohio, not far from Dayton. Although there are many Appalachians in her town, "this place is Appalachian-averse," she says.

DR. JANICE WILSON'S STORY

There are a great many Appalachians here, but they didn't want them. I came here to teach, and I started dating and then married a man whose family came here in 1796. That got me in a lot of doors. I got invited to do things locally and in the school that two of my friends who had moved up from Kentucky never got invited to because I had this legitimacy from having married into an old family.

I'd been here almost a year. It was summertime and there was a church ice cream social at the Presbyterian Church, and, whoever the minister was, he was "Dr. Somebody"—I can't remember the name . . . Anyway, my boyfriend Art took me to the ice cream social, and we get our ice cream and we go for a picnic table, and there's one where the minister is sitting.

Art said, "Let's join him," so we went over and sat down. Art introduced me to him and added, "And she's from West Virginia." And the minister laughed out loud!

Then he caught himself and said, "Virginia is a beautiful state." And I said, "So is West Virginia. You ought to go there sometime." But he laughed because I was a hillbilly.

West Virginians have more of a drawl than an accent, and Kentuckians have more twang—eastern—the farther you go into the mountains, the more you get the twang. Anyway, I had a real drawl. I spoke very slowly, and I would say things like, "Oh, my gracious!" "Bless your heart!" That's another one.

When Art told his mother that he was going to marry me—it was partly because I was from the South, but partly because she just didn't want to lose her son—the first time I saw her, I was six feet away from her and she walked right past me and didn't speak to me. This was because she didn't want him to marry me, but it was also the hillbilly accent because later, much later, one of his cousins who became one of my closest friends told me that when she told the family about Art getting married, she would say, "Janice is from the South, but she's very nice."

I'd been here five or six years, I was teaching English at Beavercreek High School, and I would give a spelling test every Friday. I would introduce the words on Monday, go over them Tuesday, Wednesday, and Thursday, and I'd give a test on Friday. I had a girl who was a really good student, but she wasn't doing well in spelling. Her father told me that the reason she wasn't doing well in spelling was that she couldn't understand how I said the words.

I didn't counter, but I thought to myself, "You know what? She's heard me say that word four times already. She's got a problem if she can't look at it on a piece of paper I'd given her and listen to me say it and realize it." So it was just an excuse, but it was an excuse for his daughter—it was my fault because I didn't speak well enough for her to understand.

Actually, at Berea College they taught us standard American speech, because in the fifties when I was there, it was still true that you wouldn't get a job because—in fact, I *didn't* get a job because I had a drawl. I applied at Reading, Ohio, a Cincinnati suburb, Little Kentucky, 80 percent of the people are Appalachians, and I applied at the high school, and the principal told me that I had too much of an accent!

Dr. Katherine Rowell had much the same experience:

You know, I had the accent until I went to college. In elementary school I had it. I used to be made fun of. In college I worked really hard not to have it, but if I could go home—even today I have to remind myself to put a 'g' on the end of words, and if I'm tired, there are a lot of words I say incorrectly, and I get corrected. I have to with my grammar. Today I don't care. In college I got corrected a lot, but now I don't care.

And Tess Little, who established the accredited Appalachian Outreach Program in 1995—the only one in Ohio—talks about attending nearby Wright State University and being told "if I didn't lose my accent, I wouldn't graduate."

Janice Wilson remembers that when she was a college student,

Every student who graduated from Berea had a required speech class. It was a semester long, three or four hours. The whole purpose was to teach us standard American speech so that we could get along wherever we went. And I can remember standing up and the teacher would hold your diaphragm and she would teach us how to breathe and we had to go around the room, breathing right, and saying "wild" instead of "wahld." That would be politically incorrect these days. . . . That was the approach that Berea had, to get you ready for wherever you want to go.

Changing the way one speaks, or "code-switching," can be a dilemma. Do you "put on airs" and deny your heritage? Or do you strive to have people listen to what you are saying, rather than how you are saying it?—as I did in a stint as a substitute teacher in Toledo.

At the Dayton Early College Academy, where most of the college-bound students are inner-city African Americans, it's a decision they face every day: "Although at home students may speak informally in the style they're used to, the teachers basically teach you how to be a chameleon, how to switch atmospheres, so when we're in a professional setting, use your professional voice," says one senior. Another student adds, "'They really instill in us using correct grammar, greeting appropriately, and making sure we conduct and carry ourselves in a professional manner.'"[15]

Ricky Skaggs understands that "there are people who change their accent, change their appearance, they do whatever they have to do to be accepted, and I think we need to celebrate where we're from!" Wouldn't it be great if we could do that?

Elmo Garrett grew up in the Upper Cumberland Mounts of Tennessee and has now retired in his home state. He recalls that discrimination was more "covert than overt," but he learned that it did exist, as he writes to me:

ELMO GARRETT'S STORY

I actually left the hills three times before I finally stayed up north for over thirty years. Three days after I graduated from high school in 1962, I and a friend hitched a ride from a semi driver that we knew and went to Indianapolis. My friend had some relatives we could stay with.

I'm still amazed at the primitive conditions that I and a large percentage of the folks in our area lived in. The night before we left, I did my usual chores of going to the woods to find dead poles to drag in and chop for our wood cookstove. There was no running water in the house although we did get water pumped up the hill from the spring a couple of years prior. Outhouses were the facilities that most everyone had.

There were very few manufacturing jobs in our area. The jobs that were readily available consisted of farming, sawmills, logging, etc. There were a couple of garment factories, but they primarily employed women. The reason I left the Appalachian area is because of the lack of jobs, and people in the North seemed to have better cars and more spending money than the folks in our area. When a nice car was spotted on our roads, everyone would comment, "They must be from up north."

The first trip to Indianapolis was not a complete cultural shock to me as I had visited my uncles in the cities, and my homesickness was tempered by the fact that I knew I was staying only three or four months, then returning home and try to go to a state-supported college. I still remember wanting to be back home to see my parents and four siblings and my dog.

I experienced some discrimination because of my southern speech, but most of the discrimination that I experienced was covert, not overt, such as hearing others talk among themselves and telling hillbilly jokes or stories.

I don't know if I was ever discriminated against when applying for a job. Both my friend and I got a job at RCA, and I rode to work with a carload of ladies that were ten or fifteen years older than I, and I guess my biggest surprise was how these ladies were more liberated than the ones that I was familiar with. I believe they thought it was their duty to make me blush, which they did. . . . I was not used to the openness they expressed.

The second trip was in 1963 when I left the hills to go to Dayton, Ohio. I stayed with an uncle and worked at Rike's Department Store downtown. I was not aware of any outright discrimination except for derogatory remarks made by some about hillbillies.

I stayed about six months and went back to college, but I could not finance it for a whole year, and I had a girlfriend and wanted to get married, so I left the hills for the third time.

Two friends and I went to Anderson, Indiana, and I got a job at a General Motors plant and soon started an electrical apprenticeship with General Motors paying for my schooling. A lot of the students would rib me about the usual hillbilly stereotypes such a moonshine runner, one leg shorter than the other, etc., but I never considered that discrimination.

It was during this schooling that I learned that there was some discrimination being experienced. I only learned this when a fellow student from the city came to me to apologize. I was fortunate enough to be in the top 10 percent or so of the class, and he said he wanted to apologize to me because he literally thought *all* people below the Mason-Dixon line were extremely uneducated and unable to learn.

He seemed sincere, but I was at a loss for words and thought he must be kidding me. He assured me he was not, and being in school with me had taught him a good lesson. He turned out to be a friend all the thirty years that I was there.

However, Elmo adds, "Discrimination can sometimes be a positive influence. A security guard at the GM plant where I worked told a carload of men looking for work (in their forties or fifties) where the employment was located and for them to tell the employment personnel that they were from the South because they thought the southerners were used to hard work, and he related that he saw one of them in the plant and he said they all got hired."

Joyce D., white-haired and perhaps in her early seventies, is a graduate of the Dayton Art Institute and a retired registered nurse, who now gives art lessons at the New Hope Methodist Church's art center. From outside, the building resembles a storefront church and the congregation is mostly Appalachian. She is from Kentucky's Estill County, noted for its beautiful Red River Gorge.

Dayton was very different from their old home: no trees or greenery, just concrete, she remembers, and many more people. They had lived in an isolated area with unpaved roads, so getting to town was not easy. Her great-grandfather had a general store, and we compare our memories: the smell of calico and burlap bags for her, tobacco and cheap candy for me.

The important thing in the country was that people took care of one another, she says. It was different in the city.

We were isolated in that area, and people did not reach out to us. When we came to Dayton, 10,000 people were in this area, in rental properties, with two or three rooms if they were lucky. In Dayton it was very crowded and there might be three rooms for a family. At that time there were big houses in the [nearby] Oregon area, with sleeping rooms. Men left their families back in West Virginia, Kentucky, and Tennessee. They always went back on weekends because they missed their families.

There was a lot of prejudice, even in schools, because when [poor] people moved in, the rich people left. Appalachian people were not educated. It was not uncommon for people not to go to school. Most went to school through the sixth grade. It was not free—you had to buy books and pay the school. When we came to Dayton, people called us "briars" or "hillbillies" and claimed we took their businesses. Most of us felt it, but a black teacher told me that I could clean up and go downtown and nobody would notice. That was a great lesson for me.

I was nominated to join a national sorority in the fifties, and I was told not to tell anybody where I was from. There is still talk against all kinds of people. They say there is inbreeding in Kentucky, West Virginia, and so on, which is nonsense. Much of that is just nonsense. They still think of us as not being the brightest.

Many have proven them wrong. Joyce's brother is an orthopedic surgeon who "used to wear a cowboy hat and boots to tease the people at Mass General, where he worked. They loved him," she says. She mentions attorneys with roots in the community, including Mike Turner, formerly Mayor of Dayton and now a U.S. Congressman.

Not all have been able to escape the challenges of poverty, however, especially when the strong traditional family support is lacking.

Randy L. lived in the Mt. Washington section of Cincinnati, a poor neighborhood on a hill sandwiched between two more affluent areas. "Four-Mile Road curves around," he says, "and the top half and the bottom half of the road went to a different school from the poor kids in the middle." And that school failed the boy in more ways than one.

Randy's father was an alcoholic who abused all eight of his children. Randy says.

When he came home, Mom always sent us out the door to stay away from him. When we walked past, we'd duck to get away from him. He'd get mad because we would duck. Then we'd get hit no matter what.

I'll give you an example. I was in elementary school, and we had to take gym and get dressed for gym in shorts and shirt and stuff. I refused to get dressed because my dad beat me the day before [for breaking a window]. So anyway, I wouldn't take gym.

What they did back then in Mt. Washington, you got a swat with a paddle if you didn't take gym, but the gym teacher made you take a shower first. So anyway, I wouldn't do it, and he grabbed me, and my shirt came off and my pants and he saw the stripes.

So he took me to the principal's office and he promised, "You will not be in trouble." The police came, the whole nine yards.

Well, they called home. Dad worked second shift, so they had to wake him up, and Mom and Dad came up. I remember standing between two cops, and one guy was an African American, big guy. Dad walked into the office with my mom and the police officer said, "Is this your child?" "Yes." "Did you do this to your child?" "Yes, and if you don't let him go, I'll do the same thing to you too." I went home and got another beating. My sisters Cathy and Jeannie went to the school and told the school that they were being sexually abused, and the school said, "Shh, shh, shh." I think they were afraid of Dad, seriously, because they wouldn't do anything about it.

Nothing more was heard on the subject; no authorities were called in. Randy continues:

I have no education. I'd been beaten so bad I just couldn't comprehend. And they always put me in a corner and they passed me from year to year. I remember in eleventh grade Mr. Eliot came in the hallway, and he said, "Can I talk to you?"

I said, "Sure."

He said, "You are a very sweet person. I don't understand. Why don't you do your work? You could become something."

I wanted to say, "I can't make it. I need help." But I had too much pride and I was too ashamed. That's when I just turned around and walked out.

But Randy wasn't finished. Years later he was determined to become literate. Every night, after working all day, he would go to the library to be tutored: "through first grade, second grade, third grade . . . and finally I went to the Church of the Savior, down in Cincinnati, where they had a program where you could study to take your GED, so I studied for that, and I took the test. And finally I got my GED. . . ."

Until recently students in Cincinnati's Lower Price Hill neighborhood have also been undereducated, says Nancy Laird, who wears many hats, one that of the director of the Lower Price Hill Prevention Initiative. As we tour the area, she explains that:

> The education part is hard, because a lot of times with the school system, you would have to go to a neighborhood that wasn't safe. In other words, right now [the local] Oyler School is K through 12, but it wasn't always that way. The students would get through junior high and then they would have to go to another neighborhood for high school and that just didn't work. They wouldn't go, because to them it wasn't safe.

There was hostility from those who lived in the middle-class neighborhood above them at the top of the hill, she says. "Like right now, people who live right up the hill to come down to Lowe Price? Heck, no. People from down there to go up there? Oh, my God! No, no."

Jan LePore-Jentleson is the director of Dayton's East End Community Center, which has served a large Appalachian population for many years. She once asked children in the Appalachian neighborhood to describe themselves. She was appalled that they used negative stereotypical terms like "redneck" and "white trash."

She laments the fact that "the urban culture has undermined the ancestral identity that may have come up from the South. As Appalachian families get more and more removed from the South, they lose sight of their roots and don't know who they are. They have taken on a complete new identity rooted in poverty."

Randy L. blames his father's violence on his alcoholism, but child abuse is also strongly associated with poverty. Although most of the immigrants would succeed, for too many the hope for a better life in the city was doomed. Too soon they would join the ranks of the urban poor, with a culture of its own, prey to predatory lenders, pawnshops, rent-to-own stores, and all the other businesses that exploit the poor. Tragically some would become more susceptible to what's sometimes called "drugs of despair."

NOTES

1. Norma Lee Browning, quoted in Albert N. Votaw, "The Hillbillies Invade Chicago," *Harper's Magazine*, February 1958, 65–66.

2. Rhonda H. Halperin and Jennifer Reiter-Purtill, "'Nerves' in Rural and Urban Appalachia," *Appalachian Cultural Competency,* Susan E. Keefe, ed. (Knoxville: University of Tennessee Press), 2005.

3. William W. Philliber and Clyde B. McCoy, eds., *The Invisible Minority,* (Lexington, KY: University Press of Kentucky, 1981), 48.

4. James N. Gregory, *The Southern Diaspora,* (Chapel Hill: University of North Carolina Press, 2005), 162.

5. Ibid., 167.

6. Roger Guy, *From Diversity to Unity,* (New York: Lexington, 2007), 104.

7. Browning, 65–66.

8. Guy, 104.

9. Guy, 68.

10. Barbara Kingsolver, *The Prodigal Summer,* (New York: HarperCollins, 2000), 11.

11. Michael Montgomery, "The Scotch-Irish Element in Appalachian English," *Journal of East Tennessee History* Vol. 65 (1995).

12. John Rehder, *Appalachian Folkways*, (Baltimore: Johns Hopkins University Press, 2004), 291.

13. Loyal Jones, "Foreword to the Fourth Edition," *Appalachia: Social Context Past and Present,* Philip J. Obermiller and Michael E. Maloney, eds., (Dubuque, IA: Kendall/Hunt, 2000), x.

14. Amie Sparks Ball, "The Effect of Appalachian Regional Dialect on Performance Appraisal and Leadership Perceptions (2014), *Online Theses and Dissertations* 203. http:/encompass.eku.edu/etd/203.

15. Nancy Brown Diggs, *Breaking the Cycle,* (Lanham, MD: Rowman and Littlefield Education, 2013), 111.

Chapter Eight

Addiction

The Scourge of Appalachia

There's no ignoring the 800-pound gorilla in the room, the monster that has destroyed so many lives and damaged many more. And that's what addiction is. While drug abuse is fairly new on the scene, alcohol has long been the scourge of Appalachia. So many families, like Sheila Taylor's, have suffered from alcohol.

The Reverend Linda Williams, ordained by the Assemblies of God denomination, pastors the Church on the Rock, the independent church that welcomes everyone. Blonde and dressed casually for this warm September day, she's waiting for me at the Big Sky Bread café, where she tells me her "complicated" family story, one in which she experienced the ravages of addiction close at hand.

My mom is from Litchfield, Kentucky. It's a long story about my mom being poor and undereducated when she came north. When she was a young girl, her father went to Middletown for work and sent the money home, but her mother liked the bar and didn't spend much on the kids—pretty much abandoned the kids—and my mom was left with a total of four children to take care of when she was twelve years old, because her mother, my grandmother, was an alcoholic.

So there was no money for them. The stories that she told seemed unbelievable to me and my sister. They seemed farfetched, but they were not farfetched.

She told one in which her half-brother Eugene, who was much older, would go out and get drunk and come home and beat up the youngest. His name was Calvin, and he had a rheumatic heart.

One day when she was ten or eleven years old, she was out gleaning in the fields for food. The farmer next to them came over to her, gave her a double-barreled shotgun, showed her how to use it, and told her to never let it leave her side, no matter where she went.

A couple of nights later, Eugene came back to the house, drunk, and burst through the door. They ran—she got everybody into another room. She had the gun, and she shot him through the door. He never came back. So that was the story.

Calvin was just a little boy, about six or seven years old. He was really sickly, Mom said. He ended up growing up and coming up to Bryan, Ohio. He became a Southern Baptist minister and eventually moved out to Phoenix, Arizona, became well known, and planted a couple of different churches. . . .

I don't know how much of all that is true. But my grandmother would go to the tavern and spend the money, and she had a poor reputation. Fortunately a farmer there assisted my mom, making sure there was stuff for her to have.

Anyway, my mom did really well. She got to Dayton and applied for a job at my grandfather's restaurant. (My dad told me this story recently before he died.) She came in, she was real gaunt and she had a little boy with her, my half-brother, and she was very poor, was how she appeared. My grandmother gave her the job knowing that she was a single mom, and eventually she and my dad got married.

Her first husband, after the birth of her child, my half-brother, abandoned her and went in the Merchant Marines. I think that's why she ended up coming up to the Ohio area, in hopes that one of her half-sisters could help her up here, give her a place to live temporarily.

So my mother—I don't think she completed grade school—did really well. She got involved with the women's Shrine, part of the Masons, actually attained a high office in that organization, for somebody who had trouble reading. She was a learner. She would force herself to learn. I think Appalachian people across the board—I know not everyone, but they're hardworking, typically. . .

I think in general society, whether you are highly educated or uneducated, there are tempters out there. I hear it every day and see it every day.

When they learned that Linda's young nephew was being abused by his alcoholic parents, Linda and her husband, newlyweds at the time, stepped up to the plate and took him in charge.

That's how Bill started to come to live with us and eventually we got custody—I wasn't twenty-one yet, was only twenty. My husband's eight years older than I am. So Bill has that history, not that that's an excuse, but it's a history, and so it seems as though those addictions—because Bill got hooked on drugs in Dayton, and at his birth mother's home, her second husband was assaulting the girls and providing drugs. There are horrible drugs. So anyway, that's how all of that kind of came together, and my son got married many years later. Because of the addictions that he had, I warned his fiancée. I said, "You know, you shouldn't do this."

"Well, I love him."

And I said, "I'm telling you, but . . ."

They finally got married and a year later they had their first child, Rachel, and then Jake, and Rachel is fine. And the boy—I just found out that he's recovering, he's clean from heroin. He's about twenty-five, I think.

The marriage didn't last. Bill's an alcoholic. Lives by himself. We had a phone call one day from Mom—when I say that Appalachian theory that I will protect my family no matter what the cost even if it is illegal . . . My mom and dad got divorced much later, and she got a double house on the street where we lived. She allowed Bill and Ann, his second wife, to move into the other half of the double, and my mom just allowed it, the stuff that went on. . . .

Linda recognizes that not only is addiction a genetic problem, but it's a matter of culture, as well.

Many years ago when we started the children's ministry one of the little boys who came—he was eight years old—showed up on a Saturday morning, kind of collapsed, and he wasn't making any sense. What is going on? Well, we finally got it out of him: "Last night my mom's live-in boyfriend found out it was my birthday, I'm going to be nine years old, and they went out and bought a twelve-pack and made me drink it."

So they learn these behaviors, and that child had trouble. I followed him all the way through juvenile jail and prison. So, you know, it's also commitment.

You have to have a commitment to working with people, regardless of how the behaviors are . . . So he's now moved out west, but the fact is that he had some bad behaviors that he was given. We got him help and got him cleaned up.

They were probably involved in our ministry six or seven years. He and his sister—his mother was an alcoholic and a prostitute. Where else are these kids going to learn?

It's how they are reared, what they see around them, and there has always been a degree of people being alcoholics somewhere . . . but it's like the Bible says, the curse will come down from the first to the second, third or fourth generation.

Ike Bowling also goes to the Bible to note that there has always been the use of alcohol: "When you go back, people always had some kind of stimulants . . . If you go way back, people always used [something]. The Bible warns about strong drink and wine." In fact, an Internet search for reference to drunkenness can lead to at least a hundred in the Bible.

Given the propensity for alcoholism in Appalachia, there's good reason for some churches to take an anti-alcohol stand. As Linda puts it:

[In my church] we look at it this way. Drinking is a behavior. It's a negative behavior, and if you want to influence people, you have to hold the standards yourself. We don't tell people that you shouldn't drink. What we do is say,

"How do you want to represent yourself? So I tell people, "There's nothing wrong with a glass of wine."

I would get in trouble, because the Assemblies of God is adamant in their ministries that when you take that vow, you will not drink. You will not smoke. You make a commitment not to do that. Well, it wasn't a problem for me. I already had that commitment. I tell them, "There's so much alcoholism." And we have recovering alcoholics and recovering heroin addicts. . . .

It's just like when your kids think they're invincible—you know, children think they're invincible: "It'll never happen to me." So people think that way, especially young people, they're not mature—and then you get people that are highly educated who do the same stupid stuff because maybe they're pushing themselves so hard that they need something.

Most fundamentalist churches take a firm view of drinking and a strict rule of abstinence, which makes sense for many. If you never indulge, you won't become addicted.

To Ricky Skaggs, it takes God to rescue someone from addiction: "I believe that the spirit of God can absolutely deliver someone from alcoholism. If we can self-help ourselves—I mean we have to take responsibility, I don't mean that—but if we can have salvation through twelve easy steps, then why did he go to the cross?" asks this devout Christian. "He went to the cross because he knew we couldn't do it."

I'm reminded that Bill Wilson was motivated to found Alcoholics Anonymous after a religious experience, and that Dave, at the Tabernacle in Jesus Name, credited his conversion for saving him from drug addiction.

The genetic component to alcohol abuse was unfortunately one that the immigrants carried to their new land. Rates of alcoholism in Scotland today far exceed those in other European countries. A BBC report claims that deaths from alcoholism in Scotland are 80 percent higher than those in the rest of Britain.[1]

Ireland, too, the source of many Appalachian immigrants, has its elevated share of alcoholics. Dr. Garrett O'Connor, in an article titled "Breaking the Code of Silence: The Irish and Drink," concedes that the stereotype of the drunken Irishman is not far off the mark: "A 2009 Irish Health Board Report showed that 54 percent of respondents (about 2.14 million adults out of a population of 4.2 million) engage in harmful or risky drinking each year, compared to a European average of 28 percent." He blames the high rates in part on "the Irish cultural DNA" as well, a reaction to long years of hard times.[2]

The old river town of Gallipolis, Ohio, is the home of the Athens County Health Recovery Services, of which Dr. Joe Gay is director. Joe was cited as an expert in the book *Dreamland*, by Sam Quinones, who described him as "garrulous."

We met in his office late in the day, when he had just returned from the state capitol of Columbus, seeking more funds for his treatment center. He was indeed friendly and forthcoming on the subject.

There is a cultural factor involved in substance abuse, for, as he says.

> There's some interesting stuff on the way people drink. The French probably drink more than the English, and the Italians drink more than the English, in terms of gallons of alcohol per year, but they have a relatively low alcoholism rate in Italy, because they have different norms about drinking. And drunkenness is shameful in Italy, to be actually drunk, and the French are not particularly tolerant of drunkenness, either, whereas, particularly in Ireland, it's expected that you drink to get drunk.

He agrees that there is a strong genetic component in alcoholism, too, "one of the very strongest factors there is," And one that is carried through to other addictions.

> I think that the Scotch-Irish predisposition to alcohol relates to the reason it took hold so strongly in Appalachia once it got here. I think there's probably some overlapping in genetics between alcoholism and drug addiction, because we now see a lower proportion with alcohol as the proportion of opiate problems has increased. [Alcoholism] apparently ran in the family. That's the way it usually is.
>
> It sometimes skips generations and even in identical twins—there have been several studies of this—among identical twins, if a person is an alcoholic and they have an identical twin, that person has a 50 percent chance of being alcoholic. This holds true even if they're reared separately. If one or both of them are adopted and raised in different families, what they call a concordance rate is still 50 percent.
>
> Although we see a few families where everybody's alcoholic or addicted, usually there's somebody who's not. There may be four siblings and three are alcoholic and the other one is a perfectly functional person.
>
> There'll be whole families of addicts. We're seeing that now. Now we've just barely had enough time to get a second generation of rural opiate addicts, but we do see them. There was a father and daughter who overdosed in Gallipolis about a week ago, and the father died.

Dr. Gay has gathered together some charts to show me the shocking exponential growth of heroin addiction in Ohio's Appalachia.

> Most of these new heroin addicts are white. So in 2001 there were eight counties that had a significant opiate problem. And at that time most of the counties were urban counties with heroin problems, and a disproportionate number of the heroin addicts were African American. By that time pills had hit [Portsmouth's]

Scioto County, and [Dayton's] Montgomery County was another county where there was an early problem with prescription opioids. That was probably some mixture of traditional heroin users and then prescription opioid users. These are roughly two-year samples. Look how it evolved.

There are just a couple of counties in Ohio that seem to have escaped the epidemic—and they're the ones with a heavy Amish population.

"Is there any good news on this depressing subject?" I ask.

Well, one bright side is overall, across the United States, not many people use heroin. The use rates are, depending on the age group and the populace, two, three, four people per thousand, but in the areas where it's concentrated, it's a big problem.

There's an organization called the Coalition for Appalachian Substance Abuse Policy. They talked about a study that showed that in certain cities the rate of opiate addiction as now about 10 percent of the population, as opposed to two, three, four per thousand in the country. So in the areas that are heavily impacted, it's much, much worse, and that 10 percent would be roughly the rate of what used to be alcoholism.

Among the African Americans, heroin addiction seems to be dropping, and I think it's because these old heroin addicts were so pitiful, the young people didn't want to do that. So the new wave of heroin addiction has not hit the black community very hard. Which is good. Part of it, too, I think is that their lack of access to health care, which was probably based on racism, protected them from the pills.

I don't know that; that's just my theory. And I think traditionally back in the year 2000 racism protected white people from heroin, because they didn't want to drive down into the ghetto to buy it. It is the new cartel that Sam Quinones talked about that started really marketing in a way that white people would buy it.

I think people do learn and eventually we'll see this—it's still growing, but [eventually] it will taper off. So the bright spots I can think of is that it is still relatively rare and it is treatable.

It costs money, and the health care costs are enormous, but they're going to be much higher unless . . . Many, many people who inject heroin have had hepatitis C, and that's a very, very expensive disease to treat.

As for hepatitis C, Appalachia is already in the midst of an epidemic: "Hepatitis cases across four Appalachian states—Kentucky, Tennessee West Virginia, and Virginia—more than tripled between 2006 and 2012. Kentucky leads the nation in the rate of acute hepatitis C, with 4.1 cases for every 100,000 residents, more than the national average, according to the CDC." And such an epidemic can "foreshadow a wave of HIV."[3]

It would seem that nothing could be worse than some of the stories we hear of families destroyed by alcoholism, but the tragedies brought about by drug addiction are even more distressing: the death of two-year-old Lee Hays, who somehow got hold of fentanyl, the baby and toddler who died in separate incidents in Columbus, Ohio, from heroin laced with fentanyl, or the airline pilot and his wife who were discovered dead in bed by their four children, the year-old baby who died of an overdose, the man who found his brother and girlfriend dead on Christmas Eve, the child who ran down the street to find his grandmother when he couldn't wake his mother. . . .

The statistics are alarming: almost 64,000 deaths yearly were attributed to drug overdoses in the United States in 2016, with the number likely to grow. Another shocking figure: the 533 percent increase in opioid addiction from 2010 to 2016. In West Virginia, the worst state for drug abuse, out of a total of 1,000 live births at Cabell Huntington Hospital, 139 babies were treated for addiction.

Our local hospital, too, has had its share of addicted newborns. I was one of the scores of those who answered the call for "cuddlers." Volunteers, who must not be judgmental, undergo a rigorous background check that includes being fingerprinted, two TB tests, references, inoculations for childhood illnesses, as well as a three-hour orientation, before holding the "cuddlees." They must also follow the strict rules for all hospital volunteers, including maintaining confidentiality.

In the orientation we learned about the increased risks for drug-addicted babies, who might have seizures, low birth weight, and other problems. In spite of the latest advances in treatment, we are taught that nothing can take the place of the human touch.

In addition, the mothers who are letting us hold their babies have been required to enroll in a prenatal drug rehab program. Each baby has his/her own room in the Neonatal Intensive Care Unit and is attached to wires that lead to a monitor. There is a comfortable chair, an electric rocking cradle, and a supply of pacifiers. The curtains are closed and the rooms are kept quiet and dark.

Usually treated with morphine initially, each baby stays until weaned from the painkillers, as well as the mother's opioids, and able to receive a passing grade on the Neonatal Abstinence Score ("NAS"), which rates symptoms like continuous high-pitched crying, convulsions, tremors, frequent yawning or sneezing, feeding problems, loose stools, and others. They may be in the Neonatal Intensive Care Unit from one to six weeks. Although the babies are getting the best care available, no one knows what the long-term effects will be.

The babies are lucky to be getting such good care, and their mothers know it. A note to the nurses on one baby's bulletin board says, "Thank you for everything you do for our sweet baby boy."

Why has the drug epidemic hit Appalachia especially hard? Perhaps this is due to work-related injuries that have been treated with opioids in the past, or because of other factors that lead to "drugs of despair": poverty, unemployment, and depression.

Cincinnati's Lower Price Hill is a prime example of what drugs can do to an Appalachian neighborhood, as Nancy Laird will tell—and show—me. Nancy has held many responsibilities in advocating for the Cincinnati area's Appalachian population. Having trained with Catholic Social Services, most recently she has directed the Appalachian Community Development Association. Not long ago her office was closed for lack of funds due to a United Way money-saving move, but she was able to move to another office provided by Santa Maria Community Services nearby.

I plan to meet Nancy at Blochead Pizza, a tiny place with three small tables, which is next door to the State Street Methodist Church, a force for good in the neighborhood. I've arrived early, not sure exactly how long the trip would take, which will give me a chance to talk with Mary J., a church member who works at the pizza stand, as her "Blochead Pizza" T-shirt indicates.

As I sat with my pizza and lemonade, a pretty dark-haired teenager came in and approached two men who were sitting at a small table. With slurred speech she begged for money because she was "so hungry." They didn't give her any but instead directed her to a shelter around the corner. I gave her half my pizza, and back she went on the street, not headed for the shelter.

When Mary had a free moment, she sat down to talk. Dark-haired and pony-tailed, she claims a Cherokee grandparent, as Appalachians sometimes do, as there was often a mixing of races in the mountains, she says.

Given the appearance of the young drug addict in the store, Mary brought up the big drug problem in the neighborhood. When I asked why she thought people start doing drugs, she replied:

I think it's a lot of reasons. I think the way a lot of the young women get hooked on drugs is because they have a boyfriend and he introduces—sometimes it's the boyfriend that is strung out. They go to parties, or keep themselves medicated for years. A lot of it is mental illness, but these guys—they're at a party, they try it, they like how they feel the first time, so then they try it again, and then they're hooked.

What they'll do is they'll usually string out a girlfriend so she can be the main source for them to get sources to drugs. You see these girls around here walking, they're not doing it just for themselves, they're supporting another drug addict. I don't know who that young woman is. Like I said, she's not from around here. Actually she's at a "trap house," where drug dealings are going on, where people come and buy dope, or they just stay there.

The men were talking about "Weightless Anchor." It's a program that BLOC ministry does right around the corner here. It's a program that tries to get the women off the street. They feed them, give them a hot meal, let them take a shower, and if they need to change clothing, they give them a change of clothing, and they have counselors on hand to talk to them. If they need to go into rehab or something, they give them information. But the women have to do it themselves. Nobody's going to make them do it.

It's hard to get into rehab. I've got one [family member] getting ready to go, thank God. She's going to be gone for thirty days and then she'll be doing an outpatient program, so I'm so thankful that she's doing that. She got hooked on prescribed drugs because she had surgery.

Well, she had open-heart surgery when she was young, and then she got hit by a car and had to be put on pain medication. They were feeding her like ninety-four Percocets a month, and I'm like, "Is this good?" but I didn't realize she was hooked on them, so she's actually going into a program. She's got five children. I'll take care of them for thirty days. They range from sixteen to five here in a couple of days.

Actually her husband's going to help, too . . .

Everyone's touched by drugs down here. But I think they get hooked just— they're at parties, they don't think it's going to be them. There's depression, they get out of a bad relationship. A lot of the women—I have a friend that I've been friends with since we were in school, and she's my age, and she's hooked on heroin. She just got hooked on heroin. Any kid in the neighborhood could tell you where to go for heroin.

Mary has given a lot of thought about how to deal with the problem.

First of all, I think there should be tougher laws on the drug dealers. I think what we're doing is we're punishing the drug users, and we're not punishing the drug dealers.

It's a lot better to pay for the rehab than not to do anything, because they're robbing everyone blind . . . People are getting shot.

I'm still friends with some of the people I went to grade school with. We raised our kids and our grandkids down here. I mean, there's still a lot of good people down here. It's almost like we're being bomb blasted. It's sort of like a war zone. You know, we're at the point that "what do we do"? We don't know what to do. You call the police on somebody, then your neighbor calls and then you just get retaliated against. And then you see them back out in three days. So what do you do?

I don't want this to sound terrible, but, you know, I'm not for any kind of drug, but if it's marijuana, you're going to prison for a long time, but if you're dealing in heroin, you go to jail for three days and you get out and you're back on the street . . .

I'm not promoting the use of marijuana, but I think we really need to—we're putting people in jail for marijuana, but we're letting the heroin dealers hold schools hostage, order hits on people, and do three days in jail? I mean, this city really needs its priorities looked at. . . .

We have a community council that just got on TV and said there's no drug problem down here! . . .

Nancy Laird arrived, gave me a hug, and offered to take me on a tour of the area. First she stops to chat with others, including "Cawley," an elderly man whom she brings with her to "help clean up the neighborhood. . . . But I'll tell, you," she continues:

Down here you're family, you're family. Like around here, people consider me part of the family. There are people who warn me about the area, but I'm perfectly safe. People look out for me. People care about me, like Tommy here, another person who comes and helps, anything I have to do. He'll come and sweep up and be part of the crew. And like Mary, we're a team.

Yes, Nancy agrees, drugs are a huge problem.

There are drug dealers everywhere. There are shootings everywhere. There are shootings down here at night sometimes. Have I been down here at night? Yeah. Do I feel OK? Yeah, but I don't mess with the drug dealers. I don't buy drugs, I don't mess with them, and they don't mess with me. But are there other people who are hooked on drugs that would take anything from my car that they could sell to get a fix? Yes, there are, unfortunately. So that's what's happening down here.

Isn't there a police presence, I wonder. Do they come when they're needed?

Let me tell you how fast they come. . . . I called the police because one of my clients was having mental issues and he was lying in the middle of a busy street waiting for someone to run over him because he wanted to die.

I called the police, and I called the police, and I called the police. Finally I demanded to speak to someone, and they said, "Well, we don't really have any cars right now. . . ." and I said, "You're telling me you can't find some way to come down and help this person?" No, the police do not respond.

Friendly and chatty, Nancy is a free spirit. Raised Catholic, she has tried various faiths, including Methodist and Church of Christ, but declares she has come up with her own. After taking classes in "nondenominational things," she became ordained, certified by the state of Ohio to marry, bury, and baptize. She's also a Reiki master.

"There are a lot of alternative therapies that are effective" she says. "I like to play with those, but my fundamental basis is my relationship with my higher power, however you see that. Whatever that looks like to you is fine."

She's also a great believer in angels. As we approach the car, she says she can visualize "an angel in each wheel, an angel on top, and she's looking like this: he hair's blowing back and it's curling—I have a vision of her—and one underneath to make sure the mechanics are working, and one inside so there's lots of harmony. . . ."

"But keep your car checked, anyway!" I say as we step into her ageing compact, filled with the clutter of a busy life.

As we drive past the crumbling facades of what were once what she calls "fantastic buildings," with the architectural details characteristic of their time, she points out the makeshift memorials for gunshot victims and a "drug corner," an old building with blacked-out windows, along with the positive forces in the neighborhood: the shelters like "Weightless Anchor"; the "Dream Center," which guides those in need to the proper resources; and the BLOC ministries building. The latter, for which Blochead Pizza is named, is the acronym for "Believing and Living One Christ." Along with a fitness center and arts and crafts, it offers mentoring, job training, and many other services in the area.

We pass by Oyler School, now K through 12, which is attracting much positive attention under its new principal. Students no longer have to go to another, unwelcoming neighborhood to complete high school.

Hardly any Appalachian community seems to have escaped the plague. Why here? Why now?

As Sam Quinones says in his book *Dreamland*,[4] the worst scourge of drug addiction in America's history can be blamed on a deadly trifecta: drug dealers from Xalisco in Mexico's Nayarit state who introduced customer-friendly business practices, greedy drug companies, and unscrupulous doctors who ran "pill mill" offices.

Appalachia was ripe for the picking, with its large working-class population suffering from the injuries of physically demanding jobs. Now those workers have proved to be in more danger of overdoses than those in other professions. One study showed that from 2010 to 2016 "construction workers were seven times more likely to succumb to a fatal overdose of pills, heroin or fentanyl than the average workers." Those in farming and forestry were not far behind.[5]

Even ethical, conscientious doctors were likely to overprescribe opioids to relive their patients' pain, partly due to the misinterpretation of a letter published in the prestigious *New England Journal of Medicine* in 1980. From observing almost 12,000 hospital patients with no history of addiction who were taking narcotic painkillers, Dr. Hershel Jick concluded that addiction was rare; only four had become addicted.[6]

Although the article was often cited, it was not intended to refer to those not under the controlled conditions of hospitalization. As Dr. Jick would say much later, "'[If] you read it carefully, it does *not* speak to the level of addiction in outpatients who take these drugs for chronic pain.'"[7]

Quinones' book *Dreamland* focuses on the old river town of Portsmouth, Ohio, where the drug epidemic first took off. Perhaps the saddest thing in this once thriving city is the number of babies born addicted; the county has the highest rate in Ohio. The nurse manager of the Southern Ohio Medical Center reports, "We're running about 12 to 13 percent of our babies testing positive at birth for some kind of substance that is either illegal or illegally obtained," with the same rate for the mothers.[8]

I paid a visit to the city to meet with the Reverend Sallie Schisler at All Saints Episcopal Church, who also pastors a church in Ironton, Ohio. Before becoming a priest in 2008, she worked as vice president of Marketing and Development at the Southern Ohio Medical Center in Portsmouth. She also did an internship at a drug and alcohol facility and now is involved with drug counseling groups. With this background, she says:

> I can probably talk more about the drug problem than anyone else. Part of the drug use comes with a culture of poverty, where you don't see a future, and no jobs for them, and living with a couple of generations without work. . . . People in poverty often will get outside influences to make them feel better, like drugs and alcohol. They think, "I want to feel better right now; I want to change how I feel right now," and of course drugs and alcohol do that very well.
>
> Unfortunately, when you wake up the next day the problem is still there. If you happen to have the addiction gene, then it's too late. . . .
>
> In the Appalachian area, people didn't really leave the mountains. They married from the next town over or the next community over, and there wasn't a lot of new blood coming into the community, and by the time the gene pools had crossed, they might have a stronger affinity for drugs and alcohol issues.
>
> I think the family is still a huge influence. Families stay here for generations, and people leave to go look for jobs and come back, even if there's no promise of work for them here. When I worked at the hospital, when someone would come to the emergency room, they would often bring with them two generations of family, and we're not talking one or two people; we're talking a crowd! If the family member was in the intensive care unit, they would camp out. They would set up camp in the lobby, with aunts and uncles and everybody. Families are still, I think, a huge Appalachian value.

It's not always a positive trait, however. In early days when there was no organized security, you'd look to your kinfolk for protection. As things change very slowly in the mountains, we still have clan loyalty outside of and superior to the law. "My family, right or wrong!" is still the theme.

> Families often cover up and enable their drug-addicted loved ones. I've heard some really amazing stories. One woman set her alarm clock every night for when the bars closed and would go pick up her husband, because she didn't ever want him to get a ticket. Just that kind of enabling. How peculiar is that?

Drug addiction has taken a toll on families in many ways, she says.

There's a lot of internal stuff among families. People have told me that they're afraid in their own homes of their children and grandchildren, because when they're drug seeking, they can be pretty unpredictable.

There is great pressure, as we've seen, on children to stay home, and the family system is that no one ever leaves. And that would certainly be true in the addicted family systems I've seen. When you ask a sixty-year-old mother why her forty-year-old son is still living at home and sleeping on her couch, she'll say, "Well, I don't want to upset him."

Treatment for drug addiction may involve just that—a stark break from a former life.

That's one of the big first things that people are told when they go to treatment, that your whole life is going to change. You think you're going to stop taking drugs or drinking, but the truth is that your whole life is going to change. You are no longer going to be able to have the same friends, go to the same places, and sometimes that means family.

If you're from a generation of people who have been drinkers and alcoholics and addicts, it's very difficult, especially in a culture that says family really, really matters, which is why you need is a strong recovery community to be a part of. So here, in this community, there's a place people can go any time of day way up into those white nights. It's like a clubhouse where you can just talk, or play games or listen to music, but you're supported, you're surrounded by all sober people.

I asked Sallie, "Have there been any cases in which you made a lot of progress?"

There were a few people that were in my earliest groups and they've been clean and sober for like twelve years now, and they have earned, some of them, not only college degrees, but master's degrees. A lot of them are drawn to social work, because they have been greatly helped by other people. One woman is working on a Ph.D.

So with the right environment and the right kind of support system, people can make dramatic changes. One of the women—she and her five children for five years had not had a home. They just spent one night here, and five nights there, and they were like gypsies. She had lost her car, she had lost everything. Just what she had in green plastic bags. And now she is married and has her degree and has a plum job, so, yes, there are people that I've worked with that have changed very much.

"How do you work those miracles?"

It takes a whole team of people to do that. It takes good health care profession-als, nurses, and doctors and psychotherapists and counselors and people like me who are willing to just sit and listen and say things like, "Oh, that sounds like you're getting off track," or "Have you thought about looking at that from another direction?" It's really more like relationship support, it's more like personal support, it's more like mentoring . . .

Sometimes they hear about the program when they come into a hospital. Sometimes the courts—the courts here are a very important piece in the recovery community. The judges are very supportive of treatment in lieu of incarceration.

She laughs as she adds:

You can wear that out! You can abuse that privilege—but many times it's very successful. Addiction is a relapsing disease, so it's not uncommon for people to have to go through treatment more than once. It's a chronic disease, just like diabetes. . . .

Columbus, Ohio, also home to a large Appalachian population, has its share of drug problems. In the city's Franklinton community, I spoke with the Reverend Doctor Lee Anne Reat. Although she is a little older, she is often mistaken for the Reverend Sallie Schisler, as they both have short blond hair, are about the same size, and do look something alike.

I join her at her workplace, St. John's Episcopal Church, where she is wearing her clerical collar and black sweater over an orange-patterned shirt. She is known for her stance against Ohio's death penalty, as well as for the services the church offers. The one-hundred-year-old building is simple in style: white walls with dark woodwork and the universal musty smell of old churches. It stands in a neighborhood that has been decaying but is now on the verge of gentrifying, much to the dismay of low-income residents.

"I would say that the members of this congregation who come from this community have Appalachian roots," she declares. "This neighborhood, Franklinton, is very much Appalachian, as is much of Columbus, south Columbus, Hilltop. Obviously that has changed over the years, but the whites in Columbus pretty much have Appalachian roots, in my experience . . ." She thinks "undoubtedly" that those roots still have an effect on them.

"You know," she continues, "Appalachians have been so denigrated and infiltrated with [terms like] hillbillies and poor white trash and all the negative characterizations, that people have said, 'Oh, that's not me. I live in Columbus, Ohio. I'm not a hillbilly, I'm not wild . . .'"

One of the services offered at the church is its free food program, which serves some 250 meals a week and emphasizes healthy eating: "One of the problems in the neighborhood is very compromised health: gross obesity, diabetes, heart disease." On Sunday she holds a street church service, followed by lunch.

Here, too, drug abuse is a major concern. She recalls a recent incident when someone called her attention on the street and said, "Look down at your feet."

I look down and there are two syringes, one full and one empty. I took the full one and squirted it into the ground; it was the black tar heroin there. It's an epidemic. And of course it drives a lot of the crime, because you've got to get your money someplace, and you're probably not working if you're addicted . . . [but] you just have to keep loving people.

A woman several years ago would come in and say, "I'm ready to go to rehab. I've got to go to rehab." And I'd say, "OK, let's go." And I'd call my contact and get her in, and she'd say, "Well, I'm going to go home and get my stuff together and I'll be back." And then she wouldn't come back. Time and time and time again. And every time she came, I'd say "OK, let's do this."

Finally one day I got her in the car. On the way up—it's maybe half an hour east, where she was going—on the way up she handed me all her crack pipes and said, "Here, would you throw these away?" So I put them in a bag that I had in the car, and we got a little farther up the road and she said, "Can't do it." She goes, "You're going to hate me. You're never going to talk to me again." I said, "Absolutely not. I love you. We've come this far. I'm not going to stop loving you, ever."

And then shortly after that she died of an overdose. I hope she died knowing that somebody loved her. . . .

We've had some success stories. Our deacon took a woman [to a program]. She came back and I think she probably had some relapses, but she had built up the resources internally to get over that and was back with her children, and hopefully life is better. We usually hear from people when their times are bad.

So often throughout the area it comes down to a question of money. According to a newspaper article, state support for county-level behavioral health services is about 40 percent lower than a decade ago, even though there is obviously a great need. And so I headed to meet with Robin Harris, who heads the Alcohol, Drug Addiction, and Mental Health Services Board for southeastern Ohio's Appalachia, which includes Gallia, Jackson and Meigs counties, located down the road from Dr. Gay's offices and not far from Portsmouth's troubled Scioto county.

I drive past it at first, because it's not the institutional-looking building I had expected, but rather a large white house on a hill, where I'm welcomed into its cozy meeting room. Robin reminds me of England's Prime Minister Theresa May—the same short wavy hair style and the same professional manner of being in charge, but she's better dressed, in a brown sweater with printed blouse, navy slacks, and black flats, and wearing a simple pendant. She tells me:

I participated yesterday in a poverty-simulation exercise which was put on by Advocates for Ohio's Future. It was designed to change our frame of reference: put us in the shoes of people living in poverty, and get all of the information from Ruby Payne's book *Bridges Out of Poverty*,[9] and understanding that there is a culture of poverty. That had me thinking while I was on the road, "Why did the opiate epidemic take on so strongly here?"

And yet, as I look back over my thirty-plus years in behavioral health, we have always had the highest rates of teen pregnancy. Anytime there's a social ill, we land at the top. . . .

We have eighty-eight counties and we run somewhat autonomously, or at least individually. Not that we don't get help from the state, but it doesn't come down equally. There are many factors in how money is distributed, so in behavioral health, there are factors where the state looks at the severity of the problem, whether it's drugs, whether it's mental health issues, or whatever.

They look at that, but when the money is actually designated for a certain problem and then allocated, it gets allocated per capita, almost always, which is a particular problem for us and causes a great deal of disparity in our ability to be able to address problems, because, you know, at certain levels, opening a program is going to have the same cost whether you're serving 100 people or 1000 people. You need to get a building and get it furnished and licensed. There are certain fixed costs, administrative costs, and the overhead, and we end up with less money because we have fewer people.

In the State of Ohio there are fifty-three county boards. We have three. But out of the fifty-three boards, there are only three of us that don't have a local tax levy. We are in Appalachia. It's Adams, Lawrence, Scioto that border us, that would be Ironton and Portsmouth, that area, and then our board and then Washington County, which is Marietta. Culturally, people here are strongly opposed to tax levies, especially a property tax. There are people who say, "Well, that isn't a fair tax, because it's unduly assessed." They are the people carrying the larger share of the burden, because we do have a lot of people on public assistance, living in public housing, and they're not paying those taxes.

The stigma is a huge problem for us, and there's still a great deal of stigma attached to mental illness, as well. We have a lot of work to do in this area in helping people understand the brain is an organ of the body that develops illness, and it's not the person's fault. There is some work with that, and we're making some progress with that, but it has a way to go, and the drug problem carries an even larger stigma because of the behaviors associated with it and the fact that at some point, initially, it *is* the person's fault.

Well, in the case of opiates, there are people who were put on pain pills because of an injury, a surgery, an illness, and the addiction developed. But if you take the greater drug problem—marijuana, cocaine, methamphetamines—all of the things that these people are using, initially there's a choice somewhere. The illness of addiction is when a person is no longer making a choice.

We have the history of our state psychiatric hospitals. When the state passed what was the Mental Health of Act of 1988 that was to close institutions and deinstitutionalize the mentally ill, the plan was and the promise was that money that had been put into those institutions would come to the communities to take care of people who were being sent back there. In fact, we currently are operating on 40 percent less funding than we had ten years ago.

That's because of budget cuts at the state level. Some of it was the turning of the economy and trying to correct—six years ago the state of Ohio was running an 8 billion dollar deficit, and now we are in the black again. The state actually has a rainy-day fund now. So I can't fault all the decisions that were made by the governor, the legislature, to increase stability. We couldn't continue the path we were on. . . .

When you think about the culture here, I often think that the things that make us charming are also the things that hurt us. Historically the people who settled here did so because they were individualists and independent.

When you asked what did I think was behind the drug problem here, I keep going back and I think back and remember conversations we had in my younger days when we were trying to address teen pregnancies, and when I sat with the kids that were either pregnant or parenting. I called them into a room and I said, "Talk to me about this. Did you not have access to birth control? Did you not know how to use birth control? Was it an accident? Let's talk about this." The theme that came out was—if the question was "Why did this happen to you?" the answer was "Why not?"

Maybe this term is too strong—I'm struggling with it—but it's "hopelessness," maybe that sense of resignation that things don't change, they aren't going to change . . .

We think about, "OK, why are we stuck?" If I'm at the state, and I know a lot about the legislature and state government and everything about funding, services, and resources here, they listen and they understand that we're in a dire position here, and then they say, "Why won't your people pass tax levies? When are your people going to take some responsibility for themselves?"

So we struggle and we come together in the community to address problems, and we talk about how we're putting out fires in this epidemic with opiates, but at what point are we going to try to get in front of this problem and do good prevention? And we start to look at what is happening to our children. Why, with all the knowledge and all of the information accessibility, why would any young person now in this day and age pick up marijuana, pick up—? We're treating a ten-year-old here in Gallia County who was shooting heroin. Ten—years—old! So those of us working in social services—there has to be that tipping point, that elusive thing that we're missing.

I've seen research that the passive entertainment--now we're handing toddlers iPads to watch movies—and the way it stimulates the brain sets that person up to no longer be able to create their own pleasure. Passive entertainment creates in a child an inability to use their imagination, and I do wonder about that. I do wonder what we're doing to the brain physiologically with the electronic kind of stimulation that we start so early. . . .

My own city of Dayton, Ohio, with its many Appalachians—I once heard an estimate of 40 percent of the population—in 2017 topped the list of the ten worst cities for drug overdoses in the country. The "epicenter" of the epidemic was said to be on the largely Appalachian east side of the city.

The police department's East Patrol Operations Division was responding to nearly twice as many calls as was its counterpart on the west side, which is primarily African American.[10] In 2017, with overdose deaths running at twice the rate of the previous year, the county mortuary had run out of room; its director resorted to requesting storage space at local funeral homes.

It's not just heroin anymore. Heroin in its more powerful "black tar" form; fentanyl, 50 times more powerful than morphine; and carfentanil, an animal tranquillizer, have added to the mortality rates.

Why is our quiet city of Dayton now such a center for the drug market? I met with Montgomery County Sheriff Phil Plummer for some answers. He, too, has Appalachian roots, his grandfather having come from Adams County to work in a factory here. At our table at a Panera restaurant, people recognize him in his uniform and come by to shake his hand. He is friendly but never seems to step out of his serious persona.

He tells me that our city has suffered the shocking invasion of the drug cartels due to our convenient location. We're a prime target because we are at the intersection of I-70 and I-75, at the crossroads of the transportation network; Mexican drug gangs come right up from Mexico and then easily distribute their wares.

When Phil attended a training session at the border, he learned that of those dealers apprehended, 80 percent are caught at border checkpoints, 20 percent crossing over illegally.

The 101 gangs that control the drugs target junior high school-age kids, where the schools, many of which are chaotic, are not equipped to help the children with this problem. Given that heroin is so cheap, it has become the drug of choice. While Oxycontin sells for $80 a pill, the equivalent amount of heroin is only $10. Phil believes that preventative education for the young people is a must.

As for marijuana, I asked, should we legalize it?

Since it is much more potent than it used to be, and is, in his opinion, a "gateway" drug, he's not in favor of legalization.

He describes an environment in which the drug culture flourishes: no opportunities, no respect for authority, no wholesome recreational activities, video games and rap music that lead young people to "hate and kill." Family structure—or the lack thereof—is also a factor: "Seventy-five percent of the kids are in single-mom homes with no dads around. Because poor families are on welfare and live off the monthly checks," he says, "dealing drugs is tempting." But it's a poor career choice: "Drug dealers live for about two years and are often robbed of their proceeds."

"We've got our work cut out for us," he adds, although "there are some good people in tune with what's going on," the basketball coach at the inner city's Thurgood Marshall High School, for example, or the Police Athletic Group, the Christian Life Center, or the "life-changing" Victory Project," which works as a "launching pad" for disadvantaged teenagers.

Not all those affected by the drug problem are poor, however. As drugs have become more accessible to the middle class, the epidemic has not been discriminating in its victims, even in high government office. Ohio Lt. Gov. Mary Taylor has revealed that her two sons, in their twenties, have struggled with their addictions for the past five years, entailing "failed drug rehab programs, two overdoses at the family's home and urgent calls for ambulances." Their problems began, like so many, with prescription drugs.[11]

NOTES

1. "Alcohol related deaths are the highest in Scotland," BBC, http:www.bbc .com/newsuk-2520065, 3 December 2013.

2. Garrett O'Connor, "Breaking the Code of Silence: The Irish and Drink," *Irish America,* February/March 2012.

3. Claire Galofaro, "Appalachia being gripped by a hepatitis C epidemic," (AP), *Dayton Daily News,* 7 June 2015.

4. Sam Quinones, *Dreamland,* (New York: Bloomberg Press, 2015).

5. Katie Wedell, "Working to recover," *Dayton Daily News*, 3 December 2017.

6. Derek Hawkins, ""How a short letter in a prestigious journal contributed to the opioid crisis," *Washington Post*, 2 June 2017.

7. Quinones, 110.

8. "Scioto leads on addicted babies (AP), *Toledo Blade*, 17 October 2016.

9. Ruby K. Payne, Philip E. DeVol, and Terie Dreussi Smith, *Bridges Out of Poverty* (Highlands, TX: aha! Process). rev. ed. 2009.

10. Cornelius Frolik, "Police: Bulk of OD calls originate on Dayton's east side," *Dayton Daily News,* 9 December 2017, B1.

11. Laura A. Bischoff, "Ohio Lt. Gov. Mary Taylor reveals sons' struggles with opioid addictions," *Dayton Daily News,* 1 June 2017.

Chapter Nine

Slaying the Monster

Substance abuse is a formidable enemy, but those who are fighting it have more than one weapon in their arsenal; treatment and prevention go hand in hand with law enforcement.

First, to understand more about the plague, I review my conversation with Dr. Joe Gay for a crash course in drug addiction and its treatment, in which he says:

One of the basics of effective treatment for opiate addiction is medication-assisted treatment, and all addiction is brain disease. Opiate addiction is particularly and strongly a brain disease. People who have used opiates have changed their brain chemistry, and so you have to stabilize that change and we do it with medication-assisted treatment, but it is medication-*assisted* treatment. You need to stabilize them with medication so they can make changes in their lifestyle.

There are three types of medication, two of which are pretty closely related. There is methadone, which is called an agonist. Methadone is a different drug, but in effect it is simply a slow-acting heroin. It makes a difference that it's slow acting, because if a drug produces its effects slowly, it's less desirable than a drug that produces an effect quickly. . . . Methadone is absorbed slowly.

And then there is a drug called buprenorphine. The trade name is Suboxone. It's called a partial agonist, and it has sort of a partial effect of an opiate. It occupies the receptors, but it has a ceiling effect. The more effect you get, the drowsier you get, and if you take too much, you'll go into a coma and stop breathing and die, but Suboxone has a ceiling effect, so if you take more, you don't get much more intoxicated. But it still is a substitute medication. And then there's a medication that blocks the opiate receptors and if it's given in its fast-acting form, which is called Maloxone—it's the drug they use to reverse overdoses, Narcan, but there is a slow-acting form of that which is injectable.

It's called Vivitrol, which is an injection that lasts about a month. That blocks the receptors, so that even if the person takes an opiate, they won't get high. They say it reduces cravings, but I've never seen in print an explanation for why it reduces cravings.

I have a theory, which is I think that cravings involve stimulation of these receptors, kind of like if you smell food, you salivate, you know. So I think that maybe in blocking the receptors for drugs of abuse, you may also block the receptors for what's sometimes called the priming effect. And that's a well-known phenomenon with a variety of drugs, that if you see stimuli that remind you of the drug, that's associated with the use of that drug . . .

Like coffee and cigarettes, I think. "But," I ask, "how about the expense? I can imagine that people would say, 'I don't take drugs. Why should I have to pay for somebody who brought it on themselves?'"

Well, the reason is that for every dollar that's spent treating addicts, you save somewhere between $4 and $7 in other expenses . . . The number of people in the court system now who are there because of the opiates is enormous, like 85 percent. So the courts and the jails are just full of people, and we're paying tax money for that.

There are significant medical costs associated with substance use and opiate use. The most dramatic is the overdoses. You can imagine what a trip to the emergency room for an overdose costs. And you've probably seen some of the news—overdoses are happening all the time.

Now the good news is that treatment works. It doesn't work all the time, but good treatment, responsibly delivered—and that doesn't always happen, with medication-assisted treatment—you may approach a 50 percent success rate for a given treatment episode. In other words, you can treat them and at the end of the treatment episode they'll go out and they won't be using, although some of them will relapse later.

Some people may think that doesn't sound very good, but the success rates for most chronic diseases—diabetes, heart disease, asthma—the compliance rates with treatment are about 50 percent. You know a lot of people—you might have even been one of these people—who had a heart attack and two months later are smoking a cigarette, and you know the doctor told them, "Stop smoking," and that's about 50 percent of the people. They don't lose weight, they're still eating . . . [My friend and I] would have breakfast together one morning a week, but he's had a heart attack. He had to take off two or three months for cardiac rehab, but he'd be eating eggs and sausage . . .

For advocacy work, trying to influence the state budget, I did an analysis of treatment funding, The counties that have the highest overdose death rates were getting the least funding from the state drug and alcohol [budget]. I started wondering, "Why is that?" And so I looked at data I got from various sources . . . I looked at all these variables across the counties and found what was related to what.

I found out that the Medicaid enrollment rate—the percentage of people in the county who had Medicaid, which relates to poverty—was positively correlated with the overdose death rate, and that was a highly statistically significant finding. And then the higher the Medicaid enrollment, the more doses of opioids were being distributed. The higher the Medicaid, the more people were in treatment for opioid problems, and so forth. The bottom line is it's related to poverty. It's negatively related to median household income.

When I give lectures I sometimes say, "Anything that common sense would tell you would increase the rate probably does," but genetics would clearly be a factor. Family dysfunction is a factor, trauma's a factor, abuse, things like that. Any of those would be a factor. And many of those dysfunctions, family dysfunctions, disruptive families, trauma, also correlate with poverty.

"And peer pressure?" I ask.

Oh, sure, sure . . . There's a concept in the prevention literature called risk and protective factors. One of the big risks is peers that use drugs. This is in general, not just opiates. Poor grades is a risk factor, lack of engagement with school. Engagement with school is a protective factor. It's what's called pro-social involvement.

As always there is a need for money.

Medicaid expansion [in 2014] was such a blessing. I do not belong to the same political party as the governor, but the Affordable Care Act encouraged states and allowed states to expand Medicaid. Before the Affordable Care Act, to receive Medicaid, a person had to be either disallowed or a person could be eligible—children up to their nineteenth birthday were eligible, and parents—and I'm not sure exactly how this went, but parents of children who were in certain risk categories were eligible. Those were all who were eligible for Medicaid.

The Affordable Care Act allowed states to base eligibility on income, and the state of Ohio said that anybody whose income was less than 130 percent of the poverty level was eligible for Medicaid, so almost everybody we treat is eligible for Medicaid.

Before Medicaid expanded, there was a period, a time with budget cuts to treatment, when we were turning away probably at least a third of our referrals. I mean, it was terrible. This was 2008, 2007, back in there. It was terrible, and Medicaid expansion really fixed that. I was no great fan of the governor, but expansion of Medicaid took a lot of courage on his part. And he and his team expanded it and worked around where they expanded it without the approval of the General Assembly. They found some administrative way to do it.

Even among mountain people—is the glass half full or half empty? Even among mountain people, it's probably no more prevalent than alcoholism was, which is like one out of ten, which is still pretty awful when you're talking about heroin.

Another bright spot is that treatment works. It doesn't work for everybody, but it works almost as well as it does for other chronic diseases . . .

"How can you prevent young people from even wanting to do take drugs?"
I ask.

It's difficult. And I think part of the problem is—this is a little bit of a digres-
sion—but I see approaches that are conventional prevention approaches, but
they don't work at all. Not very much. We need to still do them, but it seems like
most of the people we see who use heroin became addicted to pills, and when
they could no longer afford their pill addiction, they turned to heroin, which is
cheaper, but prevention strategies don't work for those people, because they're
beyond reason. I mean, prevention depends on reason.

If we could make people aware of the consequences, it would be a step forward in prevention, and so what we need to make sure of is that for the general
public, heroin continues to be viewed as very dangerous.

There's a principle in prevention research called "perception of harm." One
of the problems with prevention is it's hard to measure the impact of prevention,
because in a way you may have to wait two or three or four or five or ten years before—if you do prevention with six-year-olds, it's not very likely that they're going
to drink or use drugs. You have to wait ten years before you can measure anything.

This "perception of harm," which is a person's opinion on whether or not this
will hurt you, will predict whether or not they'll use drugs. There's still in the
general public a relatively high perception of harm for heroin, and we want to
make sure that continues. Now that contrasts with the fact that right now in our
society there's an extremely low perception of harm for marijuana.

So we want to keep the perception of harm high, and part of the problem is
the perception of harm for prescription opioids is pretty low, because "Grandma
takes them. The doctor gives them to Grandma, so they couldn't be too bad" so
people will experiment with them. . . .

Meanwhile, those same doctors who have been prescribing opioids for
Grandma's aches and pains are seeking other ways to alleviate her problems:
nerve-numbing agents, for example.[1] Ohio's Department of Health is urging
doctors not to be so quick about prescribing strong drugs for pain and to try
other treatments, like "physical therapy, ice or heat, massages or OTC medi-
cations."[2]

The Justice Department has another arrow in its quiver to aim at those
medical providers who abuse the system. The Opioid Fraud and Abuse De-
tection Unit, relying on databases that track prescription drugs, Medicare and
Medicaid figures, will focus on twelve regions most affected by the epidemic,
half of which are in Appalachia.[3]

There is good news on the science front, too, which is leading to recogni-
tion that addiction is a brain disease. "There's great research being done on
the brain at Ohio State right now," says Robin Harris, who is in charge of
behavioral health in three Appalachian counties. "I'm so excited because I
think when it all comes out, we'll be able to reduce stigma around behavioral

health all the way, and that is, actually understanding with new methods to scan the brain and actually watch how it functions."

There's no wonder that Robin is impressed by the new discoveries. *National Geographic* reports on what scientists are learning about the brain and addiction. Summing up in a few words a very complicated subject, Fran Smith says, in a section titled "Hijacking the Brain":

> New research suggests that the brain's reward system has different mechanisms for craving and pleasure. Craving is driven by the neurotransmitter dopamine. Pleasure is stimulated by other neurotransmitters in 'hedonic hot spots.' When the craving circuitry overwhelms the pleasure hot spots, addiction occurs, leading people to pursue a behavior or drug despite the consequences.[4]

The article describes one experimental treatment under study that shows promise, although it sounds right out of a nineteenth-century medicine show. Dr. Luigi Gallimberti in Italy thought that "repeated pulses might activate drug-damaged neural pathways, like a reboot on a frozen computer." So he tried applying electromagnetic pulses on the prefrontal cortexes of cocaine addicts, apparently with some success.[5]

Robin Harris recognizes that a major asset in the struggle is people, those who are helping now, as well as those who might be trained to assist in the future. Investing in more "warriors" would be a good use of the money she does receive.

> You know, here in this area, we have a university. Just nine miles up the road here is Rio Grande. We have Ohio University in Athens that is an hour away from here in Gallia County. We have Marshall University sitting there in Huntington, West Virginia, an hour from here. The availability of education in this area is rich. We are currently working with the state on trying to offer incentives for people to choose social work, or counseling, or psychology majors, because we're really suffering here with our workforce shortage, which is an odd thing to say in an area where the unemployment rate is [so high]. The one here, Rio Grande, is a community college for the first two years, and they have a bachelor's degree in social work, so we're trying to work with them.
>
> I'm the executive director of this basically $10-million system of care, when we talk about all the agencies, and all the Medicaid and all that, but I may be out at 10:00 on a Friday night with a sheriff's deputy helping him resolve something for a family. If that's what's needed, that's what we do. I wouldn't trade that for all of the resources in [Columbus's] Franklin County.
>
> So I stand here and I think I wouldn't lose the charm of our culture and the fact that we do what it takes and we understand that, and we aren't afraid to push up our sleeves and get our hands dirty in this thing, whether it's a county commissioner, or a judge, or a sheriff, directors of agencies—we're not afraid to get in the mix and figure it out, because we've learned that we will not be rescued

from the outside. And then we turn around the next day and we put on our suits and ties and dress clothes and we drive to Columbus and we go to a legislator's office and we advocate for money down here, because we need that!

It's a hard job, and we do it with a passion. So I try to take a realistic look at who we are and hold us accountable in the fact that we may in our helping have created the sense of "Who's going to fix my problems for me?" amongst a population and when are we going to stop and take a hard look at that and say, "What is truly helpful? How do we help people without inadvertently harming them?"

We go back to the way the government provides assistance, and I wonder if when government assistance first started, there would have been the people who were ashamed to have to need it and people who maybe didn't get to fall out of it, but after you pass it down from generation to generation to generation, "It's just my culture." And especially if people are in pockets of poverty, that's their community. Their community is people on public assistance.

Educating the public is important, but prevention at the youngest age is crucial, says Robin.

We're looking now at whether the [anti-drug] message could be embedded in all curriculums starting in kindergarten. With health we've managed to do a lot of that, you know, things like hand-washing, brushing teeth, personal hygiene, those messages are carried in various ways and they sort of permeate how life is, and so we're thinking prevention—first it was a high school program, now it's a middle-school program, and really we need to be in the elementary school. It might be a one-day activity or somebody coming into the health class for one week and talking about drugs. This needs to be a message they hear every day.

Money is needed everywhere—for prevention tactics for treatment, for law enforcement, for alleviating poverty—but how it is spent is crucial. Handouts from the federal government have sometimes proved to be more harmful than helpful.

Ohio's former Attorney General Mike DeWine, now governor, has followed in the footsteps of Kentucky and has filed a lawsuit against several major drug companies. The city of Chicago, counties in New York, California and West Virginia, the City of Dayton, and now the city of Columbus are all involved with litigation. Dozens of local communities in Alabama, California, Illinois, Kentucky, Ohio, Washington, and West Virginia have filed "public nuisance" suits against the drug companies.

DeWine and others are also looking at new ways to employ law enforcement personnel. As Dr. Joe Gay notes:

There was a forum at Ohio University and it was a health class. There were about 100 students there talking about opiates, and I was part of the presentation that was on the impact on families. The presentation before mine was on law enforcement, and they all seemed pretty enlightened. All of them were concerned, all of them had seen huge increases in heroin use, but all of them said, "We can't arrest our way out of this."

The police will still do their sworn duty to uphold the law, but they are in the forefront of new methods of approaching drug addiction. In Kentucky, two dozen of its county jails are offering prisoners the option of enrolling in a unit in which they receive full-time rehabilitation, including Vivitrol treatment. It's an extensive program with other offerings to prepare them for a drug-free life when they are released. After the six-month participation, prisoners can choose to become peer mentors.

I heard more about successful methods for combatting the epidemic when I met with Ohio's then Attorney General Mike DeWine, now governor, who has received national attention for suing five pharmaceutical companies for their part in the plague, a suit that is still ongoing.

DeWine's aide, Damon Morris, first joined me at a quiet table at a Panera restaurant in suburban Dayton. As we waited for the attorney general, Damon told me that he, too, has been affected—in a positive way—by the drug epidemic. He and his wife have adopted the two boys they were fostering, children whose parents had been on heroin.

While his driver waited by the door, the attorney general described some of the events that have been taking place in the state, including the county in which Toledo is located.

The Lucas County sheriff called me about three years ago, and he said, "I have an idea for a program, and I said, "What is that?" He described it for me and then he said, "I need some money," so we got some money from the attorney general's office, and he raised some other money from just the public, businesses, then he got some county money. . . . What he said was "Someone goes to the emergency room they've overdosed, they live, and," he says, "nothing's happening, or they walk out. Usually they walk out."

So what he has done is, with our help and the help of a lot of people, he's got deputies who created this unit in the department, and so the hospital now calls the deputies and says, "We've got a guy that's overdosed." The deputy comes out and uses that really as a teachable moment.

The person may have family there, may have a girlfriend there, boyfriend there. The guy or woman might be ready to try to get him to some program. So, he said, just handing them some brochures and saying, "Here's a number to call, [the deputy] then becomes almost—this is my language—almost like an AA sponsor.

So the deputy will get that person into a program, and he will be there when they get out of the program. I was up there on the first anniversary of the program, and I was talking to some of the deputies that were doing it and some of the recovering addicts. One addict pointed to a deputy and said, "See that guy over there?"

I said, "Yeah."

He said, "I call him six or eight times a day. "

I said, "Why?"

He said, "That's the only way I can get through the day." He said, "The guy takes my call at 2:00 A.M. He takes my call—doesn't matter if he's at a church picnic, it doesn't matter where he is, the takes my call—he helps me get through the day."

"How do you get someone that's that committed to help someone?" I asked.

Well, that's their job, and they have the personality that can do that. These are all deputies, full-fledged deputy sheriffs in Lucas County. It is clearly labor-intensive.

The sheriff did another thing, which is the other component part of this. The big drop-off many times is when the person gets into a treatment recovery program—when they get out of the program, what happens? So the sheriff has created what I call a half-way house. He's raised some money and it's basically not staffed by certified, trained people, but it is staffed by people who are familiar with addiction. Many of them are recovering alcoholics themselves, or recovering [addicts]. So those are the two things that Lucas County has done. That model has been used in a number of different communities in Ohio.

We also have done four or five videos—I say "we," I mean the attorney general's office—we've done videos on that program. One of the things we have tried to do is be a force-multiplier, so we take in information. If we see a program that works, we try to get that out to another part of the state, other communities, other police departments, other sheriff's' departments. . . .

The way I describe it to the national media is there's good news and bad news in Ohio. The bad news is obvious. The epidemic is continuing. It has now moved to fentanyl. Fentanyl is so much more potent than heroin, and they're mixing it with everything. They're mixing it with heroin, they're mixing it with cocaine.

The drug dealers don't really care if people die. The business model is so good than they can lose some. The business model is they get you hooked for ten bucks on heroin, and then, if you're still alive in a year, instead of a $10 a day habit, you may have a $500 a day habit, or a $1,000 a day habit.

"And how do the customers get the money?"

They steal. You take [Dayton's] Montgomery County. Well over half the crime in this county is by people who are stealing money, stealing something so they can buy drugs.

What I tell people, though, is that that's the bad news. The good news is that we're doing a lot of things in Ohio that we weren't doing five years ago or even three years ago or even two years ago. And people are being innovative and they've come up at the local level with some very fascinating programs.

When I took office seven years ago, the big problem then was—at least the way we perceived it—the pain meds. It was particularly hard along the Ohio River, which gets back to the book *Dreamland*—but what I noticed right away was that some of the communities had gotten so bad that there was a grassroots effort that just rose up. Literally from the grassroots, not from the top but from the bottom up, usually led by a mother who had lost a son or daughter, sometimes a dad, but usually a mom.

So what these groups were doing was bringing an awareness to it. Our guiding principles have been that communities first have to recognize that there is a problem, and in the affluent suburbs, that was slow coming: the Upper Arlingtons, the Oakwoods, on and on. Second, they really need to take an inventory of what their assets are, financial, everything.

We have a series of Town Hall meetings where I would go around and talk about the problem, and we would put experts up. They were true Town Hall meetings, anybody could show up, we advertised them. The best part was when you get rid of the so-called experts, push them aside, then you had the public, and people started talking.

At every single one I had, somebody would stand up in one corner and say, "Here's what we need in this county: we need 'blah-blah-blah' treatment," whatever it was. Somebody in the other corner would stand up and say, "George, that's what I do. That's my group, that's my nonprofit." I'd look over and say, "George, talk to Merritt."

What you found is when you went into those counties, is one, they wouldn't recognize they had a problem, so you had to get people to understand they had a problem. That was five years ago, four years ago, three years ago. Two, you had to get them to take an inventory: what assets do we have. You get out of the smokestacks, you get out of the silos: treatment people not talking to law enforcement, law enforcement not talking to educators, educators not talking-nobody's talking to anybody. They're all in their own world. That is typical.

To me that's not shocking. It's just the way the world works. So you have to break those down. The goal has to be in every community: One, recognize we have a problem. Two, let's inventory what our assets are. Three, let's see what we need and let's figure out how we try to get, or cobble together somehow, what we need, and let's get everybody talking to everybody. Let's get the treatment people talking to the law enforcement, law enforcement needs to be talking to the educators. So, we have examples of programs that work in Ohio.

That's what we think works. It doesn't always have scientific data behind it—or that's at least what appears to be working.

So what you find is people like Sheriff Tharp in Lucas County. You find law enforcement doing things that law enforcement never did before, and the reason they're doing it is because no one else is doing it. And because they understand that they can't arrest their way out of this problem, but you have to take a holistic approach to the problems . . . .

I asked the attorney general the same question that I had posed to Dr. Gay: "The ordinary person might think, 'Why should I pay for them? They brought it on themselves.'"

We're in a strange situation where the first decision may have been voluntary, or it may not have been, and these numbers are probably changing now, but the addiction experts would say, at least a year ago they would have told you, 80 percent of the people who are opiate addicts started with pain meds. Many of them were prescribed perfectly legally. Some of them were diverted, but many of them were like a 45-year-old laborer who hurt his back and he's prescribed pain meds and he gets hooked and then, that's it.

So my answer to people who say, "Let them die"—and we get this question most when we're talking about Naloxone, or Narcan—my answer is, well, first of all, that's the wrong thing to do. You can't do that. You can't tell EMS to go out and try to figure out whether this guy's overdosed before. EMS is trained to save people's lives. That's what they do. They need to do that.

The other thing is I'm convinced that if people can stay alive long enough, most of them will get off of it eventually. It's very difficult. I think very few people get off an opiate addiction the first time, maybe the fourth time, the fifth time, I don't know what the difference is.

"Who pays for this," I ask. "The state of Ohio? The federal government?"

Part of it was paid for with the Medicaid expansion in Ohio. The governor made a decision to run as much of this through Medicaid as possible. That was when the federal government was paying 100 percent of it.

The answer to your question is there's no one answer. [Sheriff John] Tharp is paying for his program with some tax dollars, some private business dollars, up in Lucas County, and he's raising money. So the answer to your question is everybody's paying for it.

Here's my quick snapshot of the problem in Ohio. About fifteen people are dying every day. We've got babies born every day addicted. We don't know how many, because there's no central place where data is kept on addicted babies. Our jails are detox centers today. You've got a significant cost there. Foster care—half the kids in foster care in Ohio are there because one or both parents are drug addicts. So you've got foster care bursting at the seams in most counties, but the part that no one really can calculate is the fact that when I get out and talk to business men and women, their biggest complaint is "I can't find workers."

They can't find workers for two reasons, when you boil it down. One is [applicants] can't pass a drug test, and the other is they don't have the educational skill sets. Those are the two big reasons. If you look at the problems that the state faces, you start with those two problems, long-term problems.

It's quite complex. Why was it the worst, initially at least, in our Appalachian counties? I don't know. I can guess. Maybe there's more despair, lack of jobs. Maybe part of it is that most of the people there are working with their hands and their backs and maybe they have a higher incidence of injuries than a person working a white-collar job. Maybe it has something to do with ancestry and heredity and Scotch-Irish. . . .

The governor cites the "perfect storm" that brought addiction to Appalachia.

You saw in the book *Dreamland* that about twenty years ago the drug companies started telling primary care physicians that this stuff is not very addictive. That was not a study at all. So that's number one.

Number two, the Mexican drug cartels are very good business people and they decided a number of years ago to start growing poppies in Mexico. So they grow the poppies n Mexico, they turn it into heroin down there, they get across our southern border, however they do it, in body cavities, in shipments and other ways.

As I said, it's a pretty good business model; you get people hooked for ten bucks—it's cheap, heroin's dirt cheap. They get them hooked for ten bucks, because they're already hooked on pain meds, then they switch them over to heroin. A year later, if the guy's still alive, it's a $500 a day habit, or a $1,000 a day habit. So you have that.

You also have a culture change, and I don't know what caused this, but I started my career as a county prosecutor and attorney in Greene County. That was way back in the late 1970s. Heroin in those days was something that had a real stigma attached to it. If we ever found heroin in Greene County: in Fairborn, Beavercreek, Yellow Springs, Cedarville, we'd be shocked. Heroin was confined to the inner cities, a small group of people. There was a stigma attached to it.

So you'd have people who were doing drugs. As a prosecutor, you get to know the drug dealers, you get to know the addicts, some of them at least. I would talk to some of them, and sometimes I'd ask them, "What kind of drugs do you do?"

"I'm doing this, I'm doing that."

"How about heroin? Do you do heroin, Charlie?"

"Oh, come on. I'm not stupid. I'm not doing heroin."

Now the guy just told me he just did LSD or some of that crazy stuff. But there was a stigma, a cultural stigma attached to heroin. That cultural stigma is gone. Doesn't exist anymore. Heroin is looked at by people taking it as just like any other drug.

Like Sheriff Phil Plummer, Dr. Joe Gay, Robin Harris, and everyone else who is facing the challenges of the drug problem, DeWine agrees that prevention is essential.

The thing I talk about a lot that we're not doing is the prevention side. When I was in Congress, the federal government made the decision to stop the "drug-free school" money. Pretty much stopped it, and that was a mistake. I fought against that, but I lost. So what you have today in most schools is very hit-or-miss. A school might have a DARE program for half a year for fifth-graders, but that may be all they have. They may do something in health.

I was on the national commission for drug-free schools in the 1980s under President Reagan and every expert who came in said, "If you're serious about this problem, you've got to start in kindergarten and do something K through 12 every year, do it consistently, do it age-appropriately, and also do something that has a scientific basis to show that it actually does work."

There have been more well-intended drug programs that don't do anything, because we're dealing with kids, and we're not dealing with miniature adults, and they look at the world very differently. Most fifteen-year-olds are pretty invincible; nothing's ever going to happen to them. Their brains are still developing, so what you have to do is do things that actually have been tested, that we know work.

I put a working group together a year or so ago. They came back with a report. I charged them with looking at what's needed in the area of prevention in Ohio. They came back and said, "K through 12." . . .

That's the one thing we could do, that's cheap to do; it doesn't cost very much. The schools that are doing it are not bringing in different teachers, they're using the same teachers. They're integrating it into their science curriculum. . . . What could be more important than trying to keep our kids drug-free? Look at your priorities. That's got to be near the top.

He maintains that "the kids aren't getting it. What I argue is that they should be getting it at home, they should get it at school, they should be getting it at Boy Scouts, Girl Scouts, they should get it at 4H, they should get it everywhere. . . ."

Law enforcement, he says, is well aware of the pipeline that is bringing the poison into our communities. Governor DeWine describes how it works:

Take a rural town like Circleville or Marion. The drugs come out of Mexico, they're brought up by the drug cartels. At some point they may be sold off to the local dealers. They're close to Columbus, so the dealer will come out of Columbus. They'll come out to a small town like Marion or Lima, and they'll rent a house, and they'll operate out of the house. They'll have two or three or four—depending on how big the community is—runners who are in cars with drugs. And they never carry very much because if they get busted, they don't want much possession, because the sentencing laws in Ohio are based on the quantity.

So they carry a small amount, and then it's all by cell phone. If we knew the number right now to call here, you could call and they'd meet you at a parking lot at Walmart, or a parking lot at Seven-Eleven, or they'll meet you at the parking lot of Wendy's . . . .

"Is there no good news?" I lament.

We've got a lot of good news. I mean, there really is a lot of good news. There are a lot of good people who are doing a lot of good things that are saving lives every day in Ohio. If it weren't for fentanyl, we would have turned this thing around. We would be headed in the right direction, because fentanyl is so lethal, and they don't know what they're taking, they don't know the quantity. It's fifty times more potent than heroin.

The Mexican drug cartels have moved now to fentanyl because they make more money with fentanyl. They don't have to grow the poppies, they don't have to process it. It's a synthetic that's made in a laboratory. A lot of it's made in China, and it's sent from China to Mexico and from Mexico up here. Some of it's sent in the U.S. mail from China and the profit margin is just much bigger. Very little invested and they just make more money.

"Doesn't it go through Customs?"

It gets through somehow. Think of the volume of stuff that comes in here from China today. Massive volumes. So if it weren't for fentanyl, I think we would at least be headed in the right direction. It's just so lethal, and it's so deadly. And what happens is the EMS squads will tell me that they used to bring someone back with one or two doses of the Narcan or Narloxone. Today it may be four, five, six, ten, fifteen—and that's because of the fentanyl. It's so potent, so nasty.

"You'd think people would learn. They're not thinking . . . "

Their minds are totally changed. I'm not a medical expert, but their minds are clearly changed, and their brains are altered, and they really can think of nothing but that fix. It's the reason that people abandon their children, abandon their spouses, abandon their jobs, and all they think about is that next fix, and they've got to get it every day, and they'll do anything to get it. That's the bad news.

The good news is that there are people that I see every week that I talk to who are recovering addicts who have made it or who think they have made it, and so, yeah, there is hope. I think there is always hope as long as that person can stay alive. And that's the problem.

To tell you how counterintuitive it is what people do: several times we've seen Dayton have a whole bunch of deaths over one weekend and the news media would say, "anybody's that thinking of taking this stuff had better be careful because there's a bad batch out there, blah, blah, blah."

What we found is that that increases the appetite of some of the people because they look at that and they say, "Well, it must be a good batch. I'll get a better high." It's more potent. One of the reasons they want the fentanyl is that they can sell it and say, "This is a better high. Now it may kill you, but . . . "

We really have not talked about the law enforcement side, but certainly there is more that we can do. We have a couple of task forces; one's a task force that we call a "bulk cash" task force, or "bulk drugs." Basically what they do is instead of trying to get the street guys, they try to get the bigger dealers. Part of the process is to seize the drugs coming in. What goes back to Mexico is guns and cash. You try to seize the guns and cash before they go back and try to get the drugs when they come in.

We had a drug bust that the attorney general's office was involved in two weeks ago over in Columbiana County, over south of Youngstown. And we seized enough fentanyl to kill every man, woman and child in thirteen counties around there. . . .

Another drug bust in June of 2018 indicates that the bulk task force has been so successful that it is seen as a model for the state, DeWine said. Its partners included a local township, Dayton's Montgomery County, the Ohio State Highway Patrol, Homeland Security, and Ohio's Bureau of Criminal Investigation.

Ohio has five such forces; DeWine would like for there to be ten. Sheriff Plummer praised the task force that arrested four men, one with apparent ties to a Mexican drug cartel, and confiscated $3.6 million in drugs—twenty pounds of fentanyl and more than 100 pounds of marijuana, and $150,000 in cash.

This was the latest seizure of many carried out in the past three years, which have kept thousands of pounds of drugs from the market. Says Sheriff Plummer, "They have a lot of secrets that I can't share with the public, but they're very good at what they do. The stats show that."

One welcome statistic: In 2016 it was reported that Dayton's Montgomery County had the worst overdose death rate in the country.[6] Two years later the county's overdose deaths had been almost cut in half: from 566 in 2017 to 294 in 2018. Community leaders credit three factors for the progress: the Community Overdose Action Team, a collaborative effort that has brought together those involved with treatment and law enforcement; increased Narcan availability; and rapid response teams, which follow up with overdose survivors to refer them to treatment.[7]

There was good news on the national front, too, as in October, 2018, new legislation was passed by Congress and signed by the president that, among other things, "makes it easier to intercept drugs being shipped into the country, authorizes new funding for more comprehensive treatment, and speeds up research on non-addictive painkillers."[8]

As Ohio's Governor Mike DeWine says, "substance abuse is a complex problem that requires the cooperation of all those involved: parents and caregivers, educators, law enforcement, drug abuse specialists, employers, law courts, and others." His Twelve-Point "Recovery Ohio" plan not only stresses prevention and treatment, but also would empower employers to help their addicted employees and offer incentives to hire those in recovery.

The DV8 Kitchen in Lexington, Kentucky, could serve as a model for what the governor may have in mind. "DV8," when spoken, sounds like "deviate," implying that addicted employees can deviate from their past ways. The owners, Rob and Diane Perez, have had to make some compromises, since their employees come from nearby treatment centers. Only breakfast and lunch are served, allowing employees to attend evening support meetings, but there are no compromises on food quality and professional service. A mandatory workshop is held once a week, when professionals give advice on such things as getting a criminal record expunged, financial matters, and teamwork. Employee turnover has been remarkably low, and the Perezes are looking to open another DV8.[9]

States most affected are sharing their experiences, DeWine says. "We have gotten together with our neighbors in Indiana, West Virginia. We've held joint panel meetings. We did one in Huntington, West Virginia, for example, where we brought people across from Ohio. We did one in Wheeling. So certainly there's some comparing of notes."

Huntington, West Virginia, one of the cities most affected in the state with the greatest substance problems, is also tackling the problem with innovation. Mayor Steve Williams is credited with establishing the Mayor's Office of Drug Control Policy in November, 2014, and it is showing results. In a letter to the city's residents, the Mayor wrote that although there was "no shortage of efforts and resources attempting to wrestle this beast to the ground," there was a great need to coordinate those efforts, which would be "aggressive, coordinated, and unrelenting." He appointed a team headed by the city's retired Police Chief Jim Johnson, whose holistic approach included prevention, treatment, and law enforcement.

Huntington was praised in *The Christian Science Monitor* for "its blend of law enforcement, data analysis and compassionate care," but, says William Ihlenfeld, former U.S. attorney for the Northern District of West Virginia, "If we ever climb out of this hole we're in . . . it won't be because of what D.C. does, or even the state government. It will be because of what the people are doing at the street level."[10]

With the vast array of weapons at their disposal, Appalachia is working its way toward recovery, especially as attention turns to the poverty and other social problems associated with substance abuse. If it does find a way to slay the monster of addiction, it will most likely be through the efforts of those most familiar with the problem, and not with the interference of outsiders, no matter how well intentioned they may be.

NOTES

1. Lauran Neergaard, (AP), "Hospitals explore new ways to treat pain," *Dayton Daily News,* 7 May 2017.

2. Laura A. Bischoff, "Ohio doctors get new guidelines on prescribing opiates," *Dayton Daily News,* 19 January 2016.

3. Sadie Gurman, AP, "Feds employ warning system in opioid fight," *Dayton Daily News*, 3 January 2018.

4. Fran Smith, "The Addicted Brain," *National Geographic,* September 2017, 42.

5. Ibid., 36.

6. Chris Stewart, "Dayton tops list of drugged-out cities," *Dayton Daily News,* 25 May 2016.

7. Katie Wedell, "Lessons learned from opioid fight," *Dayton Daily News,* 10 March 2019.

8. David Jackson and John Fritze, "President Trump tries to project image of bipartisan action with opioid bill signing," *USA Today,* 24 October 2018.

9. Priya Krishna, "A Kitchen Serves Up Recovery," *New York Times,* 11 July 2018.

10. "One West Virginia city's pioneering approach to opioid crisis," *The Christian Science Monitor*, 22 May 2017.

Chapter Ten

Looking Ahead

The King is Dead. . . .

King Coal is dying, and it won't be the environmentalists who deliver the coup de grâce. Not that mines are not dangerous to one's health, both that of the miners and consumers: Michael Bloomberg of the *New York Times* reports that "in 2010, airborne coal pollution was killing 13,000 Americans a year," down to around 7,500 in 2017.

Rather its death will be hastened by the fact that the energy from other sources is cheaper. "Why," asks Bloomberg, "would consumers pay more for a power source that may kill them?"[1]

And according to Coral Davenport, who writes about climate change, "the burning of coal for electricity [is] the nation's largest source of planet-warming emissions."[2] Coal, however, was well on its way to losing ground to other energy sources before the Obama administration acted to curb carbon emissions. Not long ago, coal supplied approximately half of America's electricity; now it is down to less than 40 percent.[3] By January of 2016, coal production in the country was at the lowest level since 1986.[4]

The Energy Department projects that percentage will slide further as power plants turn to natural gas and renewables like wind and solar power; "wind industry jobs surpassed coal mining jobs in 2008, as wind employment increased by 70% from 50,000 in 2007 to 85,000 in 2009."[5]

What mining there is has moved out West. Montana (with 942 coal miners) produces more coal than Virginia (with 5,262 coal miners). Wyoming (with 5,837 coal miners) produces more coal than West Virginia, Kentucky, Pennsylvania, Virginia, Alabama, and Illinois combined (with a total of 58,995 coal miners).[6]

As if interstate competition weren't enough, foreign competition has affected the market, but after a lull, exports seem to be rising. But who knows what the vicissitudes of politics will bring?

Robin Harris is dismayed over politicians' false promises to bring back coal.

What I have noticed, especially in the political ads out of West Virginia, is that people running for state-level legislative offices, or whatever, are playing on that coal-miner thing: "I'm for coal!" and that sort of thing. And I thought, "Are you doing people a disservice?" Because it is not realistic to lead people to believe that coal is going to be the strength of the economy in the future. Don't you have a responsibility as a state officeholder to help people move beyond this? I felt they were playing on it deliberately. They've adopted the mentality of coal is going to come back: "Coal, coal, coal!" If all we can do is say, "You have to bring back our coal mines . . ."

One by one, the mines in Appalachia are closing, laying off thousands of miners. Lay-offs have not been entirely due to lack of production; more efficient technology requires fewer workers to achieve the same output.

New technology has also impacted the steel industry, which had been such a large consumer of coal. Sabri Ben-Achour gives one example: "Something came along called the minimill—essentially a process for recycling scrap steel and turning it into higher quality steel," which was more efficient and cheaper than "'smelting it from scratch."[7]

What's more, the price of Appalachian coal began to increase in 2004 and is expected to continue to increase by 1.6% each year "due to declining mine productivity."[8] Factoring in transportation, power plants on the East Coast are finding it cheaper to obtain their coal by ship from Colombia.[9]

No longer can the coal companies depend upon exports, either. In 2015 "export to the United Kingdom, Italy and China plummeted by more than 50 percent. Overall, U.S. exports of coal dropped by about 21 percent last year."[10] The application of tariffs and reciprocal measures could have a very adverse effect.

The death of King Coal means the end of a way of life, when a miner could earn enough to support his family comfortably, if not lavishly. In spite of the hardships, there must remain some emotional attachment to a way of life that is so much a part of the region's history. We're told that miners liked the work, but, says retired miner Dave Dilly, "'The people who worked in the coal mines—they don't miss the work of the coal mines, because it's very hard, dangerous work. It's the people you work with. They're your brothers. . . . We stick together.'"[11]

And dangerous it is. The Bureau of Labor Statistics maintains that those who work in coal mining are more likely to be killed or injured, and their injuries are more likely to be serious, than workers in private industry as a whole. A fact sheet from that bureau states that coal miners are almost five times as likely to be killed than equivalent workers in all of total private industry.[12]

Any death is tragic, but compared to the figures of a century ago, the statistics are much better, especially when calculated by deaths per hours of work. From 1880 to 1920, thousands died in explosions and other accidents. The worst year was 1907, when an estimated 3,242 people died, 358 of those deaths due to a mine explosion in West Virginia.[13]

Perhaps because there have been fewer mines, the number of deaths have decreased, although 19 miners were killed in 2010 in an explosion in a West Virginia mine. In 2017 there were 16 deaths, which actually was up from eight in 2016; seven of the eight fatalities in the first half of 2017 involved a worker with one year or less of mine experience.[14]

My husband can vouch for the dangers to neophytes. His first assignment as a young consultant years ago was to the Blue Diamond Coal Company in Kentucky, as safe as any mine can be. Nevertheless, he claims that he was almost killed three times: once when he bumped into the high-voltage wire overhead, once when a railroad car came hurtling toward him, and finally when there was a fire in the mine. Fortunately he was being escorted by the mine superintendent, who, in this last instance, showed him how to run with his head close to the floor as they raced under the low ceiling to the exit.

As King Coal dies, many of the communities that depended on the mines have died too. Not only have those who worked for the coal companies lost their jobs, but their demise has affected those who depended upon the industry: railroads that transported the coal, those who supplied materials to the mines, and all the businesses that served the population, like diners and stores that sold consumer goods.

While traveling in eastern Kentucky, my husband decided to revisit Leatherwood, Kentucky, the scene of his narrow escapes so many years ago. The name of the town was on the map, but there was nothing there! No stores, no schools, no churches, no diners. Just a flat road, except for one thing: the liquor store.

He stopped in and learned from the owner that Leatherwood was a distant memory. All had been leveled, the tunnels sealed, the town gone, the Post Office closed, the workers seeking other opportunities in other regions. He did learn, however, that one resourceful miner had opened the "Blue Diamond Bar" in Louisville.

From mining's peak year of 1923, when almost 900,000 worked in the mines, today, due to mechanization, there are only about 20,000 in West Virginia and 16,000 in Virginia and Kentucky combined.[15]

Although the moribund patient has made a few rallies, as in 2017 when a concatenation of events led to a brief rise, King Coal's prognosis is not good.

Which leads us to the catastrophic destruction of surface mining: the open pits, strip mines, and mountain removals. More than 500 mountains have been removed. In a book titled *Missing Mountains: I Went to the Mountaintop but It Wasn't There,* prominent Kentuckians like Bobbie Ann Mason, Wendell Berry, and Loyal Jones "oppose the terrible violence being inflicted on our home planet and native state."[16] "The sanctity and sacredness of all life and the natural environment should not be destroyed in the name of corporate profit," wrote the Catholic Committee of Appalachia in 1998, while the book's photographs graphically illustrate that destruction.[17]

Not only are the tree-covered mountains gone, but the clear running streams in which Ike Bowling once fished are gone, for those mountain tops have been dumped in the valleys. More than 2,000 miles of those streams are gone, as are the fish, killed by acid runoff from exposed seams. Between 1999 and 2011, two-thirds of the fish population downstream from mountain removal projects were gone, and the ones that were left are often deformed.[18] The shaded streams and forests—1.4 million acres of them--upon which many birds depend are gone, impacting that population, as well. If it's that bad for the animals, what must it be like for people? The desecration continues. The CDC reported that in 2015 there were 1,055 surface mines still operating in Appalachia today;[19] the devastation covers over 2,000 square miles.[20]

By law, mining companies are required to restore the land, and they assured residents that they would do so. But the poor excuses for reclamation are what one resident calls like putting "lipstick on a corpse."[21] The recontoured land is sprayed with non-native grass seed, presumably to ready it for another use, but less than three percent of the reclaimed land has been used for economic development.[22]

Communities are not taking this latest outrage lying down, though. Associations like Appalachia Rising and The Alliance for Appalachia with its many member groups are fighting against destructive surface mining, especially mountaintop removal.

The Abandoned Mine Lands Project (AML), after working with regional stakeholders, in 2012 sent a delegation to Washington to meet with "potential national allies" in Washington, D.C., like The United Steelworkers, The Department of Labor, ARC, and others. It has come up with a "Shovel Ready Toolkit" to help communities access what they have learned about reclamation and reuse.

. . . LONG LIVE THE KING?

Now that coal is gone, will there be another heir to the kingdom? Never again will there be an industry so dominant as mining. Instead, many communities are taking small steps.

An alphabet soup of local associations, STAY, SOAR, SOCM, CRMW, MACED, and others are working toward promoting business and tourism in their areas and toward making their towns more attractive as places to live and work. Many of the results are small, like Whitesburg, Kentucky's tattoo parlor, cupcake store, vape shop, and record store co-op. Or Pomeroy, Ohio's antique and gift shops.

Peter Hille heads MACED, The Mountain Association for Community Economic Development, which has funded local businesses like a T-shirt company and a dog-grooming service. As he told Alana Semuels of *The Atlantic,* "There's not a silver bullet. There's just a lot of silver beebees."[23] But that doesn't mean that the states are not preparing their citizens for bigger things.

Michael Gerlach, Middleport's former mayor and history teacher, is optimistic about his region's future. He reminds me of the startling number of chemical plants like Solvay and Dow that line the Ohio River.

> They've been there originally maybe because the land was cheap and labor was cheaper, and you have river access and railroad access for hauling. I think they may actually become the replacement for coal someday, because if those fracking wells and all that stuff develops and produces a whole lot of chemicals, then your chemical plants are right there, because it's [about] petroleum-based chemicals.

He's not the only one that sees the possibilities of the Ohio River. "I think all of us see that." He says. "You're looking constantly." He hopes that the recent expansion of the Panama Canal will allow shipping containers up river for the market, for whatever they're bringing through the canal, and that the "thirty or forty barges" pushed by river boats can take the place of many of the trains and trucks now in service..

He, too, notes that gas is "a whole lot cheaper" than coal: Natural gas seems to be the future, and, he claims,

> You can switch your coal-fired plant over and have it powered by natural gas. There are already lots of smaller plants being done that way. We had a lot of natural gas even before the fracking. There are wells all around here. At one point, coal was cheaper, but the cost of getting it, the cost of it, to make the power . . . Natural gas is clean, it's a clean-burning fuel.
>
> Natural gas is all the rage, if you will, so if that's what's happening, what does it take to get those guys working—for those guys working in the coal mines, for those guys working in a plant that's making electricity using coal—what does it take to get them retrained so that they can work in the same plant but using natural gas as a fuel?

In Appalachia right now, coal is on a downhill slope. You hate that, because so much of the economy here has been tied to that. With fracking, suddenly this is bigger gas and oil than Saudi Arabia or anyplace. It's obviously a boom economy.

If you're here in Appalachia, number one, you've got to try to protect your resources, including water. Because we don't get our water from the river—we have wells—we were told get a baseline of what minerals are in your water. So we got a baseline: here are the chemicals that are in our water, so if something happens down the road we can say, "Here. This was caused by you. It wasn't here originally."

I'd say that people here generally like fracking. Now in Meigs County so far that's touched us in the fact that the waste water that's being pumped out of those wells is getting pumped into the ground down here in some places, but it has not been a hazard so far.

It is encouraging that a University of Cincinnati study found no evidence of groundwater contamination in five of Ohio's Appalachian counties with fracking activity. At the same time, says an industry spokesperson, "Given the fact Ohio is leading the country in carbon emission reductions because of the increased use of natural gas, I believe that fracking has been a win for both the environment and the economy."[24]

Mayor Gerlach is a great supporter of the Appalachian Regional Council, or ARC, the partnership among federal and state governments to support economic projects. He calls it "a lifeline." adding, "I'd say that most of Appalachia is scared to death that that will be cut off, because there are a lot of big major projects, all manner of things that get funded through the ARC. It could be anything from a village's project to build parks, infrastructure, just a ton of stuff. And then there are educational grants . . ."

There is some risk that funding will be eliminated for ARC, which has invested heavily in education and retraining, water systems, health care, telecommunications, roads, and energy projects. ARC has supported initiatives like POWER, which helps communities to strengthen their economies. In September 2017 ARC announced that to date it had invested a total of $94 million "to diversify the economies in 250 coal-impacted counties across 11 Appalachian states."[25] They are also focusing on retraining former coal workers to enter new fields.

For Dan Mosley, a political leader in eastern Kentucky, mechanization in the coal industry has been a two-edged sword. Although jobs have been lost through its introduction, he agrees that coal workers' talents can be transferred to other industries, for mechanization "gave workers broad set of skills—part miner, part electrician, part engineer—that equips them to handle surprise at every turn."[26]

After decades of depending upon a nineteenth-century industry, Appalachia has now entered the twenty-first. BitSource, located in Pikeville, Kentucky, is a software development company that has trained former coal workers in how to code. In Ashland, Kentucky, the state has created the Ashland Area Innovation Center, a partnership among technical colleges, business and the state. It's the first of sixteen planned in the state.

Solar industry is another contender for the "now economy," and one to which former coal workers could adapt. Joshua M. Pearce writes in the *Harvard Business Review* that:

> For each type of coal position, we determined the closest equivalent. For example, an operations engineer in the coal industry could retrain to be a manufacturing technician in solar and expect about a 10% salary increase. Similarly, explosive workers, ordinance handlers, and blasters in the coal industry could use their sophisticated safety experience and obtain additional training to become commercial solar technicians and earn about 11% more on average.
>
> Our results show that there is a wide variety of employment opportunities in the solar industry, and that the annual pay is attractive at all levels of education, with even the lowest skilled jobs paying a living wage (e.g., janitors in the coal industry could increase their salaries by 7% by becoming low-skilled mechanical assemblers in the solar industry). In general, we found that after retraining, technical workers would make more in the solar industry than previously in coal. However, managers and particularly executives would make less.

Although most coal workers would need some training, and some, like engineers, would need more education, Pearce says that some could almost step right into their new jobs: "For example, a structural engineer in the coal industry would not need additional schooling to work as one in the solar industry. And for some coal employees, the retraining would only amount to a short course or on-the-job training."[27]

Solar energy, however, also has its challenges, since 95 percent of solar panels are imported. Imposing tariffs in order to protect American manufacturers may do more harm than good to the industry and to companies dependent upon it, since the cost of solar energy would be increased.

At any rate, the genie is out of the bottle. The world is moving away from coal toward cleaner, cheaper forms of energy.

As states look to the future, they are turning their attention to education for, as Kentucky's Dr. Bill Brundage says, "21st Century Americans are working with their brains, not their brawns."[28]

Schools at all levels are gaining new importance. A "huge piece of the puzzle for communities seeking to reinvent their economies is education," says Alan Greenblatt. "Any county with a community college is talking about using it to train residents to suit any job that might come along, whether it's a skill such as welding or an effort to turn coal miners into digital code writers."[29]

Virtually every state is working on education improvement. West Virginia has received federal approval of their plan for achieving student success; the state reports a high school graduation rate that has risen to almost 90 percent. Cognizant of the importance of early education, West Virginia will offer pre-school to essentially all four-year-olds.

When I was going to school in Kentucky, we often heard "Thank God for Mississippi," for Mississippi, rather than Kentucky, ranked at the lowest level. Today Kentucky has risen to about the midpoint.

Elmo Garrett is proud of the fact that his daughter is the principal of an award-winning school in rural Tennessee.

> This school used to be considered as an entry level for teachers hoping to eventually be assigned to other schools; now the opposite is true. This school has been involved in a national TAP grant program and last year won $10,000 in federal money for their school at the yearly meeting in New Orleans. The federal program also used some of the teaching videos from her school in some nationwide seminars.

Whatever businesses succeed, and wherever the money comes from, it will be the Appalachians themselves who will be calling the shots. "Few people here want to see coal replaced by another extractive economy allowing outsiders to get wealthy off the sweat of local workers," says Alana Semuels. "Many of the people returning to the region say that any lasting, successful economic program is going to have to be home grown."[30]

Jeff Hawkins, director of the Kentucky Valley Education Cooperative, agrees: "We have to break the pattern of people coming from somewhere else and telling us what we need to do, and then leaving three or four years later."[31]

That remark includes government interference with projects that are counter-productive. Robin Harris, the beleaguered head of the Alcohol, Drug Addiction, and Mental Services Board for three of Ohio's Appalachian counties, describes just such a situation.

> When change came along, the solution that got offered from outsiders here was government programs, handouts, and government assistance. I'm all about compassion, but I wonder. . . . One of my brothers has lived among the Native Americans out in South Dakota for years, and I almost liken us to them as far as "Did your help impact our culture in a way that made it worse for us instead of better?" Because what I see now is people that have become very passive.
>
> The most energy they put into improving their lives is figuring out how to get more of that assistance, and I wonder what happened to that pride of "I provide for myself." We see people who have been multi-generations with the pride of

"I provide for my family," but now it's "We're really good at getting disability payments. We have figured out how to get disability." . . .

I'm careful what I say, but we have a social services system that is more about handing out than giving a hand up, and it has become a disincentive. We don't "incentivize" moving off the system. Instead, the incentive is to stay in it and try to get more of it.

Ohio's Governor Mike DeWine is well aware of the problem, too. He says, "Look, we have people in Ohio who have children who are making a decision that 'Well, I don't want to take that job. I'll lose my health coverage.' Historically what happened is if your income is above a certain amount, what we used to call 'welfare benefits' would drop off. If you get more than X numbers of dollars, you no longer get X, Y, Z. That's an incentive not to work. We have to somehow figure that out."

Independence, resourcefulness—both respected values. But those values have been misdirected as people learn to beat the system. Consider the efforts that Robin and her staff have made to combat teen pregnancy.

The message overwhelmingly from the kids was "I really didn't have a reason not to have a baby. I'm ready to go ahead and start my adult life and this gives me independence."

Yesterday in a discussion on poverty, a vocational counselor—these are eleventh and twelfth graders—used an example of talking to a young lady that she was trying to keep engaged in vocational education, something to help her make a living, and the child just wasn't connecting with the need to have a means to make a living.

So finally the woman said, "You want to get out of your parents' house. You want to live independently. How will you do that?" And she said, "Well, you can sell food stamps for fifty cents to the dollar."

The counsellor said that this has become a survival skill. Embedded in our culture is a survival skill that is about government handouts being manipulated to your advantage.

Sometimes it's a question of government ignorance. "I think there are well-intentioned state leaders who would love to help us. They don't know what to do with us!" She describes the problem.

They come down here and they meet some resistance, but they also tend to come, in my field, if we apply for money, let's say, to do more prevention. The first thing we're met with is we must use an evidence-based program. That's a program that's been studied and found to be effective, with fidelity, of course, and inevitably it will not fit.

There are national standards, but, you know, for any program or curriculum, the demand is that you must choose something that is evidence-based. They're almost all tested in suburban areas, urban areas, California!—so when it comes to implementing here, we run into everything from programs that are not designed to be implemented in an area that does not have public transportation, where people are spread out all over the place with difficulty to convene and congregate, where it's assumed that people have a certain reading level or a certain education. We have a great deal of difficulty implementing evidence-based programs.

At times we try to present an argument: "We have something that will work here. We can show you it will work here, but it's expensive to . . ." The answer back is "Well, make it an evidence-based program."

So that's expensive, and time-consuming, and requires so much study and everything that we end up going, "Well, OK, we can't make it an evidence-based program. We don't have enough people, we wouldn't have enough research into it, all of those things. . . ."

Michael Gerlach describes how local citizens depend on themselves, rather than put their trust in the government when there is a crisis.

Despite their poverty, they are proud of helping friends, neighbors, or others from Appalachia in times of disasters. They will sacrifice money, labor, and time in the effort. They like to point out "famous" people who have made it "out" but come back to help in time of disaster.

Over many years, I have seen the riverfront stores of Pomeroy flood. The merchants watch the water rising. When it hits a certain level, friends start helping move the merchandise to the second floor. When the water starts to recede, the merchants hose the mud out. The store dries and the merchandise comes back down.

By the time TV news crews get here to cover the "disaster," businesses are open as usual. And nobody has contacted FEMA.

Sam Morgan is no fan of "government interference" either when he says, "Now, I don't like people in the government telling people what the minimum wage should be. I think the cost of living in New York City is a hell of a lot more than it is in Hyden, Kentucky, so let the states determine what the minimum wages are and get the government out of people's lives!" Sam adds that it has been hard to get employees for his large company because "they wanted to work part-time so they could continue to get welfare. So this is a problem . . . ."

We'll recall how important Sam thinks it is for people to have the pride that comes from work; with no work, the pride is gone.

Or, as Ricky Skaggs says, "It steals the dreams." He remembers that:

When I was a kid, Bobby Kennedy and the whole Kennedy organization came to Appalachia and to eastern Kentucky with what I guess they thought was a good thing, [but it] was just welfare, and what people needed was jobs! They didn't need welfare. You know, there's a lot of pride in those people, and so that whole thing of entitlement now has grown to full blossom, full fruit, and that's one of those things that has killed the growth and the integrity and the dreams! That's the thing that it steals: the dreams.

We're no different from people in Latvia, Finland—I mean, we're no different from people in Japan, China. People want to work, because they want to be productive.

Not to be considered "outsiders" who have rushed in and out with ineffective notions of how to help are those I think of as the "Champions," people who in effecting change have chosen to become a permanent part of the community:

CHAMPIONS, OR "WHAT'S A NICE JEWISH LAWYER LIKE JOHN ROSENBERG DOING IN APPALACHIA?"[32]

The answer to the question above, posed in a *New York Times Magazine* article in 1997 was, and is, a lot. The director emeritus of AppalReD, the Appalachian Research and Defense Fund legal aid society, is as enthusiastic as ever about the organization he founded almost fifty years ago and which has helped thousands of low-income clients over the decades. John claims his perky wife Jean is especially skilled in persuading lawyers to volunteer their services. He has received many awards for his work, including the Muhammad Ali Kentucky Humanitarian Award.

At the presentation of this latest award, he recalled that he's also a holocaust survivor. He remembers, as a seven-year-old in Magdeburg, Germany, being herded from the family home while Nazis burned the adjacent synagogue's Torahs and prayer books, then dynamited the building. His father and hundreds of other Jewish men were sent to Buchenwald concentration camp. Miraculously, his father was among those released after eleven days and told to leave the country.

After a year in a detention camp in Holland, the family was able to get on what he says was "virtually the last ship to leave for the United States." He was "eternally grateful" to America, a gratitude expressed by enlisting in the Air Force, later attending law school on the G.I. bill. There must be many in Appalachia who are equally grateful for what he has accomplished.

Headquartered in Prestonsburg, Kentucky, AppalReD is proud of its many successes: obtaining black lung benefits for a disabled coal miner, saving the home of an elderly woman from foreclosure, requiring a landlord to restore electricity for a family when it had been turned off illegally, and much more.

I've met the Rosenbergs, as well as other Champions in Kentucky, thanks to my friend, diminutive dynamo Dr. Carole Ganim. She's a former Catholic nun who has written a book about leaving the convent titled *Being Out of Order.*[33]

One warm July morning we wave goodbye to our husbands and head out for what Carole calls our "Thelma and Louise" road trip. Carole is an easy travel companion and a knowledgeable guide, having spent several years teaching English literature at Alice Lloyd College, while living in a "holler" not far away. The college, sometimes referred to as the "Miracle of the Mountains," still offers a quality education at a low cost. All full-time students work from ten to twenty hours a week, depending on financial need, and their income is applied toward their education cost.

It was here that Carole encountered her first "language problem." As she was moving into her new office at the top of a hill, she asked a student if he could help carry some of her boxes of books up the stairs.

She was surprised when he answered, "I don't care to." Later she learned that in the local vernacular that means "Sure. I'd be glad to."

Carole is eager to visit her old friends at the ecumenical Mt. Tabor Monastery. Like John and Jean Rosenberg, the sisters here have also become a permanent and integral part of the community.

Following a steep and winding road through the woods, we come to an even steeper and more winding road that leads to the monastery. The simple wooden buildings at the top of the hill overlook the valley and mountains beyond.

Each of the ten or so sisters must hold an outside position, as well as perform their duties at the monastery. Some serve as teachers and childcare workers. Sister Cathy gets up at 4:00 A.M. to do janitorial work at Lowe's, while Sister Judy, the former prioress of the monastery and paramedic with the Fire Department, is now the Reverend Sister Judy Yunker, Order of Saint Benedict, and an Episcopal priest. She serves as the vicar of Prestonsburg's Saint James' Church, noted for its soup kitchen, food pantry, clothing store, and well-attended Narcotics Anonymous meetings.

When I met her, she had just finished serving on a committee to right a community wrong. An unscrupulous lawyer had inveigled people to come to him to get disability payments and had recruited four crooked doctors to pronounce them disabled. When the government became aware of the large number of claims coming from the county, it cut off all disability payments, including those to many who were truly disabled. I'm told that 1,500 people were affected, 900 of them cut off without a hearing, while 600 were being reviewed. Perhaps because of the committee's efforts, now the stoppage has been postponed pending reviews.

The sisters dress in practical clothing: T-shirts and Capri pants, which they cover with white robes for the evening service. The surrounding trees throw a moving pattern of light and shade through the large windows encircling the octagonal chapel. A meditation room off the front entrance invites us to contemplate the cross and a painting of St. Benedict.

Sister Eileen is now the prioress of the monastic community. Cheerful, with a lively sense of humor, she serves us a lunch of chicken salad, fruit salad, lemonade, and homemade bread and cookies. She'll accompany us on our tour of the region.

The sisters of Mt. Tabor have a close relationship with their Catholic counterparts at the St. Vincent Mission down the hill in nearby David, Kentucky, led by Sister Kathleen. She's a big woman with a big smile, and she, too, dresses informally: blue shorts, sneakers, and a green T-shirt with the mission's logo. St. Vincent's, in addition to having a food and clothing outlet, sells locally made arts and crafts. Other services include working with the "GrowAppalachians" project, teaching gardening skills to those who have lost their traditional ways.

When we arrive at St. Vincent's, Sister Kathleen is on the phone with a client who has called for a ride to the bank to get $250 to make a payment on her overdue electric bill of $650, since, she says, she has a broken leg and her husband has a bad back. Sister Kathleen, no pushover, tells her to make her own way to the bank to get the $250 and then come out to the mission, where the caller and her husband can do six hours of service to earn the additional $400.

"I bet they won't do it," she says. "Because they won't want to work--even though they're getting paid more than I am!" she adds with a laugh.

Close to the mission is the small village of David, Kentucky, which made the news when the former coal town suffered a "blow-out" at the closed mine. Water and mud had built up behind the closed openings and burst out, filling the roads with mud. A lot of the dirt was removed to flatten out a valley near The David School, our next stop, to serve as a field for sports.

The David School, featured in the *Frontline* PBS documentary series *Country Boys,* offers a second chance for those who have not succeeded in traditional schools. Here students prepare their own lunches and clean the facility, as well as learn a trade. Their star alumnus, after studying heating and air-conditioning there, now has his own successful repair business.

There's no dearth of Champions in other states, too, like Mayor Stephen Williams of Huntington, West Virginia, who has received accolades for his innovative anti-drug program, and like Loren Howley and her late husband Bill.

Lorie and Bill, both Yale graduates, moved to West Virginia in the back-to-nature times of the seventies to help the people of that impoverished region. Lorie, an attorney, has been honored by the state for her services, which have included serving on the Board of Legal Aid of West Virginia and on Calhoun County's mental hygiene and fiduciary commissions.

Bill dedicated his life to energy activism and was the newly appointed program director of WV SUN, an organization that promotes solar cooperatives, when he was killed in an accident on his way to a meeting at the state capital.

Lorie had warned me that it might be hard to find her "off-the-grid" house. Driving beyond the small town of Arnoldsburg, I turned at the even smaller town of Chloe (pronounced "Clo"), not much more than a church, a hardware store, and a post office. There the road became rougher and more narrow, and the GPS deserted me: "*You have reached an area . . . .*"

"Go about 3.6 miles on Oka Road, also known as White Oak Road, over a low gap," I read in Lorie's directions. "On the downhill side of this gap, there is a major slip in the road, so be careful going around it. . . . Turn right onto Beech Road, but the road sign has been knocked down, so watch for a large red-sided gambrel-roofed barn and turn left . . ."

Here the ruts got deeper and deeper, the road almost not wide enough for two cars to pass. "Turn left on Redbud Road, where there may still be a road sign . . ." There wasn't.

Fortunately a pick-up truck was creeping so slowly toward me that I could roll down my window and ask for directions.

"Loren Howley? She's my neighbor," said the driver, "Just follow me." He waited patiently while I drove another quarter of a mile or so to find a spot big enough to turn around. As he entered the driveway toward his big graying farmhouse, with the usual assortment of farming machinery and old cars, he waved me past toward Lorie's, just beyond another ageing house next to a rusting trailer and four or five junked cars.

The "off-the-grid" house, with its dark wood and surrounded by gardens, blends with the naturescape of the hillside. It seems as though it is from the Europe of another century, with its many rooms at different levels, built at different stages. The outhouse still stands at the end of a short path, but indoor plumbing was installed at some point. While gas is available and cheap, electricity is another story, and cell phone service requires a special adaptor.

The view is spectacular, especially when we walk up the hill across the road, past the terrace with its large pond that the Howleys had created, big enough for two canoes. On this winter day we can see row after row of mountains from the top.

Since their father's death, Lorie's sons have urged her to move closer to them on the east coast, but she hesitates to leave her beautiful surroundings and the community that has been her home for so many years. Jewish by background but not religious, she was finally able to convince well-meaning churchgoers that she was not interested in being converted.

Lorie invited me to spend the night and to attend the local bar association Christmas party in Spenser, the county seat, reached by another narrow, winding—and dark—road. There I met some of the brightest and best of the region, or of any region—judges, prosecutors, and attorneys—all speaking with the accent of true Appalachians.

I don't have to look far to find other unsung heroes. I once heard a motivational speaker claim that self-esteem was the most important key to success. Many in communities throughout the region are doing what they can to instill pride in the Appalachian community.

The Appalachian specialists at Dayton, Ohio's Sinclair College, along with those in other communities—Cincinnati's well-known expert and advocate Michael Maloney comes to mind—are not the only ones who have extolled the good in Appalachia. I hear time and again of Lela Estes, longtime president of Our Common Heritage, known among other things for its annual "Mountain Days" celebration.

I met with Lela at the Sanctuary assisted living facility, and, while she enjoyed showing me her albums of old family photographs, she could recall little about her accomplishments. She died just a few weeks later. It would be up to others to tell her story, like Tom Ritchie, who is a champion in his own way.

Long active in union affairs, the Hazard, Kentucky, native is Director of Field Services for the AFSCME [American Federation of State, County and Municipal Employees, AFL-CIO]. He's a big man with a white beard, who was very friendly and helpful. When we met in his office, he was also very busy, having some "400 locals to supervise." I had a chance to look at the numerous awards displayed on the wall as he stepped out frequently to take phone calls.

He is also an ardent Democrat and a great supporter of former U.S. Congressman Tony Hall, for good reason. Tom's father was a veteran and a long-disabled coal miner who had not been able receive compensation for black lung disease until Tom was fourteen years old. It was Tony Hall who helped him get the pension he deserved.

Tom says, "I can remember the day that my dad got his check, the first thing he did was get in the car and we drove to Congressman Hall's office and made an appointment to see him. My father was a very simple man, and he wanted to give a contribution to Congressman Hall's campaign. And from that day on, I worked on every campaign that Congressman Hall ever ran. We became friends, and I worked with Tony."

Tony Hall also helped with an Our Common Heritage event, as Tom describes.

What it was, it was also an Appalachian organization, and there were no jobs, so if they could get the people from the Athens [Ohio] area to Columbus for training, they would guarantee them employment. Congressman Hall helped us get the bus from RTA [Regional Transit Authority], one of their older buses, big bus—and I got the city to agree to let the mechanics at the city garage donate their time to work on the bus, and Our Common Heritage bought all new tires and all the parts for that bus. . . .

I'll never forget it. When we started into this little town, people were lined up. It was misting rain. Congressman Hall was on the bus with us, along with four or five people from Our Common Heritage, and when we started into this little town, there were just hundreds of people along the street with flags. Unbelievable. So thankful, and for a long time they used to keep us posted on how people had done. It made a difference in that community.

Tom tells me about Lela Estes.

She was a tough lady. Her husband deserted them, and she moved to Dayton and raised her children by herself. She worked for the city of Dayton and retired from there. She specialized in helping citizens with housing issues, especially the poor. They had a fund at the city called the "Lela Estes Fund," and what would happen was this: You know, our inspectors have to write up people who were not up to code on their housing issues. We had some of our inspectors who by law had to write up the violations during the day, and then in the evening Lela and some of us would get together and literally go make those repairs in the evening: screen doors, broken lights.

The president of this local, Ken Selfridge, who is retired, used to do the same thing. If we had some electrical things, he would volunteer and go do it. We had the AFL-CIO literally adopt some houses and we made some repairs, because, you know, at one time the major unions in this valley were represented by all Appalachians.

The aim of Our Common Heritage organization, founded in 1971, on which Tom served as vice president to Lela Estes' president, has been to help others. In a presentation that Tom makes to community groups, he says, 'The purpose of the organization is to address the social and economic concerns of Appalachian people as well as lending our support toward the improvement of our community life. . . .' Part of its mission is also:

To help the several generations of Urban Appalachians now living in the Miami Valley recollect, retain, and celebrate the rich cultural tradition that they carried north, where it can continue to enrich not only them but their non-Appalachian neighbors. The Mountain Days Festival held every August is one expression of how we celebrate our Appalachian heritage in music, art, dance, fellowship, and song . . .

The festival has attracted some of the biggest names in country music: Bill Monroe, Johnny Paycheck, the Oak Ridge Boys, the Gatlin Brothers, Neal McCoy, and many more, including, most recently, Ricky Skaggs. Sundays would feature preaching and gospel music.

Tom tells me that his wife Ruth grew up near Paintsville, Kentucky, near "Old 23, the country music highway." The Skaggs' farm was next to her grandmother's farm, and Loretta Lynn and Crystal Gayle grew up nearby.

Tom suggests I talk to Ruth, who serves as the treasurer of Our Common Heritage and is very knowledgeable about its history. So a few days later I arrive at the door of the Ritchies' brick suburban house with its beautiful hanging baskets and flower-lined driveway. Among the many family photographs, there are more flowers inside. Ruth, with short wavy gray hair and wearing a bright turquoise top, is as friendly as her husband.

She tells me that Our Common Heritage has run into a problem with continuing the Mountain Days festival. The usual venue is no longer available, and they're seeking another place. Not only does the event "keep the spirit alive," but is an important source of funds for the organization and the scholarships it offers.

There is still a lot of pride and dignity in the majority of the people that I know that keep that spirit alive," she says. "They're very family oriented, with family values."

And then there are the ordinary people of Appalachia who can themselves be counted among the nation's assets, for they are, to Ricky Skaggs:

UNMINED BEAUTIFUL DIAMONDS . . .

For all their challenges, he says, Appalachians "are almost like unmined beautiful diamonds, but because of tragedy, because of setbacks and because of disappointments and that sort of thing, I think our eyes sometimes turn toward looking at defeat . . ." And yet, he says, "the Appalachian spirit is a survival kind of spirit."

"In Kentucky," he continues, "we were raised to share what we had with others and give to someone who needed help," like most Appalachians. Even though I have met so many good and friendly people, we agree that, as everywhere, there are some bad eggs, too, some "mean ones," and I think of Randy L.'s abusive father.

Not that there haven't been some real successes from Appalachia. Ricky recalls that "I had a map one time, and I took a silver dollar, and I put this silver dollar over an area where Kentucky, Tennessee, Virginia and western North Carolina all kind of come together, and I just drew a circle on that map, and I got to looking and thinking about all the great musicians, the great authors—even actors, actresses, creative people, teachers that had come out of that circle."

Not to mention the nineteen presidents with Scotch-Irish roots.

As Dan Mosley, a political leader in eastern Kentucky says of those in his part of the country, "'Their work ethic is second to none. These people will crawl into the side of a mountain and never see the light of day to feed their family. Imagine what they could do for a company with good working conditions.'"[34]

Robin Harris believes that

We are incredibly resilient in coming together and problem solving. It may be in small pockets, but I have seen young leaders emerging who are no longer saying, 'I'm getting out of here. There's nothing here . . .

There's a group in Pomeroy, in Meigs County, called "Imagine Pomeroy" that was started by a young man named Brandon who got into photography. People were telling him, "If you're going to be a photographer, you've got to get out of Meigs County. You've got to go to where people will pay to have their pictures taken."

He decided to stay: "No, there are people here who would appreciate a good photographer, but I have to do it in a way that fits the community." And so he and his wife went into what was considered to be a dying town and opened a photography studio. Then they started doing things like organizing community events and taking pictures of people.

He started holding people together and said, "Let's stop talking about how bad we have it. Let's talk about what we could do." That's how they came up with this title, "Imagine Pomeroy," and it's caught on immediately because of the energy behind that. . . .

We worked with a group of kids who had made their way into juvenile court because of behavior problems, and then it was determined that there was some mental illness or social, emotional kinds of things going on. So we had groups of people working with these kids. We decided to do a summer project and let them begin to express themselves, and we chose photography.

We called Brandon and we said, "Brandon, if Walmart will donate some cameras, and we have these people, would you come and just do an hour with the kids on how to look for things to take a great picture of?" "Oh yes, I would."

The judge in Jackson talked about sending one of his juvenile delinquents to do this, and the kid had one request of where he wanted to take his picture. Jackson High School has a football stadium that looks like it belongs at a university. . . . The boy said, "Can somebody get me in the football stadium to get down on the fifty-yard line?" His juvenile prevention officer said, "OK. I'll arrange that."

He took the kid to the stadium, he stood on the fifty-yard line and took the picture, printed the picture, and brought it back to the judge. The judge said, "Why? Why there?" And he said, "Because in my school, there are about twenty kids that ever stand on that fifty-yard line, and they are the only kids that matter."

The judge took that statement and he used it. It's probably been five years ago, but you stand there and you think, "Is that why this kid started engaging in delinquent behavior and just kind of gave up: 'I'm not going to be a good citizen, because I don't matter?'" So how do we make everybody feel like they matter?

"Imagine Pomeroy" would have the unexpected result of leading to a mentoring program called "Connectors," which aims to better the future of young lives.

While Appalachians work together to solve problems and promote the new economy, the traditional attractions of Appalachia are not being neglected: the music, mountains, and waterways that have long attracted visitors. Tourism will continue to be important, in spite of the blight created by surface mining. West Virginia anticipates that its once polluted Cheat River will soon rival the New River as a draw for whitewater rafters, and the fish population is thriving again.

Traditional arts still flourish, promoted by culture centers like Berea College and Appalshop. The latter states its mission as "to document, disseminate, and revitalize the lasting traditions and contemporary creativity of Appalachia," which it does through theater, music, and film.

With Appalachian resourcefulness, Ohio University environmentalist and professor John Sabraw creates paintings with transformed toxic sludge. While incorporating the vivid yellow, red, black and brown colors into his art, Sabraw is also removing pollution. He and science professor Guy Riefler, also of Ohio University, having learned how to create the pigments, are now working on making them marketable. They hope that other countries will be able to adapt their process to their own pollution problems.

Scientists at Duke University, too, are looking at unexpected benefits from waste generated by coal production. Researchers discovered that coal ash is very rich in rare earth elements like "neodymium, europium, terbium, dysprosium, yttrium and erbium, . . . used in a variety of clean energy technologies, as well as electronics." Locating them and finding a cheap extraction method are the first steps. Then, says one scientist, "We can tap into this vast resource that is currently just sitting around in disposal ponds."[35]

YOU CAN GO HOME AGAIN

"As bad as it is, and the poor economy, there's something about Appalachia that makes people like it here," says Michael Gerlach. "This is a nice place, less crowded, it's really pretty, to be quite honest, and now that's the water's clean, and the air's clean and all that, people like it." What's more, he says:

There's a strong sense of home. Because people with families scattering all over the countryside get here later, and we have people with families that are still here. It's down home, so people come back when they retire. They want to come back here. You're now having people here saying, "Look, I can sell my house in Columbus that I had to pay $200, 300, 400,000 for—sell it, come down here and buy a house just as nice for $70,000. The tax rate is really low. So they come back.

Because we put out a lot of really good students, and they have become very successful, a lot of them are the backbone of your communities: the attorneys, teachers . . . Those are just local kids who say, "OK, I've found a job here, I can make it here."

I think that's true of the other areas, too. It's not a bad place to be. So you have in Appalachia that closeness to family, and if you can get back now because you can operate from a computer, you can come back home. You don't have to go to Columbus. . . . I think you'll likely see some businesses start wanting to locate here, because we have access to the river, we have access to the Interstates here close.

Elmo Garrett of rural Tennessee thinks his state is also attractive to newcomers. He writes to me that

It is obvious there has been a huge change in the rural way of life here, but still the way of life here is different than the metropolitan way of life. So much so that it attracts many (the Internet makes it easy to research what's available). A California couple just bought the farm and home of a friend of ours just seeing it by a walk-through camera.

Within three miles of where I live, I have met five families that have newly located here in the past few years. They are from Florida, Pennsylvania, Atlanta, Mississippi, and Canada. Their reasons usually have to do with the more isolated area, the natural beauty, the weather, and more often the imports say the kindness of the people prompted their move.

I will relate what one store clerk in Cookeville who said she was from Florida told me was her reason to relocate. She said she was on a trip traveling on Interstate 40 through Cookeville, TN, when she stopped and went through a fast-food place to order something. She said the person who waited on her thanked her so much for her business and asked her to come back. She said it was so sincere and so much different from what she was used to that she said to herself, "This is where I want to live." She has been here a while and was not disappointed in her decision.

My next-door farm neighbor is a surgeon originally from Mississippi. He works at two different hospitals and his hobby is farming the old-fashioned way with mules. In the fifties this would have been commonplace. Now people come from miles around and park on our roads to watch this. . . .

It is not just young working people who are staying or heading back to Appalachia. Older people are finding that with its lower cost of living, beautiful scenery, and friendly people, Appalachia is an excellent place to retire. Many, like Lorie Howley's helpful neighbor, have left the cities and returned to the mountains. According to Thomas Wolfe, you can't go home again. But there are those who are proving him wrong.

* * *

As writer and politician Jim Webb says, the Scotch-Irish "are all around you, even though you probably don't know it."[36] I would add that, as in my case, you may even be unaware of the influence of long forgotten ways, but, as Ruth Ritchie says, "The roots of your raising run deep in Appalachian people."

Now that I understand where they—and I—are coming from, I'm embracing my inner Appalachian with pride. Someday may this time-honored culture be met with the celebration it deserves.

NOTES

1. Michael R. Bloomberg, "Climate Progress, Without Trump," *New York Times,* 31 March 2017.

2. Coral Davenport, "U.S. Pledges to Ease Pain in Closing Coal Mines in Shift to Cleaner Energy," *New York Times*, 16 January 2016.

3. Clifford Krauss, "Coal Miners Struggle to Survive in an Industry Battered by Layoffs and Bankruptcy," *New York Times,* 18 July 2015.

4. "U.S. coal production drops to lowest level since 1986," *Dayton Daily News,* 9 January 2016.

5. "Coal and jobs in the United States," Source Watch, https:///sourcewatch.org ./index.php/Coal_and_jobs_in_the_United States.

6. Ibid.

7. Sabri Ben-Achour, "Steel's decline was about technology, not trade," *Marketplace,* https://www.marketplace.org2016/08/09/world/steels-decline.

8. Alison Cassady, "Complex Market Forces Are Challenging Appalachian Coal Mining," *Center for American Progress,* 6 October 2014.

9. Cassady, 8.

10. "U.S. coal production . . ."

11. Jessica Wehrman, "Coal miners at risk at losing pension money," *Dayton Daily News,* 11 May 2019.

12. "Injuries, Illnesses, and Fatalities," Fact Sheet/Coal Mining/April 2010. https//www.bis.gov.iif/oshwe/osh/os/osar0012,html.

13. "Injury Trends in Mining," MSHA Fact Sheet, http.//arlweb.msha.gov.

14. John Raby, "US coal mining deaths surge in 2017 after hitting record low," AP, http://www.wpxi.com/new/Pennsylvania/us-coal-mining-deaths-surge. 2 January 2018.

15. Jedediah Purdy, "The Violent Remaking of Appalachia," *Atlantic,* 21 March 2016.

16. Kristin Johannsen, Bobbie Ann Mason, and May Ann Taylor-Hall, eds, *Missing Mountains: I Went to the Mountaintop But It Wasn't There,* (Nicholasville, KY: Wind Publications, 2005), 1.

17. Ibid., 44.

18. "Ecological Impacts of Mountaintop Removal," *Appalachian Voices,* http://appvoices.org/end-mountaintop-removal/ecology.

19. "Statistics: Coal Operators," Centers for Disease Control and Prevention, http://cdc.gov/niosh/mining/statistics/coaloperators.html. April 11, 2017.

20. Rebecca Schmoyer, "Surface mining's price," *(Albany) Times Union,* 26 July 2014.

21. "How the Coal Industry Flattened the Mountains of Appalachia," *New York Times,* 16 February 2016.

22. "Mountaintop Removal 101," https:voxpopulisphere.com/017/08/08/appalachian_voices_mountaintop_removal_101/

23. Alana Semuels, "Imagining a Post-Coal Appalachia," *The Atlantic,* 8 April 2015.

24. Thomas, Tanisha, "Study: No evidence of groundwater contamination from in state," *Dayton Daily News,* 13 June 2018.

25. Appalachian Regional Commission, http://www.ac.gov/news/index.asp "Appalachian Regional Commission Announces Nearly $2 million in Additional POWER Investments in central Appalachia," September 2017.

26. Alan Greenblatt, "In Life After Coal, Appalachia Attempts to Reinvent Itself," http://www.Governing.com/topics/finance/gov-coal-trump-appalachia-economy.html. December 2016.

27. Joshua M. Pearce, "What If All U.S. Coal Workers Were Retrained to Work in Solar?" *Harvard Business Review,* 8 August 2016, 3.

28. "New Economy," http://www.migration.Kentucky.gov/Newsdroom-one=ky/New Economy1.htm., 2.

29. Greenblatt, 10.

30. Ibid, 8.

31. Greenblatt, 12.

32. Michael Winerip, "What's a Good Jewish Lawyer Like John Rosenberg Doing in Appalachia?" *New York Times Magazine,* 29 June 1997.

33. Carole Gamin, *Being Out of Order,* (St. Petersburg, FL: Vandamere Press, 2013).

34. Ibid., 11.

35. Brooks Hays, "Appalachian coal ash richest in rare earth elements, study finds – UPI.com. http://www.upi.com/Science_News/2016/05/27 . . .

36. Jim Webb, *Born Fighting*, (New York: Broadway Books, 2004).

Observations

Mountain people
can't read,
can't write,
don't wear shoes
don't have teeth,
don't use soap,
and don't talk plain.
They beat their kids,
beat their friends,
beat their neighbors,
and beat their dogs.
They live on cow peas,
fatback and twenty acres
straight up and down.
They don't have money.
They do have fleas,
overalls,
tobacco patches,
shacks,
shotguns,
foodstamps,
liquor stills,
and at least six junk cars on the front yard.
Right?

Well, let me tell you
I am from here,
I'm not like that
and I am damned tired of being told I am.[1]

NOTE

1. Jo Carson, "Observations," *Stories I Ain't Told Nobody Yet*, (New York: Orchard Books, 1989), 28–29. Reprinted with permission of the publisher.

References

"Appalachian Regional Commission Announces Nearly 5.2 million in Additional POWER Investments in Central Appalachia." Appalachian Regional Commission. http://www.ac.gov/news/index.asp. September 2017.

Bailyn, Bernard. *Voyagers to the West.* New York: Vintage Books, 1986.

Ball, Annie Sparks. "The Effect of Appalachian Regional Dialect on Performance Appraisal and Leadership Perceptions." (2014). *Online Theses and Dissertations 203.* https://encompass.eku.edu/etd/203.

Baseler, Marilyn C. *"Asylum for Mankind": America 1607–1800.* Ithaca: Cornell University Press, 1998.

Ben-Achour, Sabri. "Steel's decline was about technology, not trade." *Marketplace,* http://www.marketplace.org2016/08/09.world/steels-decline.

Berry, Chad. *Southern Migrants, Northern Exiles.* Urbana: University of Illinois Press, 2000.

Biggers, Jeff. *The United States of Appalachia.* Berkeley: Counterpoint, 2006.

Bischoff, Laura. "Ohio doctors get opiate guidelines." *Dayton Daily News,* 20 January 2016.

———."Ohio Lt. Gov. Mary Taylor reveals sons' struggles with opioid addiction." *Dayton Daily News,* 1 June 2017.

Bloomberg, Michael R. "Climate Progress, Without Trump." *New York Times,* 31 March 2017.

Brown, Stephen, Elizabeth Hirschman, and Pauline Maclaran. *Two Continents One Culture: The Scotch-Irish in Southern Appalachia.* Johnson City, TN: Overmountain Press, 2006.

Callahan, Richard J. "The Work of Class in Southern Religion." *The Journal of Southern Religion.* Vol. 13 (2011). http://jsr.fsu.edu//issues/vol13/Callahan.html.

Cash, Johnny, with Patrick Carr. *Cash: The Autobiography.* San Francisco: HarperSanFrancisco, 1997.

Cassady, Alison. "Complex Market Forces Are Challenging Appalachian Coal Mining." *Center for American Progress,* 6 October 2014.

Caudill, Harry M. *Night Comes to the Cumberlands.* Boston: Little, Brown, 1963.

Chernow, Ron. *Alexander Hamilton.* New York: Penguin Press, 2005.

Clark, Sandra H.B. "Birth of the Mountains." USGS: Science for a Changing World. Pubs.usgs.bov/gip/birth/pdf, 2009.

"Coal and jobs in the United States." *Source Watch,* http//www.sourcewatch.org index.php. Coal and jobs in the United States 26 June 2015.

Davenport, Coral. "U.S. Pledges to Ease Pain of Closing Coal Mines in Shift to Cleaner Energy." *New York Times,* 16 January 2016.

Dawidoff, Nicholas. *In the Country of Country.* New York: Pantheon/Random House, 1997.

Day, Ronnie. "Pride and Poverty: An Impressionistic View of the Family in the Cumberlands of Appalachia." Robert J. Higgs, Ambrose N. Manning, and Jim Wayne Miller, eds., *Appalachia Inside Out.* Knoxville: University of Tennessee Press, 1995.

Diggs, Nancy Brown. *Breaking the Cycle.* Lanham, MD: Rowman and Littlefield, 2013.

————. *Looking Beyond the Mask: When American Women Marry Japanese Men.* Albany, NY: State University of New York Press, 2001.

Dunn, Durwood. *Cades Cove: The Life and Death of a Southern Appalachian Community 1818–1937.* Knoxville: University of Tennessee Press, 1989. 13th printing 2015.

"Ecological Impacts of Mountain Removal." *Appalachian Voices.* http://appvoices.org /end-mountaintop-removal/ecology.

Eller, Ronald D. *Miners, Millhands and Mountaineers: Industrialization of the Appalachian South 1880–1930.* Knoxville: University of Tennessee Press, 1982.

Friedman, Lisa. "Cost of New E.P.A. Coal Rules: Up to 1,400 More Deaths a Year." *New York Times,* 21 August 2018.

Frolik, Cornelius. "Police: Bulk of OD calls originate on Dayton's east side." *Dayton Daily News*, 9 December 2017.

Furmanovsky, Michael. "American Country Music in Japan: Lost Piece in the Popular Music History Puzzle," *Popular Music and Society*, July 2008.

Ganim, Carole. *Being Out of Order: The Prophetic Generation of Nuns and Sisters.* St. Petersburg, FL: Vandamere Press, 2013.

Garrett, Elmo. *Memories of Rural Life in the 1950s.* Unpublished memoir. Undated.

Greenblatt, Alan. "In Life After Coal, Appalachia Attempts to Reinvent Itself." http://www.Governing.com/topics/finance/gov-coal-trump-appalachia.11. December 2016.

Gregory, James N. *The Southern Diaspora.* Chapel Hill: University of North Carolina Press, 2005.

Gurman, Sadie. "Feds employ warning system in opioid fight." *Dayton Daily News,* 3 January 2018.

Guy, Roger. *From Diversity to Unity.* Lanham, MD: Lexington Books, 2007.

Halperin, Rhoda H. and Jennifer Reither-Portill. "'Nerves' in Rural and Urban Appalachia," Susan E. Keefe, ed. *Appalachian Cultural Competency.* Knoxville: University of Tennessee Press, 2005.

Hawkins, Derek. "How a short letter in a prestigious journal contributed to the opioid crisis." *Washington Post*, 2 June 2017.

Hays, Brooks. "Appalachian coal ash richest in rare earthy elements, study finds." UPI.com.http://www.upi.com/Science_News/2016/05/27.

Hicks, Deborah. *The Road Out: A Teacher's Odyssey in Poor America.* Berkeley: University of California Press, 2013.

Higgs, Robert J. introduction and ed. "Chapter 1: Family and Community." *Appalachia Inside Out.* Vol. 1: Conflict and Change. Knoxville, TN: University of Tennessee Press, 1995.

———. Ambrose N. Manning, and Jim Wayne Miller, eds. *Appalachia Inside Out.* Knoxville, TN: University of Tennessee Press, 1995.

"How the Coal Industry Flattened the Mountains of Appalachia." *New York Times,* 16 February 2016.

"Injuries, Illnesses, and Fatalities," Fact Sheet/ Coal Mining/April 2010 https://www.bls.gov/iif/oshwe/osh/os/osar0012.html.

Johannsen, Kristin, Bobbie Ann Mason, and Mary Ann Taylor-Hall, eds. *Missing Mountains: I Went to the Mountaintop But It Wasn't There.* Nicholasville, KY: Wind Publications, 2005.

Jones, Loyal. *Appalachian Values.* Ashland, KY: The Jesse Stuart Foundation, 1994.

———. "Forward to the Fourth Edition." *Appalachian Social Context Past and Present.* Philip J. Obermiller and Michael Montgomery, eds. Dubuque, IA: Kendall/ Hunt, 2000.

Kennedy, Billy. *The Scots-Irish in Pennsylvania and Kentucky.* Belfast: Causeway Press, 1998.

Kephart, Horace. *Our Southern Highlanders.* Knoxville: University of Tennessee Press, 1913.

Kingsolver, Barbara. *The Prodigal Summer.* New York: HarperCollins, 2000.

Krauss, Clifford. "Miners Bracing for a Future of Ever-Dwindling Demand for Coal." *New York Times,* 18 July 2015.

——— and Michael Corkery. "A Bleak Outlook for Trump's Promise to Coal Miners."*New York Times,* 19 November 2016.

Krishna, Priya. "A Kitchen Serves Up Recovery." *New York Times,* 11 July 2018.

Leyburn, James G. *The Scotch-Irish: A Social History.* Chapel Hill: University of North Carolina Press, 1962.

Lynn, Loretta, with George Vecsey. *Coal Miner's Daughter.* New York: Knopf Doubleday, 2010.

Mann, Charles C. *1493: Uncovering the New World that Columbus Created.* New York: Knopf, 2011.

Manzoor, Sarfraz. "Scottish roots of Johnny Cash, the man in black tartan." *The Guardian.* 6 February 2010.

Matheney, Ann Dudley. *The Magic City: Footnotes to the History of Middlesborough, Kentucky and the Yellow Creek Valley.* Middlesboro, Kentucky: Bell County Society, 2003.

McClatchy, Debby. "Appalachian Traditional Music: A Short History." http://www.mustrad.org.uk/articles/appalach.htm.(accessed 18 February 2018).

McNemar, Richard. *The Kentucky Revival.* Lawton, OK: Trumpet Press, 2012. Originally published in 1808.

McSwain, Harold W. *Appalachia: Similarities to the Third World.* Columbus, OH: Rural Resources, Inc., 1986.

"The Mine Wars." *American Experience: TV's most watched history series*, PBS.org.

Montgomery, Michael. "The Scotch-Irish Element in Appalachian English." *Journal of East Tennessee History. Vol. 65 (1995)*

"Mountaintop Removal 101." *Appalachian Voices.* http://appvoices.org/end-mountain top-removal/ecology. 8 August 2017.

Neal, Jocelyn R. *Country Music: A Cultural and Stylistic History.* Oxford: Oxford University Press, 2013.

"New Economy." http://www.migration.Kentucky.gov/Newsroom-one-ky/New Economy1.htm.

Obermiller, Phillip J., and Michael E. Maloney, eds. *Appalachia: Social Context Past and Present.* Dubuque, IA: Kendall/Hunt Publishing, 4th ed. 2002.

"One West Virginia's city's pioneering approach to opioid crisis." *The Christian Science Monitor.* 22 May 2017.

"Passage to America, 1750." *Eyewitness to History.* www.eyewitnesstohistory.com, 2000.

Payne, Ruby K., Philip E. DeVol, and Terie Dreussi Smith. *Bridges out of Poverty.* Highlands, TX: aha! Process. Rev. ed. 2009.

Pearce, Joshua. "What if All U.S. Coal Workers Were Retrained to Work in Solar?" *Harvard Business Review,* 8 August 2016.

Philliber, William W., and Clyde B. McCoy, eds. *The Invisible Minority.* Lexington, KY: University Press of Kentucky, 1981.

Portelli, Alessandro. *They Say in Harlan County: An Oral History.* Oxford: Oxford University Press, 2011.

Puckett, Anita. "Language and Power." *Talking Appalachian.* Amy Clark and Nancy Hayward, eds. Lexington, KY: University of Kentucky Press, 2013.

Purdy, Jedediah. "The Violent Remaking of Appalachia." *Atlantic,* 21 March 2016.

Quinones, Sam. *Dreamland.* New York: Bloomberg Press, 2015.

Raby, John. "U.S. coal mining deaths surge in 2017 after hitting record low." AP, http://www.wpxi.com/new/Pennsylvania/us-coal-mining-surge . . . 2 January 2018.

———— and Bruce Schreiner, "Toyota investing $750M in 5 plants." *Dayton Daily News,* 15 March 2019.

Rehder, John. *Appalachian Folkways.* Baltimore: Johns Hopkins University Press, 2004.

Ritchie, Fiona, and Doug Orr. *Wayfaring Strangers.* Chapel Hill: University of North Carolina Press, 2014.

Sample, Tex. *Hard Living People & Mainstream Christians.* Nashville, TN: Abington Press, 1992.

Schmoyer, Rebecca. "Surface mining's price." *(Albany) Times Union,* 26 July 2014.

Schroeder, Kaitlin. "Brown says bill links drug recovery, job training." *Dayton Daily News,* 11 June 2018.

Semuels, Alana. "Imagining a Post-Coal Appalachia." *The Atlantic,* 8 April 2015.

Sharrett, Luke. "A Kitchen Serves Up Recovery." *New York Times,* 11 July 2018.

"Scioto leads on addicted babies." (AP) *Toledo Blade*, 17 October 2016.

Skaggs, Ricky, with Eddie Dean. *Kentucky Traveler: My Life in Music.* New York: HarperCollins, 2013.

Smith, Fran. "The Addicted Brain." *National Geographic,* September 2017.

Spargo, John. *The Bitter Cry of Children.* New York: Macmillan, 1906.

Stanger, Dorothy. *Diamonds in the Dew: An Appalachian Experience.* Bloomington, IN: 1st Books, 2003.

"Statistics: Coal Operators." Centers for Disease Control and Prevention. http://cdc .gov/niosh/minin/statistics/coaloperators.html. 11 April 2017.

Sutherly, Ben. "Area county claims highest drug overdose rate of urban areas in state." *Dayton Daily News,* 30 January 2016.

Theroux, Paul. *Deep South.* New York: Houghton Mifflin Harcourt, 2015.

Thomas, Jason. "Mining a Rich Lode of Ideas." *edible.* Louisville and the Bluegrass, edition, August and September 2016.

Thomas, Tanisha. "Study: No evidence of groundwater contamination from in state." *Dayton Daily News,* 13 June 2018.

Votaw, Albert N. "The Hillbillies Invade Chicago." *Harper's Magazine,* February 1958.

"U.S. coal production drops to lowest level since 1986." *Dayton Daily News,* 9 January 2016.

Webb. Althea. "African Americans in Appalachia." Oxford AASC, www.oxford aasc.com./public/features/archive/0213/essay.jip. (accessed 22 March 2017).

Webb, Jim. *Born Fighting: How the Scots-Irish Shaped America.* New York: Broadway Books, 2004.

Wedell, Katie. "Lessons learned from opioid fight." *Dayton Daily News,* 15 March 2019.

Wehrman, Jessica. "Coal miners at risk of losing pension money." *Dayton Daily News,* 11 May 2019.

———. "Senate Oks bipartisan opioid bill." *Dayton Daily News,* 19 September 2018.

Weller, Jack E. *Yesterday's People.* Lexington: University of Kentucky Press, 1965.

Williams, John Alexander. *Appalachia: A History.* Chapel Hill: University of North Carolina Press, 2002.

Winerip, Michael, "What's a Nice Jewish Lawyer Like John Rosenberg Doing in Appalachia," *New York Times Magazine.* 29 June 1997.

Index

Note: Photospread images are numbered *p1, p2, p3,* etc.

About the Author

Nancy Brown Diggs' long interest in other cultures is reflected by her PhD in East Asian Studies, by her language skills, and by the books she has written, which include: *Breaking the Cycle: How Schools Can Overcome Urban Challenges, Hidden in the Heartland: The New Wave of Immigrants and the Challenge to America, Looking Beyond the Mask: When American Women Marry Japanese Men,* and *Steel Butterflies: Japanese Women and the American Experience.* Having authored books on other cultures, she decided to write about one closer to her own: the Appalachian, never dreaming that it *was* her own, and that the roots of those long-forgotten ways could run so deep. Refuting the stereotypes of the media, she discovered that this time-honored culture merits admiration.